12/89

your
FOUR-YEAR-
OLD

your FOUR-YEAR-OLD
Wild and Wonderful

by Louise Bates Ames
and Frances L. Ilg

Gesell Institute of Child Development

Illustrated with photographs

A DELTA BOOK

To our daughters,
Joan and Tordis,
and our grandchildren,
Carol, Clifford, Karl, and Whittier

Published by
Dell Publishing Co., Inc.
1 Dag Hammarskjold Plaza
New York, New York 10017

Photo credits appear on page 152.

ISBN: 0-440-59479-0

Reprinted by arrangement with Delacorte Press
Printed in the United States of America
Second printing—January 1981

CONTENTS

chapter one
CHARACTERISTICS
OF THE AGE

The Four-year-old is a funny little fellow, and if you can accept him as such, you will appreciate and enjoy him for what he is. If, on the other hand, you take a sterner stance and feel that his boasting, his swearing, his general expansiveness, and his often out-of-bounds behavior is *wrong*, both you and he may have an unnecessarily hard time of it.

For the most part, we have found the boy or girl of this age to be joyous, exuberant, energetic, ridiculous, untrammeled—ready for anything. What a change he offers as compared to his more difficult, demanding, Three-and-a-half-year-old, just-earlier self! If at times he seems somewhat voluble, boastful, and bossy, it is because it is so exciting for him to enter the fresh fields of self-expression that open up at this wonderful age.

The child at Three-and-a-half characteristically expressed a strong resistance to many things the adult required, possibly because in his own mind the adult was still all-powerful. Four has taken a giant step forward. All of a sudden he discovers that the adult, though still quite powerful, is not *all*-powerful. He now finds much power in himself. He finds that he can do bad things, from his point of view, and the roof does not fall in.

More than this, following its seemingly built-in plan

1

of interweaving, nature sees to it that whereas the Three-and-a-half-year-old was rather withdrawn and insecure much of the time, Four operates on the expansive and highly sure-of-himself side of life. Four, as Figure 1 shows, is an age when the child is characteristically in a nice state of equilibrium.

Emotional exuberance has its positive as well as its negative side. The typical Four-year-old *loves* adventure, loves excursions, loves excitement, loves *anything* new.

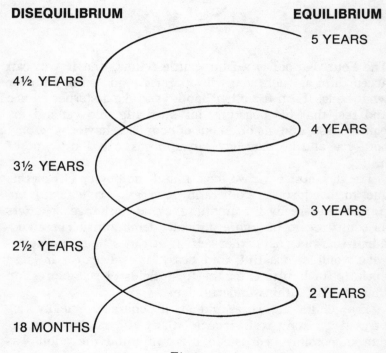

Figure 1

Alternation of Ages of Equilibrium and Disequilibrium

He adores new people, new places, new games, new play-things, new books, new activities. No one is more responsive to the adult effort to entertain. He will accept what you have to offer with delightfully uncritical enthusiasm. So, it is a pleasure to provide the child of this age with new toys, books, clothes, experiences, information—because any of these things make his eyes sparkle so, because he is so wholeheartedly appreciative.

In fact, Four *loves* many things, but his emotions tend to be definitely extreme. He loves a lot and he hates a lot. In fact, his hates may be equally as strong as his loves. One can never be quite certain what it will be that will stimulate his hate, but whatever it is, his feeling should be fully respected, at least within reason.

With those children who have a tremendously strong attachment for their mothers (and that is most) there may be especially strong hatred expressed for anything that changes her in the child's eyes. He may hate certain jewelry she wears; he may hate it if she changes her way of wearing her hair. Or, he may especially hate a special look on her face that tells him that she is displeased with him.

He may hate squash, or any other food to which he takes a dislike. Or, he may (alas) hate certain people. He especially hates things that he considers *ugly*, and may at times express a quite remarkable aesthetic sensitivity.

Four loves things that are *new*. The Three-year-old has a conforming mind. Four has a lively mind, and new thoughts and ideas or bits of information may please him as much as do new toys. That is why it is so much fun to talk with him. His incessant "whys" may sometimes pall, but often they lead the way to enthusiastic information-giving on the part of the adult. It is fun to inform some-body who so enthusiastically wishes to be informed.

The key to the Four-year-old's psychology is his high drive combined with his fluid imagination. Four is, indeed, highly versatile. What can he not do? He can be quiet or noisy, calm or assertive, cozy or imperious, suggestible or independent, social, athletic, artistic, literal, fanciful, cooperative, indifferent, inquisitive, forthright, humorous, dogmatic. He is many people in one.

The typical Four-year-old is also speedy. Each thing he does, he does quickly, and he is also speedy as he moves from one interest to the next. For the most part, he does a thing once, and *that's enough.* He isn't interested in perfection; he is interested in getting on to the next activity. Behavior is fluid, and if he does stay with a single activity, that single activity may change so rapidly as to make your head spin.

A good example of the often quite remarkable fluidity of Four's imagination can be seen in his drawing. A Four-year-old in spontaneous drawing may quite typically start with a tree, which turns into a house, which turns into a battleship. Or, even more fluidly, his "person's foot" can grow so large that it develops large toes that turn out to be the back of a bird. And that turns out to be a roller coaster. And that turns out to be the *back* of the roller coaster. (At that point, your Four-year-old may very likely run out of paper.)

Fluidity can be expressed in media other than pencil and paper. For instance, two boys, playing in a sand-pile, decide that they are making volcanoes. However, when it is suggested to them that the volcano's *erupting,* as they had planned, might be too messy, they themselves spout a little and then give up the volcano plan and decide they are digging for dinosaur bones. No bones being forthcoming, they talk awhile about how old dinosaurs get to be (nine thousand years, they think) and then turn their sand into imaginary snow and make snowballs (which do not stick together very well even with the addition of water). So, they turn their snowballs into rotten eggs and say that the last one to talk is a rotten egg. (All this within five minutes of play.)

It is no wonder that adults have to keep on their toes to keep up with speedy, fluid, fanciful Fours. But, fluid as they are, there still remains some of Three's "me-too" quality. If you ask one child in a group what street he lives on, each child in the group then wants to tell where he or she lives, and all may be surprisingly patient and polite until everyone has had a turn at giving this interesting information.

It may be that Four's expansiveness is sometimes a little too much even for him. At any rate, he likes and respects boundaries and limits, which he does not always have within himself, and which, therefore, often have to be supplied. In fact, we find that many Fours like very much the verbal restraint of "as far as the tree," "as far as the gate." Others can be reasonably well contained if told, "It's the rule that you do (or do not do) so-and-so."

In fact, many seem to seek for regularity and rules in the happenings around them. Thus, a Four-year-old may come up with the spontaneous conclusion, "It's always so-and-so." This "always" seems to give him security. He may sometimes break the rules, but he likes at least to know what they are.

Also, he sometimes spontaneously restabilizes himself, even in his wilder play. Thus, two boys may pretend they are in a cave (a large pasteboard box) with monsters, but then they protect themselves by pretending that the monsters have disappeared and that they (the boys) are "all safe and sound."

And, for all his expansive and often out-of-bounds tendencies, Four can, when he puts his mind to it, sometimes be very reliable. Many can go on small errands outside the home if these do not involve crossing the street. And many, by Four-and-a-half, have reached the point where they can be trusted to play outdoors without much supervision or checking.

However, when his customary expansiveness combines with his exciting need to see just how far he can go before the grown-ups call a halt, the Four-year-old generously and characteristically very often expresses what we consider the outstanding trait of his age—his love for going out-of-bounds.

A normally vigorous and well-endowed child of this age may seem out-of-bounds in almost every area of living. Motorwise he not only hits and kicks and spits (if aroused) but may even go so far as to run away from home if things don't please him. Whether he is happy or not, his motor drive is very high. He races up and down stairs, dashes here and there on his trusty tricycle.

Emotionally, too, he tends to be extremely out-of-bounds. He laughs almost too hilariously when things please him; howls and cries more than too loudly when things go wrong. (But he laughs more than he cries, and he loves laughter in others. In fact, he may tell you of his parents, or of other adults, "When they're happy they always laugh." He can, on frequent occasion, be extremely silly.)

But it is his verbally out-of-bounds expressions that are most conspicuous. He exaggerates: "as high as the sky," "ten million bugs," "as big as a house." He boasts: "I have bigger ones at home," "I can do better than that," "My father is stronger than your father." Along with his boasting, he swaggers. Boys like to emphasize their own masculinity by calling each other what they consider to be very masculine names, not their own: "Bill," "Mike," "Joe."

There is much interest in both the products and the process of elimination. Children are especially fascinated by bowel movements. Out for a walk, they may spot every deposit of a dog's bowel movements. Their own buttocks are especially important to them, and when asked what they think with, they may even point to their behinds.

Elimination swearing has its beginning at Four. When angry with a friend, the child may call him an "old poo-poo." In fact, in general, nouns and adjectives tend to be on the unacceptable side, and there is considerable talk about "wee-wee" and "doo-doo." (Even though right in the midst of such a conversation by one child, another may criticize and say, "That's not nice.") There is also much reference to garbage.

This concern about elimination is also seen in the child's great interest in bathrooms, especially in other people's houses. The minute he enters a house, Four may want to see the bathroom. But, though he is much interested in bathrooms and other people's toilet functioning, he tends to be extremely private about his own. He may even go so far as to lock the bathroom door, and many a Four-year-old has locked himself into the bathroom.

And (alas), all too often Four lapses into outright profanity. "Jesus Christ!" is a not-uncommon expletive, even though Four may not fully appreciate what he is saying. When one Four-year-old was heard to repeat the phrase "Goddamn it to Hell!" for each step as he climbed the stairs, his father got the message and became more careful about his own language.

And we have the (supposedly true) story of a little Boston girl whose mother, discouraged by her profanity, told her that if she swore once more, she (the mother) would pack the girl's suitcase and ask her to leave home. The little girl did swear once more. The mother did pack the suitcase and put her and it outside the door. After a few minutes, feeling guilty, the mother went to look for her daughter. The child was still sitting on the steps.

"I thought I told you to leave home," said the mother.

"I would have if I could have thought where the Hell to go," was her daughter's reply.

True or not, this story is all too typical. Or, if not with actual profanity, the child may criticize the adult with epithets and threats: "You're a rat," "I'll sock you." And, not content with unacceptable language, all too often a Four-year-old departs from truth to an extent that any literal-minded adult can label only as outright prevarication. If you meet this, as any other exuberance, with a calm "Is that so?" or with a knowing wink rather than with anger and admonition, he tends to come rather quickly back to reality.

FOUR INTO FIVE

And just in case you are curious about what happens next, here's a word about that interesting transition time —Four into Five.

We know that the typical Four-year-old girl or boy tends to be, as we have told you, extremely exuberant, enthusiastic, outgoing, out-of-bounds. We also know that at Five the same child will in all likelihood be, much of the time, calm, collected, quiet and self-contained, adaptable, conforming, well-adjusted, easy to get on with, happiest and most comfortable while engaged in conservative, close-to-home activities.

How does he get from Four to Five? What is the transition like? Does he all of a sudden one day simply forget his earlier exuberant ways and settle down? Or, is the change more gradual?

It tends to be rather gradual, and sometimes the child

himself seems a bit confused, as if he really does not know whether he is a wild Four-year-old or a calm and quiet Five. At any rate, adults often find his behavior highly unpredictable.

A clue to his own uncertainty is the strong interest of the Four-and-a-half-year-old in whether or not things are "real." Making a drawing of an airplane, he may include a *real* electric cord so that people can plug it in. "Is it real?" is a customary question.

At Four-and-a-half, the child does tend to be a bit more self-motivated than he was just earlier, and he tends to stay on the job better than he did before. Children of this age are much interested in gathering new information, in perfecting old skills. Play is less wild than at Four, and most are better able to stand frustration. But emotions may be quite uncertain, with laughter and tears following each other in quick succession.

And, the child may be less easily shifted than he was just earlier. Some Four-and-a-half-year-olds can be persistently demanding, especially to secure certain objects such as sparklers for the Fourth of July. This kind of demand may be so persistent that it becomes obnoxious. In fact, when crossed, the child of this age may become obnoxious, sticking out his tongue and making dreadful faces. It may now be less easy to distract him with humor than it was when he was just Four.

At Four-and-a-half, the child is becoming aware of authority, and a new kind of confused but listening expression, mixed with a bit of fear, crosses his face when a parent reprimands him. Parents may like to temper their demands when they see this expression. This may be a time for bargaining.

Now the awareness of "good" and "bad" things begins to dawn. Nothing delights a Four-and-a-half-year-old more than to hear real true stories at bedtime, either about himself or about his parents. He loves stories about how bad his parents were when they were little, and also stories about how good they were.

Prayers, especially spontaneous ones, are welcome at this age and often allay children's bedtime fears. The thought of God the Father, and the thought that He is everywhere, can be comforting to some. Children of this age may like to tell God about their troubles and why they happened. They like to bless all who are near and dear to them or tell God about the people they love.

All in all, the Four-and-a-half-year-old is unpredictable. But if you will keep in mind where the child has been and where he is going, it can help you to define and to understand where he is now.

WARNING!

Here, as at any age, we give you an important warning: *Do not take too seriously what anybody (we included) tells you about how your child will or may behave.*

Child behavior, for all reasonably normal children, does develop in a highly patterned way. Stages of more mature behavior follow those of less mature behavior in a remarkably predictable manner. To a large extent, when we see a child expressing some one certain kind of behavior, we can tell you what will very likely happen next.

We can also, on the basis of having studied thousands of children at every age, give you an estimate of when, *on the average*, your child may be expected to reach each stage.

Almost every child does go through almost all of the stages, and in a rather standard order. What we cannot tell you for sure is *exactly* when your own child will reach each and every stage.

Age norms (our story of what behavior is like at the different ages) are only *averages*. Your child may quite normally be ahead of or behind these averages. So, if we say that a certain behavior is characteristic of Four years of age, and your Four-year-old has not reached this stage yet, you should not feel that you have cause to worry. Your child may be, and quite normally so, a little slower than the average in his development (though the quality of his behavior might be quite superior, indicating that a fine potential will express itself in time.) *Every child has his own timetable. Do not expect that your own child will always perform right on our schedule.*

And then, of course, there are individual differences. Not all Three-year-olds are gentle; not all Four-year-olds are wild.

We tell you about behaviors that are characteristic of the different ages not so that you will check and worry. We tell you what behavior is usually like so that you can, within reason, know what to expect and then *not* worry when your own child's behavior sometimes departs from your ideal.

It is comforting to many parents to know that children do not always behave in a desirable, conforming way; that many perfectly "good" children are often, at some stages, quite normally less than good.

"Now I know he's normal" is what many parents say when they read our often seemingly somewhat lurid descriptions of what behavior can be like at different ages. This is why we write for you—hopefully to prepare you for, and to make you feel comfortable with, the many sometimes rather remarkable ways in which even completely normal children behave as they grow older.

Then you can protect yourself from feelings of guilt, or simple embarrassment, at your child's sometimes unorthodox behavior. Or, you can protect yourself from striking out at your child in an unknowing way or in aroused anger. With knowledge, you can appreciate what the laws of growth are expressing through your child, can smile within yourself at his forms of expression, and can act with confident and loving authority, knowing that this, too, will pass.

chapter two

THE CHILD WITH OTHER CHILDREN

The typical Four-year-old loves adventure, and other children, for him, can be a big adventure. Especially if they are of his own age they will be, as he is, exciting, active, enthusiastic, out-of-bounds, always ready for something new. And, like him, they will be somewhat unpredictable. This adds spice to playtime.

Children at this age enjoy each other so very much that often playtime goes smoothly without too much interference, though it may go much better if a mother or teacher is in the offing to settle disputes, patch up quarrels, provide something new when play bogs down.

Any two Four-year-olds still express the tendency to exclude some unwanted third, but somewhat less than just earlier. Now friendships may be quite positive and based on shared activities and not merely on the exclusion of some unwanted other.

Cooperation, sharing, taking turns now tend to come quite easily to most. Interest may be directed more to the excitement of shared, cooperative activity than to attempts to control the actions of other children. In fact, the Four-year-old's love of big projects often makes the help of several other children necessary.

There is much less difficulty than earlier about owner-

ship of possessions as several can now play cooperatively
with the same material.

Children of this age enjoy the notion of "friend," and
a nursery school teacher can often stimulate a friendship
simply by announcing to a child, "Here is your friend
who wants to play with you."

Fours are not as rigid about interpersonal relations as

they were just earlier, so a mother or teacher can often solve any momentary tangle by humorous verbalization, by shifting the scene of play, or merely by suggesting some interesting elaboration of any current activity.

Or, the child himself may solve his own social problems: "First let me have a turn," or, "It's my turn now. OK?" Or, "Pretty soon will you let me use that red?" or, "Please, may I have my iron now?"

Four-year-olds, obviously, have all the words they need for any and all social relations: "Let's play with this. OK?," "I'm the dairy-farm man. Want some dairy cream? Who goin' help me get milk? Who goin' help me unload the barn?," "Put it on top. Yes, that's pretty good," "Feel my forehead. It's so hot," "My belly button's sticking out." Or, cuttingly, "Richard, you have big ears."

If, in a play group, several should sit at a table, crayoning or playing with clay, there is much interchild interchange. They may quarrel mildly over materials, show the teacher what they have made or what others have made. Or, while they work with their hands, they may discuss topics quite unrelated to what they are doing.

Four's typical violence and exaggeration express themselves in play with friends as in other activities. "I just set your coat on fire," a quite usual Four-year-old may say to his friend. When his friend ignores this bit of (untrue) information, he may repeat, "Can't you see? I set your coat on fire!"

(As a matter of fact, Fours tend to be obsessed by fire. A fire engine may be a favorite Four-year-old present. Or, the child wants a fireman's hat. And above all he may want to be a fireman when he grows up. But at the same time he might be deathly afraid of the fire alarm and need to be protected from his fear.)

Violent and excitable as he may often seem, the child of this age mostly wants his friends to like and approve of him. "OK?" is a frequently used expression: "I'll just take this one now. OK?," "Let's build a garage now. OK?"

In a group situation at this age there is very little isolated play. Children are now tremendously interested in each other as people, and they are also tremendously interested in, and ready for, group activity. Most children in any play group will spend most of their time in rather elaborate constructive or imaginative cooperative play. Frequently, now, children can organize a cooperative activity by themselves, without adult help or suggestion.

They may, as earlier, emphasize imagination. Or, they may emphasize actual construction and activity. One group may, spontaneously and without help, build a large block church and then conduct a service. They may build a store and then sell groceries. They may build a boat and then go for a sail. But their talk about any of these activities may be more important to them than the activity itself.

Friendships are strong at Four. Children not only like to play with their special friends but like to sit with arms around each other and whisper. Even boys can be seen hugging and kissing each other. If one of a pair of friends initiates an activity, such as painting, his friend will probably want to paint, too.

This warm interest in others can, and often does, lead to sex play if children are left unsupervised. Such play is probably not particularly harmful to children, but most parents don't like it. And obviously it can be overindulged in if not put in its right perspective. When it does occur, no one special child should be *blamed*, since any child, no matter how nice his mother may consider him, could be the one who starts it. Careful supervision can usually prevent such play.

But parents need to remember that tensional overflow often does have its outlet through the genital region at this time, especially in boys. Grabbing the penis in a socially tense situation is quite usual. This is no time to tell the child to "stop that." Better to direct the child's mind toward something of interest, such as going on an excursion through the house or yard.

In older Fours, especially in boys, certain children tend

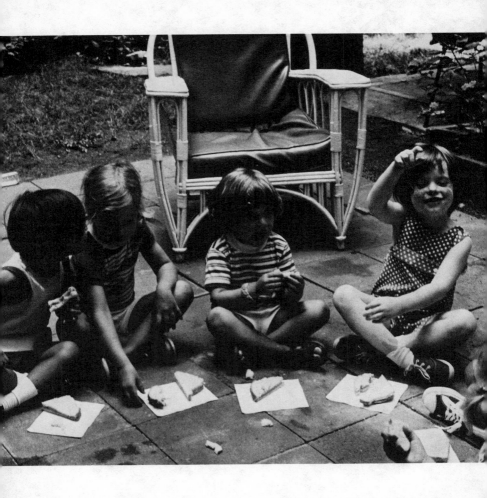

to stand out as leaders. Others in a group quite willingly carry out their orders and do what they say. Girls tend to lead in a more romantic way. In a nursery school group, one or more of the boys may consider that they have fallen madly in love with some special girl, and these friendships may last for several weeks.

In a nursery group there tends to be strong identification with the group. Children will bring in food to share with everybody. They like to invite other children, as

well as teachers, to their homes to visit them. They love parties, and like to celebrate their birthdays, either at school or at home.

SIBLINGS

The Four-year-old can be an aggressive little fellow, with brothers and sisters as well as with those outside the family. Actually he may get on less well with siblings than with others. In a play group he tends to gravitate to those other children who appeal to him and whom he likes —his friends. At home he may be involved with children he has not selected and may not always like—his siblings.

A Four-year-old is usually old enough that unless he is having real emotional problems in growing up and in being superseded by somebody younger, he will much of the time be reasonably good to a baby sibling. But even now he should not be trusted alone with a baby, at least not for any long periods of time, as he is still not entirely predictable. (And if he is one who actively dislikes his baby sibling, they should not be left alone together for even a short time.)

With other siblings, Four is unpredictable. He may play nicely, but he may be extremely quarrelsome and rambunctious, even with those somewhat older than he. It is often surprising to parents that a Four-year-old can, on occasion, get into real trouble with a brother or sister considerably older. In fact, Fours can, for their own reasons, sometimes unfathomed, become extremely aggressive and directive toward much older siblings. Perhaps their own sense of superiority is threatened by greater competence. At any rate, a quite typical command, by a Four-year-old to an older sibling, may be: "Don't do it like that. That's wrong. If you do it again, I'll cut you in pieces and throw you in the garbage."

And though often good to those much younger, a Four-year-old may be surprisingly mean even to a baby, like the boy who, quite unprovoked, said to his little sister, all dressed up in a new pink dress, "Pink, pink, you stink." (Perhaps here he is exercising his sense of superiority.)

Households vary, and children differ. Some, especially quiet little girls, may get along with their brothers and sisters a good part of the time. Others are extremely quarrelsome and "always fighting." When such fighting occurs, parents should: 1) appreciate that fighting among siblings is not only normal but tends to be much enjoyed by them, no matter how much they scream; 2) separate them when possible; 3) figure out what times of day or what situations bring the most difficulty, and then, so far as possible, avoid or minimize those situations.

NURSERY SCHOOL

Though nursery school attendance is not essential for a happy childhood, one of the most satisfactory and exciting opportunities you can offer a Four-year-old is the opportunity of attending a lively, lovely, nonacademic nursery school.

Your normally endowed, characteristically exuberant, bursting-with-energy-and-with-a-desire-for-new-experiences Four-year-old may all too quickly exhaust your own most enthusiastic and generous efforts to keep him entertained. A good nursery school teacher has that second wind so necessary to keep up with the vigorous and demanding child of this age.

Equipment in a good nursery school can, quite naturally, be both more abundant and more varied than even a well-equipped household can be expected to provide.

Teachers, unlike mothers, are not looking after the child in the midst of other duties. Setting up a situation in which the child can fully express his own creative and dramatic interests is her job, her full-time job. And she is less likely to be called on to take part in his play than is his mother at home.

Not only is equipment more plentiful, adult help and guidance more available in a good nursery school than in the ordinary home, but there are all the other children.

Other children at times excite but also at times calm down the sometimes too exuberant Four-year-old. There is perhaps no better learning situation for any child of this age than one in which he finds himself at the tender mercy of his contemporaries. Here, rather than from books or in forced learning situations, is where the child of this age *really* learns.

However, there are some children who either resist going to nursery school or who tend to develop one cold after another to such an extent that the disadvantages of the school experience may seem to outweigh its advantages. Three is the ideal nursery school age. Four demands more of school, and if it is not up to his liking he may prefer to stay at home.

There is much at home to please the child of Four. He loves all the things that happen there—the arrival of the deliveryman, the milkman, the garbageman, the mailman. He re-enacts all these activities in his own yard with such simple props as big cartons or boxes and odds and ends of toy equipment.

And, above all, whether nursery school is part of his life or not, he likes to go neighborhood visiting, just to talk. How he loves to talk to an older person who has the time and interest! But limits must be set even to this, and a parent must see to it that such visits do not last too long.

chapter three
TECHNIQUES

The techniques with which one can best handle the bouncy Four-year-old stem directly from a knowledge of his basic personality. Obviously, the better you understand him, the better job you will do in helping him behave in ways that will please you rather than grieve you.

To begin with, Four is one who loves adventures. Share them with him. Create them for him. A simple trip around your own neighborhood, with its inevitable points of interest, takes on new luster when seen through the enthusiastic eyes of a Four-year-old. And when you plan an excursion, plan it with him in mind. A short walk, perhaps past a spot where a new building is going up (or, better still, being torn down), and an ice-cream cone on the way back will be a lot more satisfactory to a Four-year-old than a cultural expedition to a nearby town.

The best way to calm Four down when some of his wilder ways (his profanity, his boasting, his supersilly way of talking) bother you is to ignore him. "He only does it to annoy," as the old rhyme tells us. So, if you show that you not only are not annoyed but do not even notice, the thrill of profanity or exaggeration dies down, in most, rather quickly.

An opposite technique, and one that is more fun and perhaps equally effective, is to join in and enjoy. You will

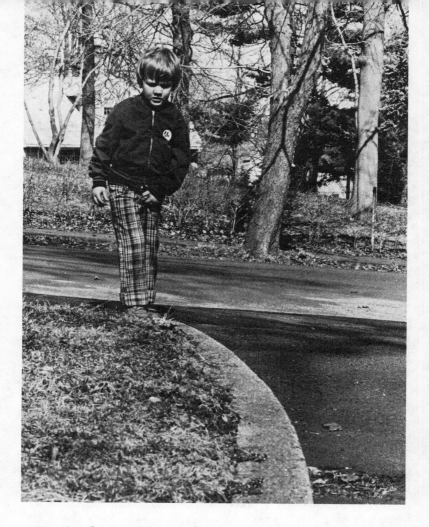

not enjoy his profanity, but you can often enjoy his exaggerated stories by countering with your own—obvious—exaggeration. That is, rein in when you feel that you absolutely need to, but do not always rein in.

Certainly you can join in with and truly enjoy some of the wonderfully silly poems and stories now available for the Four-year-old. You haven't lived if you have never shared with a Four-year-old the delightful nonsense of a book such as Ruth Kraus's *I Want to Paint My Bathroom Blue*, which tells you of

26

A doorknob a doorknob, a deer little doorknob.
A deerknob a deerknob, a door little deerknob.

Or, try some of the gorgeous rhymes in *Somebody Else's
Nut Tree*, also by Ruth Kraus:

> There was a girl
> and she had a cat
> and a dog
> and a chicken
> and she wanted a horse.
> On her birthday
> she got a horse
> and that day the horse had horses.

Four loves his own familiar stories and songs, but, unlike the just-earlier child who must have everything just
so, he may enjoy having a familiar story or song read or
sung in a silly way. Thus, "Twinkle twinkle little star"
might become "A bat and a rat sat on a hat." With each
repetition, the song may be sillier and sillier. Many parents find that they are better at these games and exaggera-
tions than they thought they were.

A very important thing for any parent of a Four-year-
old is to try not to be aroused in a negative way by his
often unacceptable behavior. If you appreciate that this
kind of behavior is potentially there, you are less likely to
be thrown by it.

If your child attacks you, as he sometimes will, with
rude remarks, play a game of "insulting" to release his
(or your own) pent-up feelings as though your name calling were real. Try such foolish epithets as, for instance,
"You're a toasted marshmallow," "You're a squashed
worm," until laughter takes over.

To be certain that you take the time for the excursions
and adventures that the Four-year-old so loves, especially
if you are very busy with his younger brother or sister,
you may like to set aside one afternoon a week, or part of

an afternoon, that will be *his*. He may choose (from a list prepared by you to be sure that things don't get *too* wild) the destination or activity that will please him for that particular week. He (or she) may even like to keep a little notebook, with considerable help from you, of course, that tells about these weekly excursions.

Since the child of this age does tend to go out-of-bounds, you will need, for safety, to find the most effective way of containing him within what you consider to be acceptable physical limits. Environmental restrictions such as gates or closed doors are not as effective as earlier, but most at this age do respond pretty well to verbal restrictions, such as "as far as the corner." In fact, the Four-year-old seems to like and respect boundaries and limits, which he doesn't have within himself. He seems to appreciate it when you supply them.

Most respond rather well to the statement, "It's the rule that . . . ," even when they do not understand why it is the rule. The statement "It's the rule" can, of course, apply to almost any situation throughout the day. It is wise, however, to use it only in fairly big and general situations, such as, "It's the rule that we don't hit other children," or, "It's the rule that we don't grab other people's toys." Don't waste this good technique or fritter it away on single situations, such as by saying, "It's the rule that you mustn't hit Johnny."

"It isn't fair" is another similar stricture that many will respond to even when they don't fully understand it.

Boundaries, or at least *shape*, can be provided if you give your Four-year-old a structure within which he can function. If, for example, he is visiting his grandmother, and his behavior becomes a little too wild, she can help him by telling him, "You are the *guest*." She can then outline a few restrictions that pertain to *guest*'s behavior, and it may be interesting enough to him to be a guest that he may to a large extent conform to reasonable restrictions.

With some boys and girls, a very good technique at this

age is bargaining. If it bothers you to do this, or if it seems too much like bribing, don't do it. But with Fours many parents find that a little bargaining goes a long way. That is, you give a little, and your child may be willing and able to give a little in return.

Since this is an age when children love "tricks" and new ways of doing things, sometimes, if a child balks or stalls, you can motivate him by suggesting that he hop or skip toward some desired destination.

Transitions do not present the difficulty they did some six months earlier, but if there is trouble with transitions this can often be countered by enthusiastic talk about the next proposed activity.

One general rule that may save you and your child much anguish is to try to avoid known trouble areas. There may be some things you do together, or some situations, that almost inevitably spell trouble. When you have identified such an area, do what you can to change the whole situation, instead of allowing it to arise and then disciplining on the spot.

One thing that from now on can make a great deal of difficulty is that most children *hate* it when their mother is on the telephone, especially when her conversations run on and on. They hate it; they behave badly and get into trouble and then make a fuss; and then their mother scolds and yells and punishes.

It is probably hard for a mother who may feel that she has little enough fun or time to herself during the day to appreciate how shut out a child feels when his mother is gossiping on the phone. It would be an act of great kindness, and would prevent much bad behavior and the accompanying need for punishment, if long, chatty phone calls could be restricted to some time when your child is having his nap or is otherwise out of the room.

A child of this age, since he so loves silliness, may respond better to some silly noun, adjective, or verb than to a more conventional instruction. If you tell him not to push a friend, he may go right on pushing. If you tell him, "Don't be a goober [pusher]," he may respond more positively.

Although positive instructions tend to work better than negative—that is, tell him what you want him to do, not what you do *not* want him to do—the negative can at times be used effectively. An exaggeration of the negative, such as "Never, never, never!," if expressed forcefully, may engage his attention and his compliance.

It's best, in general, though, to keep things positive if you can. If you tell a child how nicely he is going to behave, he sometimes does so.

As just earlier, the child tends to respond very well to the notion of newness. Such words as "different," "surprise," "guess what" are still highly effective as motivators.

Or, some made-up word that has specific meaning only to the child and his mother, such as "cushalamacree," may at times be extremely useful. Such a word can roll off Four's tongue with ease and enjoyment. And when its meaning is secret, it can produce magic results, to the astonishment of those not in the know.

Thus one girl of Four always ran and hid when her mother came to fetch her from a friend's house. But just the saying of that special word, by her mother, helped her to organize at once, helped her gather up her things and walk out the door holding her mother's hand, feeling safe in the knowledge of this word that nobody else understood.

Whispering may, as just earlier, be more effective than shouting. At least it calms the child and catches his attention.

Distraction, at any preschool age, can be, as some have put it, a truly "magic wand." This technique will be less necessary with a fluid, fast, ever-changing Four-year-old than with the child just younger. But even at Four your boy or girl may sometimes get stuck on a point, and the two of you may find yourselves at loggerheads. If this occurs, rather than fight things through, you may be best advised to change the subject or the scene very quickly by any distracting device that may occur to you.

Since Fours love exaggeration, in your efforts to motivate or restrain, as well as in your efforts to entertain, you will find exaggeration to be very effective. "As big as the world," "in ten million years," or just plain silly language, such as "mitsy, bitsy, witsy," "goofy, woofy, spoofy," can often interest or distract when distraction is needed.

At Four, perhaps even more than at other ages, praise and compliments work wonders. Later on, children may be aware of exaggeration; but no compliment and no amount of compliments seem too much for Four's insatiable appetite. You can comment on a handsome shirt, a pretty dress, nice new shoes. Or, you can praise the way the child accomplishes any given task or any creative activity. Or, if he is playing with others, you can praise his relations with others: "I bet he appreciated the way you helped him with that."

In fact, if you don't praise enough, he will praise himself. You can often hear your Four-year-old expostulate, "I'm smart." You can smile and agree with him.

You can always win by telling the child how much you love him. It is easy and natural to criticize and to try to improve your child. If words of praise come less naturally, then they need to be cultivated.

Along this same line, remember that at this or any other age the simple act of conversing with your child can work wonders. Almost any child loves to feel that he has his parent's full attention, and he loves to talk. If you want to know what is on your child's mind, you don't necessarily need to ask directly. Just talk with him. Good communication is vital in those difficult teen years soon to come, but it is important even here. So, listen to your child and talk to him. Conversation provides one of the best routes to a good relationship, and in the final analysis *it is your relationship with your child even more than the use of good techniques that gets you smoothly through the day.*

There is one special aspect of the world today, often criticized and seldom praised, that can nevertheless help you out beautifully, especially on a rainy day. Do take advantage, freely though carefully, of one of the great new things society has to offer for the preschooler—television. All of a group of Four-year-olds recently studied by us did watch television.

All parents of boys and nearly all parents of girls felt strongly that TV did add to their children's lives—if only to their enjoyment. So, don't be afraid, within reason, to take advantage of what your television screen has to offer. It can be one of your best techniques for filling some of the day and for meeting Four's high demand for excitement, activity, and drama.

The choice of suitable programs may be difficult, especially if there are older siblings. So, try to select some one program that you consider good for your child that will become *his* program. Then he can be more easily controlled in not being exposed to other programs that may be both frightening and beyond his comprehension.

And if some program he watches attempts to teach letters and numbers or sizes and shapes, and he responds to this teaching, let his interest be your guide. It won't make him smarter, and it probably won't make him read any earlier than he otherwise would have. And it is just as well not to encourage him to show off any such skill to friends and neighbors. But if you and he enjoy this exercise, fine!

Last of all, remember that once you appreciate what a child of this age (or any age) *is* like, it helps you to appreciate what he *will* like. You can tailor your techniques accordingly.

DISCIPLINE

This discussion of techniques attempts to convey, at least implicitly, our attitude about discipline. Discipline, as most of you appreciate, is not the same thing as punishment. Discipline, rather, is a way of setting up the child's life situation so that good, effective, desirable behavior becomes possible. Techniques themselves are a form of discipline.

As to your own *philosophy* of discipline, you may be an old-fashioned, authoritarian parent who expects your child to do what you tell him to, regardless, even when the demand may be unreasonable or beyond his ability. You may be a *permissive* parent who permits anything and allows the child to follow his own whim.

Or you may, as we recommend, follow a policy of what we call *informed permissiveness* (or controlled flexibility). That is, you try to fit your demands and expectations to things that it is possible for a child with the maturity level and personality of your own to perform. Knowing that your demands are reasonable, you make them, firmly and consistently.

The more effectively you manage this, the better your discipline, the fewer will be the incidents of rebellion, disobedience, or "bad" behavior, and the less need for punishment. (Though no parent succeeds entirely. There will, in any family, be some unhappy incidents.)

As to what kind of punishment you should use, if and when punishment becomes necessary, this depends partly on your own temperament and partly on what works with your child. Temporary isolation works with some. Deprivation of privileges works with others. Some respond to scolding, some to more physical measures. An occasional spanking, if it works, is not immoral; but spanking should never be relied on as a chief form of punishment.

The so-called behavior-modification people hold that you can get any child to do anything you want him to by praising the good and ignoring the bad. This kind of handling seems complicated or unnatural to some, but for those of you who would like to try it, we suggest that you read *For Love of Children* by Roger W. McIntire.

Other disciplinarians have used (for some sixty years now), with reasonable success, a common sense kind of discipline called "logical consequences." That is, if the child does something he shouldn't do, or fails to do something he should, he must take the consequences. For example, he leaves his tricycle outside, and it gets stolen.

Each of you will, of course, work out your own philosophy of discipline and methods of discipline, keeping in mind both your own temperament and that of your child. Most important of all, perhaps, is that, if possible, Mother and Father agree, if not about every detail, at least about the basic approach. Two parents working together, especially if they have a reasonably good understanding of what it is reasonable to expect of their particular child, have a very good chance of helping him to behave in a comfortable and effective manner, at least much of the time.

THINGS TO AVOID

1. Don't worry excessively if your Four-year-old, as he very likely will, goes out-of-bounds. A certain extra exuberance is natural, usual, and quite probably necessary at this age to give balance between uncertain Three-and-a-half and quiet, adaptable Five.

2. Don't fuss too much and certainly don't worry if your boy or girl lies, swears, and/or exaggerates. Such behaviors are almost the essence of Four-year-oldness. You can, and undoubtedly will, discourage and disapprove of such behaviors, but try not to worry about them.

3. In fact, try to avoid excessive "moral" judgments about your child's often somewhat antisocial behavior. In another year he or she may be as conventional, as docile, as conforming as you please.

4. Avoid that wild search for things that will motivate an uninterested or underactive child. *Success* is the best motivator at any age. The likelihood is that any child will be motivated to activity if you provide for him materials and opportunities that by his temperament and matu-

rity level he will be able to cope with and to deal with effectively.

5. Don't worry that you should be doing something to increase your child's IQ. Basic intelligence level is, so far as we know, largely determined by genetic factors. You can and should give all children reasonable stimulation, but don't be self-conscious about level or quality of intelligence.

6. Don't feel that you should be teaching your Four-year-old to read. Read to him. Make books available. And when the time comes that he starts picking out initial letters in books or asking, "What does S T O P spell?," by all means respond. But don't push. Be sure that any interest in reading (or in numbers) that may be shown is his and not merely your own.

7. If your child is still sucking his thumb, fondling his blanket, or indulging in any other earlier tensional outlets, try not to feel that it is now "time" that he give these up. Another few months may see the behavior ended.

8. Don't feel that you have a "bed-wetting problem" if your child still wets the bed at night—some nights or even every night. Many quite normal children do not develop the ability to stay dry until they are Five or even Six, or even later. (Pad them up good and tight to save on laundry, and don't fuss or worry.)

9. Don't blame your child's playmates for behaviors in him or her that you don't like—exhibitionism, bad language, sex play, and the like. Today it may be a neighboring child who initiates the activity. Tomorrow it may be your own!

10. Don't fail to enjoy this extremely amusing, lively, enthusiastic age while it lasts, even though some aspects of your child's behavior may not be entirely charming.

chapter four
ACCOMPLISHMENTS
AND ABILITIES

As long as your boy or girl is developing in what seems to you a reasonably normal way, if he behaves about as other children in your family have at his same age, or about the way other children in the neighborhood seem to do at his age, you should not be too self-conscious about specific abilities and inabilities.

It is important to remember that intelligence and maturity are two separate things. A child may obviously be very bright, but young for his age. Or, he may be not so bright, but mature for his age. And whether he is bright or not so bright, mature or immature, keep in mind two important things.

First of all, remember that intelligence is to a large extent an inherited capacity. You will, of course, want to give your child all the reasonable stimulation possible, make his life full and interesting. But even your best efforts will not, in all likelihood, make him more intelligent than nature intended. Even if he is not one of the more superior, intellectually, there can be a very good life ahead for him if you do not make his lack of A-quality intelligence a matter for major concern.

The same with maturity. Our expectations of what a Four-year-old should be able to accomplish are only averages, and a child might be quite a bit ahead of, or quite a bit behind, any time schedule that we or others set up, and still be perfectly normal. If your Four-year-old by chance does not seem quite up to usual Four-year-old maturity standards, this may mean that, when the time comes, you will want to have him go a bit more slowly in school than the law permits, but it still is not necessarily a cause for anxiety.

Any listing of the activities and accomplishments of the supposedly typical child of any age should be preceded with the clear warning that perhaps there actually *is* no truly "typical" child. When we describe Four-year-old behavior (or, for that matter, behavior typical of any age), we mean that most or many children of that age do behave that way.

But there will be many children who, because they follow the usual path of behavior change at a faster or slower rate than the average, will reach the behavior in question sooner or later than the average time. There will be many others who, because of their own individual personality, may actually never behave in quite that special way.

Consider an age characteristic such as the expansiveness and out-of-bounds behavior that we think of as so highly typical of the Four-year-old. If you have a gentle, quiet, moderate, restrained little boy or girl, he or she will in all likelihood be more expansive at this age than at Three or Five, but may not even at this lively age go to any great extremes. Or, if his or her whole rate of development may be a little on the slow side, even though intellectual endowment may be fully adequate, it could be on toward Five before the customary Four-year-old expansiveness appears. That is, the behavior in question may come in early or late.

As to specific abilities described in this chapter, here, too, you must allow your boy or girl considerable leeway. A child could be as much as a year ahead of, or behind, any supposed "average" and still be quite within normal limits.

For instance, interest in books and in formal learning varies tremendously. Or, a child may be ahead of age in some one behavior (language behavior, for instance) and not up to age in motor behavior. Each child has his own individual rate and pattern of growth.

MOTOR BEHAVIOR

Your typical Four-year-old, with his high drive, enthusiasm, expansiveness, is a motor person *par excellence.* He loves to run. He loves to climb. He loves to gallop. He loves sheer movement for its own sake. And, he loves to talk, to shout, to carry on. He loves exaggeration, of sound and movement as well as of actual words. He loves to talk about big (or enormous) things, and he loves to make big things. His drawing strokes are dashing, and he needs lots of room for his productions.

His drive seems boundless. There is strength and push behind everything he does, and he gives the impression of being ready for anything. A difficult motor situation, which may have brought out all his sensitivity and insecurity six months earlier, is now a welcome challenge. He loves the difficult and the daring. He loves the different. He loves to show that he is master of space and incline.

As we've said before Four is speedy. There is a quickness of decision and of action apparent in almost everything he does. He moves quickly and with very little wasted motion.

Four coordinates the movements of the parts of his body much better than formerly. In fact, he often shows a remarkably good ability to move his body effectively and to move it in relation to other things in the world. His increasingly good sense of balance allows him to play games requiring complex motor skills and to enjoy bodybuilding skills and stunts. This may be a good time to introduce a few body exercises such as toe or knee touching, or making angels in the snow. The child appears especially to take pleasure in stunts that stimulate the semicircular canals: whirling, swinging, somersaulting.

In fact, there seems to be an inner awareness of what he or she can do. More feelings seem to be unfolding now, combining the control of physical ability to move with the awareness of self and feelings inside one's body. This is why a child of this age enjoys creative movement, with perhaps the addition of drumbeat or song. (An inner awareness is also evident in his interest in stomach, heart, and bones. His frequent reporting of stomachaches makes one aware of this concern.)

At times, his motor drive is so extreme that if he is *not*

given opportunities for motor activity, for blowing off
steam, he may become a difficult young person for those
in charge to manage. If any Four-year-old is giving you
trouble with his exuberant demand for action and variety,
see to it that he spends as much time as possible out-of-
doors, and hopefully that he is provided with plenty of
physical equipment that will give him the opportunity to
use and display his muscular effectiveness. He feels his
muscles in activity, and he also wants *you* to feel his
muscles and to tell him how strong he is. He may like to
tell you, "I'm tough!"

Specific motor abilities of both balance and action have
improved impressively in the past few months. The child
not only walks upstairs a foot to a step but also walks
down a foot to a step, at least on the last few steps. He
can stand on one foot from four to eight seconds, can skip
on one foot. He can accomplish either a running or a
standing broad jump. He can jump down from a two-foot
height with feet together. He can hop on his toes with
both feet off the ground at the same time, seven or eight
times in five seconds.

Many can learn to use roller skates. And some of the
better coordinated can even ride a small bicycle if it is
equipped with training wheels.

By Four, most children have acquired strength, ease,
and facility in the use of their legs, which lend considerable grace to their movements. Most walk with long, swinging steps, in the adult style.

Boys, especially, and some girls, are rapidly becoming
athletic, and take real pride in attempting motor stunts
that require delicate balance. In ball play, most now use
their hands more than their arms in catching a small ball.
They can judge their direction of throwing better now
than they did just earlier. Boys throw a ball overhand with
a horizontal motion from above or to the right of their
shoulder; girls from above the shoulder with a downward
sweep.

Fingers are now much more skilled than earlier and

under better control. Children can handle small objects, button or unbutton buttons, lace shoes, string even rather small beads. Most can cut on a line with scissors and can carry a cup of water without spilling. They enjoy games that involve many little pieces that need to be manipulated.

Though the Four-year-old is by nature active and athletic and loves to cover considerable space both on the level and in climbing, his increased attention span means that he can stay longer than he could before in a single area of activity. In fact, though he so greatly loves physical activity, he is able to sit for relatively long periods of time at an especially interesting manual task.

Hyperactivity. We hear a good deal nowadays about a way of behaving that has probably always been with us but that currently has a new name. When a child is over-active and seems never to stay still, can't quiet down, can't stick with one thing, can't turn his motor off even if he wants to, we label his behavior *hyperactivity.*

The truly hyperactive child finds it almost impossible to slow down and concentrate. As a preschooler he wears everybody out, and as he grows older he frequently finds it difficult or impossible to behave "properly" or to succeed in school because of his overactivity.

It is often difficult for parents of the active preschooler who is quite normally "always on the go," always "into everything," to distinguish between normal preschool activity and real hyperactivity. Your best bet is to check with your own doctor or child specialist.

If no such help is available, you may like to use a checklist offered by Dr. William Crook. In *Can Your Child Read? Is He Hyperactive?* he lists thirty-five behaviors characteristic of hyperactivity (or hyperkinesis) and suggests that you rate your own child as to how often he displays each of them.

Give a score of 0 if your rating is "rarely or never"; a score of 1 if it is "occasionally"; a score of 2 if it is "often"; a score of 3 if it is "usually or constantly." The highest

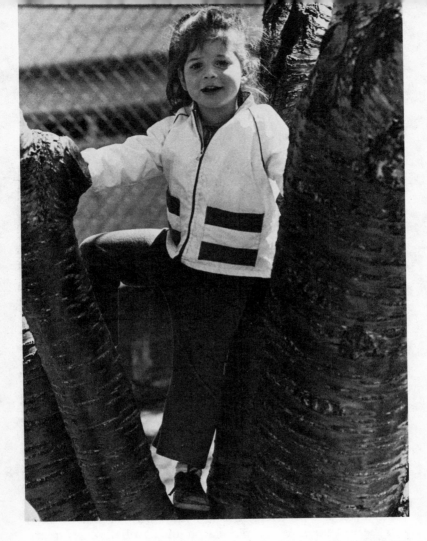

score possible would be 105. Any score over 60 suggests the probability that your child is hyperkinetic. (But remember, any child at times may be expected to show almost any of the behaviors characteristic of hyperkinesis. It is the extent and frequency of his behavior that determines the diagnosis.)

The kinds of questions asked include the following: Is he overactive? Does he not finish projects? Does he have trouble sitting still at mealtime? Does he wear out his toys? Is he generally destructive? Is he impatient, accident-prone, clumsy? Does he get into things? Is he always on the go?

VISUAL BEHAVIOR[1]

There is a fluidity, flexibility, and looseness in the visual patterns of the typical Four-year-old. He is definitely more stable visually than he was at Three, and definitely more outgoing in his visual response. His attention is to the horizon, and he often goes far afield in his pursuit of that horizon.

As his space world enlarges, he enjoys outdoor play, while indoors he prefers not to be confined to a single room or play area. In nursery school, his activities spill over from one room to the next, and even into hallways. Outgoing he is. Boundaries need to be carefully established lest he go too far and endanger himself, such as following a dog across the thin ice of a pond.

Four's high energy drive results in a new burst of physical activity. He is a charmer who has trouble telling the difference between fact and fable. He exaggerates as he practices using new and big words. He may roll his eyes in a delightful manner as he talks.

There is greater interest and participation, now, in both gross and fine visual-motor activities. Outside, he likes climbing equipment, ball play, a tricycle, and sometimes even a two-wheeler. The availability of plastic bats and balls makes a simple game of baseball even more fun. The newer, small-size two-wheel bikes make learning to ride without training wheels easier. If the youngster can touch the ground while the bike is upright, he will have less trouble learning.

The secret to balancing on a bike is through the hands, which tend to be in better control if the trunk is bent forward. Once a child can trust his hands, he'll be able to ride. Newer versions of the old-fashioned tricycle, with the sitting area closer to the ground, reduce the danger of

tipping. The heightened motor activity is not limited to boys alone. Girls enjoy it, too.

Drawing, coloring, and painting are becoming more successful for the Four-year-old than they were earlier. A good pair of blunt scissors is appreciated by the young craftsman or craftswoman. Puzzles, blocks, and other building materials are enjoyed. Four may try his hand at hammering nails—best into a log that does not demand precision.

Seeing is now action oriented. For this reason, the child may like to sit close to the television as if participating in the action on the screen. Parents should remember that television viewing is a poor substitute for activity at this action-oriented age.

Spatial language is well developed. The child can now react correctly to such prepositions as "on," "under," "in back of," "beside" or "in front of," when asked to place a ball in relation to a chair. And the child is now better than he was at following directions at home. He can find his own clothes. He understands about picking up toys and putting them away.

If there has not yet been a visual or eye examination, now is a good time to have it. Four can attend to directions, answer questions, and he is capable of concentrating for a period of fifteen to twenty minutes while such an examination is being made. When he has had enough, he may get down from the examining chair and leave the room. He escapes!

Good cooperation is possible if the examiner works quickly. The Four-year-old responds well to the simple E letter test, or he may know some of his letters, especially those in his name. Both of his eyes participate in the total act of seeing. There is better eye teaming and less need than earlier to support vision by bringing hands into the seeing act. There should be a normal amount of farsightedness measurable. His visual acuity may be close to 20/20 if not already there.

ADAPTIVE BEHAVIOR AND PLAY

Wild as your Four-year-old may be in motor ways, and even emotionally, when it comes to working with his hands you may be surprised to find a beautiful fining down. Eyes and hands coordinate with increasing skill, and fingers increase in their ability to make even rather fine and intricate adjustments.

Four can do many things that his Three-year-old self could not accomplish. Building with cubes becomes so increasingly skillful that he can now imitate a four-cube gate with delicately tipped center cube. By Four-and-a-half, he can make such a gate from a model, without watching it being built.

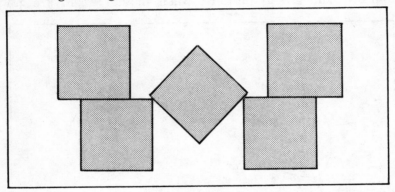

Figure 2

With pencil or crayon, too, he is becoming increasingly skillful. Whereas at Three he could imitate a cross, he can now *copy* a cross if you show him a drawing of one. And, at Four-and-a-half he can copy a square, a rather mature skill.

Or, he can copy the order of a group of things, such as stringing differently colored or differently shaped beads in the order provided in a model. Many can match all shapes, such as square, circle, star, etc., in a ten-hole formboard.

If asked to draw a person, the child can make a recognizable person, though it may still have a potato-shaped body and facial features may be included inside this body. Or, he may be able to draw a man with head and eyes, body, arms, and legs.

If asked to complete an Incomplete Man, most can now add five parts, including, usually, leg and foot, arm and hand, eyes or hair or ear. At Four-and-a-half, most add seven parts to the Incomplete Man—those seen at Four, plus, in many, a body line in the neck area—and their man often appears rather wild, with longish hair, longer arm and leg than six months earlier. Many now, with their characteristic special interest in bathrooms and belly buttons, add a belly button to their man. (*See* Figure 3.)

Four years   Four-and-a-half years

Figure 3
Typical Response to the Gesell Incomplete Man Test

Most children now really enjoy drawing things, and many enjoy coloring books, filling in the outlines reasonably well. Many adults feel that coloring books deaden the child's presumably innate artistic ability. We feel that they are not harmful if you are careful also to permit the child free artistic expression. Actually, many Fours especially enjoy tracing over the lines of the figure in a coloring book. They also enjoy drawings that provide dotted lines that when linked up make a picture.

The use of scissors is becoming rather effective. Many can cut on a line well enough to cut out pictures and then paste them onto paper or into a notebook in consecutive order. Or, they can cut a picture into parts and then put it back together again, puzzle-fashion. They also enjoy large and not too complicated picture puzzles, response to such puzzles becoming increasingly adept as they move on toward Five.

Adaptive behavior that also includes language expression may now have developed to the point that the child can give likenesses and differences between familiar objects. Or, he can tell the biggest and the longest of three things, and can order five blocks from the heaviest to the lightest, with few mistakes. He masters form both in matching and in placing.

Some Fours, especially older Fours, are becoming much interested in trying to print their letters and numbers. Some may even be able to print their whole first name, though usually in large, two-inch-high, capital letters. Though children should never be pushed into this kind of activity, when it occurs *spontaneously* it should be supported and encouraged, as should early efforts to read.

Play. Four's playtime is seldom a problem. He is ready for anything. Almost any kind of toy or material appeals, and whatever is lacking can often be made up for by his vivid, fertile imagination.

But he moves so rapidly, running through materials and situations and even space, that he may need a rather large quantity of whatever it is that he (or she) is using. Parents need to budget larger supplies of material, such as paper, at this age, but at the same time they need to determine limits of use. They will also find that it is better to set these limits prior to an activity than to clamp down when it is in full swing.

Fours may be happiest with rather active gross motor play, preferably out-of-doors. Most enjoy fully any opportunity for outdoor play. This does not have to be constructive or planned for. Almost any Four-year-old, with his exuberant energy, his vivid imagination, and his ability to turn almost anything into a good play opportunity, loves to be outside where space permits him the kind of activity he so much enjoys.

By Four, or certainly by Four-and-a-half, most can play outside in their own yard unsupervised, with only occasional checking by a parent.

One can readily see why the freer, more outdoor-oriented activities of the usual nursery school are better for the Four-and-a-half-year-old than the more structured and confined, indoor, kindergarten types of activities offered by some schools.

A Jungle Gym provides ideal equipment for the Four-year-old to climb on or on which to perform interesting tricks, such as hanging upside down or holding on with one hand. A slide for sliding, a good place to dig, a flat surface on which to ride his trusty tricycle will obviously add to his enjoyment, but even a relatively unequipped yard can be turned, by him, into a joyous place to play.

Hopefully, in summer there may be a short visit at the beach or in the country. Four is not too young to begin to appreciate the birds and trees and flowers—even though, unfortunately, many children in our cities are, and remain, far away from all the wonders of nature. Watch a Four-year-old hold a flower in his hand. Or a bug. He is full of awe and wonder.

In fact, for many, religious stirrings are there, and God may become a part of the child's vocabulary, his being, and his thinking. One Four-and-a-half-year-old boy, when asked what he liked best, summed up his feelings with "I love the sky and the mountains and the flowers and the whole world." The concept of wholeness now includes the

world, and Four may even think that the Fourth of July is the whole world's birthday, not just that of the United States.

Both boys and girls, but especially boys, relish almost any vigorous physical activity, such as riding their tricycle fast, sliding, digging. Building with big blocks is also a favorite physical, as well as constructive, activity. Big blocks are often combined into impressive structures—houses, stories, forts. The child's big muscles seem to want to lift heavy objects. Once such structures are built, children often play imaginative games inside. (Or, they love any corner of a room, any secret place where they can have privacy to giggle and whisper.)

Or, big blocks may be combined with trucks and wagons, or cars and trains. Boys, especially, may construct elaborate roads and tunnels or tracks, one or two leaders often bossing a "gang" of workers. Whether they combine them with block structures or not, boys love cars and trucks and trains and airplanes—anything with wheels.

Fours, also, in their search for adventure and for anything new, very much appreciate excursions, exploring trips, visits to museums, or even simple walks in their own neighborhoods.

Four's vivid imagination often leads to dramatic play of the most creative sort. No kind of "pretend" is beyond him. Within half an hour, children in a group may be monsters, astronauts, robbers, storekeepers. Or, the child may pretend he is a photographer taking somebody's picture with a Polaroid camera, waiting a minute, and then showing the imaginary result.

Of course, inevitably, they play house, little girls usually taking the part of mothers, grandmothers, and babies; boys of fathers, grandfathers, or people coming to sell something. (Or, if no better role is available, that of the family dog.) Playing store is almost as popular as playing house, with everyone wanting to be the salesperson behind the counter.

Or, less imaginatively, children love to "help" wash cars, wash floors, wash windows. In fact, almost any sort of water play is extremely popular. Parents tend not to be too friendly toward this. They are afraid that their children will spill the water or get themselves wet. With a little effort and ingenuity, most could make more readily available this interesting, satisfying, and soothing kind of play. Blowing bubbles is especially delightful to Four and can as a rule be quite easily controlled.

Doll play, the most conventional form of imaginary play, is becoming increasingly elaborate. Dolls go to a picnic, go to nursery school, or even move to another city.

Dressing up is very big at Four. Boys as well as girls love to dress up, preferably in adult clothes. Boys, as a rule, prefer cowboy hats and holsters; girls love long gowns, veils, hats, handbags. Boys are less likely than earlier to dress up in high-heeled shoes or women's hats. Make-believe weddings, with the bride, especially, dressed elaborately from the old-clothes box, are popular.

All the usual creative activities are still great favorites: crayoning, painting, fingerpainting, cutting, pasting. Some are starting to make letters and numbers spontaneously. Play-Doh and clay are still much used by younger Fours, but as children move on toward Five this kind of play may seem too tame for them.

Many other forms of earlier play are still enjoyed. Children like to build with plastic blocks or tiles or Lego or Tinkertoys or small wooden blocks. Most Fours like dominos or puzzles or simple card games. As they move on toward Five, they may begin to like games where points are scored, though it will require a mother or teacher to tell them how many points they have earned. Also, winning and being first are very important.

Books are still great favorites with most and make up a big part of the lives of many Four-year-olds. Whether being read to or "reading" for oneself, many now have special favorites and can stay a long time with a single book. This is the age when humor in stories is especially appreciated. Nearly all love such silly books as *I Want to Paint My Bathroom Blue, Somebody Else's Nut Tree*, or Stoo Hemple's *Silly Book*.

By Four, tastes in reading, aside from the general love of the ridiculous, are often rather individual and well defined. Some like whimsical or imaginative stories like *Curious George, Mulberry Street*, or *McGillicut's Pool*. Others prefer books about "real" things.

Since Four is an "out-of-bounds" age, it is not too surprising to find that the Four-year-old has a voracious appetite for the dramatic, and that no storied situation seems fantastic enough to overtax his constantly inventive imagination. Thus, complexity of event and even horror of situation seem to add value to many of the Four-year-old's favorite stories. Executioners and miraculous rescues from destruction have much the same appeal that the

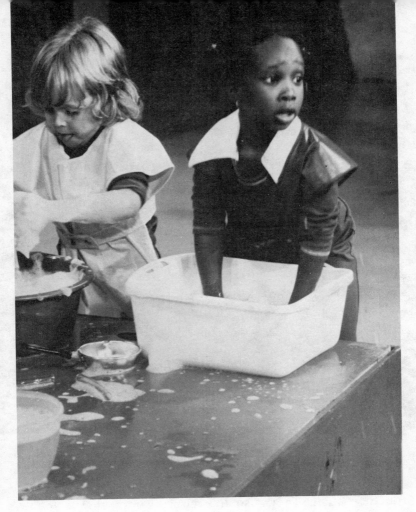

Grimms' fairy tales afford. However, caution must be exercised to protect the vulnerable child who cannot tolerate a fear- or tension-provoking story.

Children of this age like complexity in illustrations. They enjoy an abundance and diversity of tiny details. Whereas the Two-year-old preferred a single large picture to a page, the Four-year-old delights in searching out minutiae in illustrations to stimulate and satisfy his constantly expanding interest and imagination.

Music is now a source of great enjoyment for many— not only the somewhat passive pleasure of listening to

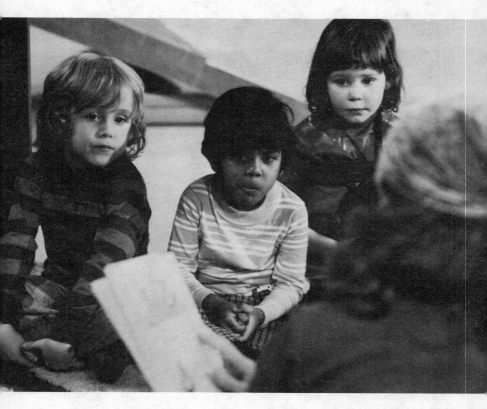

favorite records but, especially in groups, more active participation. Older Fours can beat out a rhythm rather well and may like to "conduct" group singing with a conductor's stick. They also like circle games that combine singing and skipping around.

Television, as mentioned earlier, is becoming of increasing interest. Nearly all Four-year-olds do watch television except in those rare instances where there is no set in the household. Girls, usually more amenable, as a rule accept their parents' ideas of what and when to watch. Boys, too, usually accept parents' decisions as how long they should watch, though they may on occasion object to their parents' choice of programs for them.

Most parents do admit that, though it may create some problems, television viewing does add to the young child's life since it keeps him quiet and entertained. Many do feel that it must be limited or it becomes too engrossing. Some object because they feel that it is a passive activity. Others complain that it gives a distorted view of life. Most adults, however, do appreciate the relief it gives them, even while they may complain.

Programs watched most at this age include (1975) in order of popularity: cartoons, "Lassie," "The Brady Bunch," "Captain Kangaroo," "The Lucy Show," "The Flintstones," and "Sesame Street."

Pets provide a good deal of pleasure and experience about life for Fours as for children of other ages. There is much to be learned from pets, and if not too much is expected from him the young child can learn a great deal not only about living and growing but also about responsibility from the care of simple and relatively undemanding pets. But if the parent will not take the major responsibility, it may be best not to have a pet.

Short-time pets—snakes, frogs, caterpillars that can be contained in a terrarium—can offer much interest and excitement and may need not too much care. And turtles are all-time favorites. They may even develop a personality for the child and are often much loved.

Even less demanding is the care of sturdy plants, which still require a certain amount of responsibility. Even a Four-year-old can identify strongly and can enjoy the fact that his plant is surviving and growing partly because of the care he may be giving it.

LANGUAGE AND OTHERS

The Four-year-old tends to be an egocentric little person, but his egocentricity, perhaps happily, includes his contemporaries. Any Four-year-old who may be playing in a group that includes other children and one or two adults directs nearly all his conversation to the other children and is also reasonably responsive to conversation directed to him by the other children. Though he may from time to time speak to an adult, or acknowledge something the adult may say, his chief and outstanding interest tends to be in other boys and girls.

At this outgoing age, there is relatively little solitary play, and even when there is, it is accompanied by very little verbalization. Even when a child is not talking to others, what he says tends to have a social implication, as when a boy comes into a playroom and remarks, "Oh boy! What a noise!" Or, mimicking an adult's admonition, he may remark, "If I don't stop that noise!" Four is a noisy age—the Four-year-old is loud and active in most things he does.

Children by no means ignore an adult who is present or playing with them. It is merely that they are much more interested in other children than in adults. Thus, a child may give what he considers interesting information to the adult: "I don't mind anything. Anything 'cept when Mommy washes my hair," "I live next door to a haunted house."

He may tell or boast of his own abilities: "I can write," "I can count," "I can swing by my knees," "I'm awful strong," "Watch me jump. Awful high." And he boasts about possessions, comparing them favorably to any that others may have: "I have bigger blocks at home," "I got more blocks than the other children have."

He still is not above asking the adult for help: "How do you do this, anyway?," "Will you put this somewhere it won't get lost?" He may still, for all his improved social skills, sometimes ask for help *against* other children: "They won't let me have my car," "They won't let me come in."

If no other children are present or available, he may carry on elaborate imaginative play with an adult. Thus, a boy may initiate an elaborate game of telephone repairman, telling the adult what he is going to do and then carrying it out elaborately, with appropriate verbalization.

But his chief conversation now is definitely with other children. As at Three, he is most interested in conversation he initiates himself, though he is now highly responsive to things that other children say to him. And, conversation now reflects a much more secure sense of self. The child no longer seems to need to protect his every product or possession.

So, there is less talk about ownership, more asking permission to use things that others are playing with, more use of the word "let's," more friendly suggestions in cooperative play: "Could I have those tickets?," "First let me have a turn?," "Let's play with this," "Shut dat door. You see, we don't want any germs to come in," "May I please have the iron?" ("Please" is a favorite word for many at this age.)

Imaginative play tends to involve delightful verbal fantasy: "I'm the farmer. Who's going to help me unload this hay?," "I'm off to work. You put the baby to bed."

Or, cooperative play may involve the use of real objects, especially constructive materials, and practical conversation: "Put a roof on that house, why don't you?," "Ready?," "That's pretty good, but we need another one," "I'm holding it so you can get down." In cooperative play, Fours are quick to accept suggestions from each other. Any one incident of cooperative and/or imaginative play may continue for as much as twenty minutes, with good, sustained reciprocal conversation throughout.

As six months earlier, some children still seem to define those they like by emphasizing those they do *not* like, so excluding and rebuffing remarks are still very strong: "You can't come in," "Get outta here." Or, when one child, in imaginative play, remarks, "I need some more milk," another may retort, "That's not milk. That's only blocks."

They exclude children they don't like but often verbalize strong expressions of friendship for those they *do* like (of either sex): "You're my playmate," "I'm sitting with you," "I like you." They may show jealousy of a friend: "Barbara, don't you talk to him."

Fours love whispering and secrets. They now seem to have fun with language. They enjoy rhymes, and most adore silly language: "My mother's gone goo-goo," "Ready weady, steady weady."

The Four-year-old is, above all, a boaster: "I'm bigger than you are," "I can jump higher than you can." He boasts about his parents, or quotes them as ultimate authorities: "My mother says you can't have that truck." (Sometimes this boasting gets him into trouble with Five- and Six-year-olds. A fight may be the only way out, and the poor Four-year-old usually ends up in tears.)

Silly language is so loved by many that it provides an excellent technique for getting cooperation. Four seems captivated by any silly approach. And, language of any kind is extremely important now. In fact, in some episodes of imaginative or cooperative play, there may be more talking than action.

VARIANT BEHAVIOR

Inevitably at stormy Four, some violent physical resistance and even an occasional tantrum may be expected when things go wrong. For the most part, though, when he does not wish to comply or conform, the child's objections can be expressed quite effectively in his colorful language. He tells you in words, rather than in actions, why he doesn't want to do as you wish.

The child of Four, in a standard behavior examination situation,[2] which permits a fair comparison from child to child and from age to age, as just earlier, refuses with words and not with deeds. As Figure 4 shows clearly, at Four the child refuses things that do not interest him or look too difficult, in very close to what will also be his Five-year-old manner. Quite maturely, he neither fights nor cries. He just talks.

LANGUAGE AND THOUGHT

The child of Four loves language. He loves to talk, to rhyme, to whisper, to sing. Or even to shout. He is his

Figure 4

*Age Distribution of Different Kinds of Variant Behavior,
from Eighteen months to Five years*

own self-appointed commentator and often his own audience. He loves words, likes to try them out, likes to play with them. He likes new and different words. He likes to do silly things with words, such as to say "smarty-warty" or "batty-watty" or "ooshy-wooshy." He even likes to talk to his play objects, especially if they don't do just what he wants them to: "You silly red ball," "You foolish block."

He especially loves the word "big," a word that is soon superseded by "enormous" or "gigantic." Four just naturally exaggerates, as we have mentioned: "as high as a mountain," "five million years," "as long as the world." In fact, much of his prevarication, which his parents probably call lying, may at times result from his tendency to exaggerate.

By Four, most children begin to use most of the sounds in their language fairly well. Some estimate that most English-speaking American children use about 90 percent of the American English vowels at this time.

Vocabulary has now increased by leaps and bounds. Some estimate that an average Four-year-old vocabulary may contain as many as 1,550 words. Most Fours can express themselves freely and well. They are now even more interested in stories than earlier, will look on when read to, may even ask what certain letters spell. If the child has been a television watcher, he may even be surprisingly good at saying letters and numbers, though it should be of no concern if he cannot.

The Four-year-old doesn't really *need* to know his letters and numbers, though as children move on toward Five, many quite naturally become much interested in written words and in knowing what certain combinations of letters spell. In fact, many can print their own names in capital letters.

Sentence structure, grammatical usage, and correctness of tenses is improving. As Laurie and Joseph Braga[3] point out, "Children do not learn to speak by copying adults. They listen to adults, learn the rules, and then make up their own sentences based on the rules they have at the time. Children seem to have a built-in language-learning device that lets them learn to use certain rules about their language from what they hear. They even make mistakes in a systematic way."

For example, when they begin learning the rules for making plurals, children who previously had used the correct plural forms for "mouse" and "foot," now, at Four, say "mouses" and "foots." This is called overgeneralization, and is a sign of growth, a sign that they are learning the rules. Later they will learn the exceptions to the rules—again through listening, not through lessons, and will again say "mice" and "feet."

Somewhere around Four, most begin to learn the following word-changing rules: 1) When using "she" or "he," there is an *s* added to verbs in the present tense. Thus, "She walks," "He runs." 2) An *-ed* added to the verb means the past tense. Thus, "Today I walk to school; yesterday I walked to school." 3) An *s* added to a noun indicates more than one: "one dog; two dogs." 4) When something belongs to somebody, you use words like "my/ mine," "your/yours," "his/hers," "their/theirs."

Irregular verbs come in due time. But Four goes by his own simpler rules; thus, he "builded a house" and "knowded" he was right, before he takes on the irregular verb forms of "built" or "knew." He also adds extra *s*'s for possession, as "This is hers house."

All these things come in in their own good time, and some children, especially boys, are slower than others. Enjoy these transition forms as a part of growth, and be concerned only if the child doesn't move on to the usual forms by Five or Six. *It is important not to correct your child's language.* Fear of failing can make a child anxious and might even lead to stuttering or not saying anything. If they make a mistake, you can answer them, or repeat what they have said, correctly, but don't emphasize their own mistakes.

Between Four and Five, most learn to say some of the more difficult speech sounds such as *l, r, s, t, sh, ch,* and *j.*

And what they say is now largely intelligible even to those outside the family. Children who have trouble with these sounds can be helped to hear and say them through special books such as those by Jan Slepian and Ann Seidler (*see* page 143).

This is a top age for questions. Endless "whys" and "hows" are uttered, partly in pursuit of knowledge, partly just for the fun of keeping a conversation going, and partly in resistance, such as "Why?" meaning "Why do I have to?" However, the word is used most as a request for information: "Why does the wind blow?," "Why does the sun shine?," "Why does it rain?"

Since children of this age tend to be insatiably curious and avidly seeking for information, try to answer these "whys" as long as you feel that real curiosity and interest motivate them. Don't hesitate to cut short their conversation when they use their "whys" for stalling or resisting.

Not only does the child ask the adult for information, but he, too, likes to *give* information. He has a great deal to say, to adults as well as to other children. He likes to tell outsiders about things at home, and he especially likes to talk about his mother: "My mommy has a brand-new washing machine." He likes to provide facts: "Dogs can run very fast," "A pencil is a simple thing."

Or, he makes extremely touching personal remarks, like the little boy who said to his teacher, "You know, I often think of you. You could come to my house some time, and we could play ball."

Words aplenty he now has under his command. Conversation now truly enriches his life and his relationship with others.

By Four, most children can even define a few words by telling how they are used. Thus, they can tell you that an apple is to eat, a coat is to wear. Most also know four prepositions, such as "off," "in," "next to" or "beside," and "on." They can also repeat after you a short sentence, say their numbers from one to ten, count three pennies with correct pointing. They can also carry out somewhat complex commands. A "test" that most Four-year-olds can pass is the instruction to "Close the door, put the book on the chair, bring me the key," or some variation of this kind of command.

Also, the child of Four usually has enough understanding of the relationship of parts to wholes to be able to tell you when something is missing from an ordinary object, such as an arm from a coat, or a leg from a table or chair. Or, he can tell you what everyday objects are made of, such as a chair is made of wood or a window of glass. Somewhere between Four and Five, on the average, comes the ability to name correctly the four basic colors, though actually some children are able to do this much earlier. Color naming seems to be a highly individual matter.

Most Fours can also respond correctly to such questions as "What cries?," "What swims?," "What sleeps?," "What bites?" And they can also answer correctly one of two such questions as "What must you do when you have lost something?" or "What must you do before you cross the street?" Language has come a long way for most.

chapter five
THE FOUR-YEAR-OLD BIRTHDAY PARTY

Four is perhaps the first age when the very characteristics of the age lend themselves ideally to party giving and party going.

The average Two-year-old is not really certain what a party is. Is it the cake? The ice cream? The guests?

Three enjoys a party more or less as he would a morning at nursery school or an afternoon of play with a friend. He is on the verge of awareness that a party is something special and exciting, but often only on the verge.

Four, however, can be an ideal party age. The Four-year-old tends to be a creature of boundless energy, enthusiasm, and appetite for the new and different and exciting. He *loves* an occasion!

Though Four's enthusiasm can sometimes go out-of-bounds, he can be truly cooperative if things are exciting enough and are going his way. He tends to be extremely appreciative of adult attention. He throws himself fully and positively into plans for his own entertainment.

It is easy to entertain a party-giving or a party-going Four-year-old if you yourself have time, energy, goodwill, and imagination. He tends to accept quite uncritically the games you suggest, the food you serve, the favors and surprises you provide. (Five may say, "Oh, I have one of those." Thirteen may mutter, "Oh! One of those!" Not so with the Four-year-old.) Four's demand for something special or something new and different is easily satisfied by simple favors or attractive decoration.

Discipline should not yet be a major problem, at least for the mother who understands children of this age. She knows that a party is not the place for lessons in sharing, behaving, minding. Quarrels should be settled as quickly and inconspicuously as possible by removing one of the quarrelers or by providing some different but acceptable toy for one of two grabbers.

KEYS TO SUCCESS

The keys to a successful party at this age are speed, simplicity, and novelty. Speed is necessary because Fours react quickly and they tire rapidly if the party drags or if it lasts too long. Simplicity is important because children of this age are not mature enough to understand or to participate in complex games. Some novel element is important because Fours, unlike Threes, have a general notion of what a "party" is and expect something to go on other than just to go and play. This surprise should be something quite simple, such as a distribution of favors.

Number of Guests. Six guests is a good number and definitely not more than eight (both boys and girls). It may be safe to invite one or two extras, or at least to have some in mind who can be invited at the last minute. There are apt to be casualties among invited guests, so that they do not get to the party. They may be ill from overexcitement, their mother may not be able to get a baby-sitter and so cannot bring them, or other difficulties may get in the way.

Number of Adults. The host or hostess's mother and one adult helper need to be available. One or two of the mothers may need to stay as at Three—that is, mothers of children who are extremely shy or extremely aggressive, or who for other reasons may need to be there.

SCHEDULE

One and a half hours is plenty, ideally from 3:30 to 5:00. This timing allows for a nap beforehand for those who still need one, yet doesn't bring the refreshments too near dinnertime.

3:30–4:10   Guests arrive and play with toys. Parents bring, or earlier may have brought over, something for each child to play with (in addition to what the home may provide) for this initial period. So, the living room somewhat resembles a nursery school playroom, with a good assortment of toys, including big cars and trains, a rocking horse, dolls and carriages, stuffed animals, Blockcraft, Tinkertoys, big musical tops. Children play, usually quite individually, with these toys. The host or hostess opens presents as they come.

4:10–4:15 As children go into the room where refreshments are waiting, each one is given a favor. Fireman's hats and badges make good favors. These may be available on a table, and are given to each child as he or she goes into the dining room.

4:15–4:40 Refreshments have all been set up in advance on card tables or on low children's tables. (Tables may have to be borrowed.) Use a paper tablecloth, napkins, plates, and bright cups. And provide some kind of favors—for instance, little toy frying pans filled with candy. Balloons—all blown up—hang in a cluster on the wall. These are given to the children toward the end of the party.

The refreshments can consist of simple small sandwiches, the smaller the better, but in interesting shapes. Better for children to eat several small sandwiches apiece than to half-eat one big one. Or, sandwiches can be omitted and you can have just ice cream, cake, and milk. Individual frosted cupcakes may be better for eating, but there should be a central cake with four candles on it, which can be blown out.

4:40–5:00 Informal play period. Children play with the toys in the living room and with balloons, which have been distributed. (If balloon play becomes vigorous, it may be necessary to push toys to the edge of the room to allow space.)

If the children are on the other side of Four, some slightly organized play, such as singing games, play with instruments, marching, or dressing up in costumes, could be introduced at this time. Also, this is a good time for giving out special surprise favors. These are wrapped separately and may be presented in a big cloth bag that the children reach into, taking turns. They unwrap and play with these. Good favors include small figures of animals or humans, small balls with elastic, toy wristwatches, toy rings, fire trucks.

5:00   Departure. Mothers who are already there leave with their children. Other mothers call for their children. However, by the end of the party most Fours are tired and excitable and may cry or go to pieces if they have to wait to be called for. Thus, it may have been arranged for the mothers already there to take all the children home.

EXPENSES

This can be an inexpensive party. Favors might cost around $4, refreshments $7, balloons $2, extras $2. Total around $15.

HINTS AND WARNINGS

Remember that you can count on only minimal group activity. Individual informal play is better than organized games for most. In fact, it is not only unnecessary but may be dangerous to introduce even simple games. Ring-Around-the-Rosy or Farmer-in-the-Dell would be better than something complex, such as Pin-the-Tail-on-the-Donkey, if games must be played.

Every child is likely to think that it is *his* birthday, wish it were his birthday, or pretend that it is his. So, all may want to blow out the candles. If someone other than the host or hostess gets there first, you will simply have to relight the candles.

There are almost bound to be some tears, some spilling, some disagreements or quarreling. Be especially careful that the party does not last too long. Fours tire easily and become overexcited.

As to favors and gifts: If you have hats, sturdy homemade ones are better than purchased ones, which are apt to rip and tear. Blowers may become a menace as children blow them into each others' faces. Don't have favors, surprises, hats, etc., all at the refreshment table. It makes for too much confusion. Have the surprises spread out a bit through the party instead of giving them all at once.

chapter six
HELP WITH ROUTINES

EATING

By Four, most children can feed themselves completely except for cutting. They are competent enough now at feeding themselves that they don't have to think so much about it or try so hard. Most can talk and eat at the same time now, though, in some, talking may definitely interfere with eating.

If the child's incessant talking interferes with adult enjoyment of the meal, some families still find it works best for the child to eat apart from the family. If he does eat with others, he tends to become restless long before the meal is over, and may need to interrupt his meal to go to the bathroom.

If parents are relatively relaxed about what the child eats, and unless a feeding problem has been built up in the past by poor management, there should not be much fuss about *what* is eaten. But many parents still worry about *how much* is eaten and may insist too much on quantity.

It is important to remember that the Four-year-old appetite may still be only fair, even though as the child moves on toward Five appetite may increase. Refusals and preferences are not quite as definite as earlier, but the child may still go on either food jags (insisting on the same thing over and over) or on food strikes (certain foods or types of food being definitely refused).

By Four-and-a-half, most can pour milk from a pitcher without spilling, and most drink their milk rapidly and well.

Those who eat alone are apt to dawdle, but they do not need to be fed, merely encouraged to speed up a little. Sometimes such incentives as eating to get big, racing with the baby, finishing within a certain time, or working toward a dessert goal may help. However, in general, the less gimmicky things become, and the less emphasis is put on the whole thing, the better. If children think that their eating matters a good deal to their mother, they are likely to use the power this seems to give them. A very casual attitude on the part of the adult usually works best.

By Four-and-a-half, children not only feed themselves nicely, but may even help to set the table. Both speed and appetite pick up. The child can usually manage more meals with the family, and is beginning to find a reasonable balance between talking and eating.

Though it is not within the scope of this book to discuss in any detail matters of either diet or health, and we do not wish to make any parent overly anxious about the kind of food eaten, we would like to give one warning. This is that some of the foods your child may like best may conceivably be harmful to him.

Obviously, if they make him sick to his stomach, or make him break out in a rash, you will know it and will avoid such foods. But as physicians concerned about child behavior[4] are now pointing out, many foods harmful to the individual child may do no observable physical harm but may have a disastrous effect on his *behavior*.

Food or drink, or even things that are inhaled, may produce hidden allergies, which, in turn, can cause extremely deviant behavior. In some children, dizziness, listlessness, fatigue, irritability, violence, and hyperactivity all can be induced by foods liked best.

Doctors report many striking examples of this, like that

of the boy who at Five had for two years been wetting his pants several times a day as well as having to get up several times during the night. This urinary difficulty, as well as other symptoms of overactivity, cleared up when he stopped eating tomatoes. Unfortunately, in this case, as so often, the boy craved the very food that was harmful to him. For two years he had had tomato soup for lunch every day, and would eat five or six ripe tomatoes at a sitting. His symptoms returned when (as an experiment) he was given tomatoes again, and cleared up when they were once again removed from his diet.

Or, even without there being an actual allergic reaction, harmful food products, especially artificial colorings and flavorings, have been shown to produce dizziness, listlessness, fatigue, irritability, violence, and hyperactivity, and, in school-age children, problems usually described as learning disabilities.

If your child seems healthy and happy, and if his behavior is reasonably satisfactory to you and to him, that is, if he or she is getting along all right in major ways, chances are you don't need to worry about all this. But if behavior is disappointing or unsatisfactory in major ways, and you can't find the reason, at least consider the possibility that something in your child's diet may be at the root of his difficulties.

SLEEPING

Bedtime is now relatively uncomplicated in most. In fact, some seem to know when they are tired and may even ask to go to bed. As at earlier ages, the child will enjoy some special attention, as a story read by his mother or bedtime singing. He may also enjoy half an hour alone in bed with books or crayoning, and often takes dolls or toy animals to bed with him.

The highlight for many a Four is that he is old enough to have earned the right to sleep in a big bed. Parents often produce their own bedtime problems by moving the child from crib to big bed too soon, as early as Two-and-a-half, especially if a new baby has come along. It would have been better to have two cribs, one for each.

Parents can often utilize this momentous experience of having a big bed at Four for potential transitions into release of younger behaviors. The crib shaker and head banger may even be cured overnight. The bed wetter may suddenly become dry. And the lovely, cozy expanse of a big bed may encourage a happy going-to-bed time, with room for a parent to lie down, too, as bedtime stories are read or prayers are said.

Bedtime is usually around 7:00 or 7:30 though with daylight saving time it may be later. If the child can read the time on the clock, and some can, he may respond better to the fact that the clock says it's time to go to bed than if Mother tells him.

A few children need to have not only a going-to-bed time but also a putting-out-the-light time. Without this extra few minutes to settle down in their beds with the light on, they may be very demanding.

Most sleep well, waking only, if need be, to go to the toilet. Some can manage this by themselves; others need substantial help from a parent. And still others resist being wakened and therefore should not be disturbed. This is not a big age for nightmares, though especially around Four-and-a-half some do have troubling dreams.

Many sleep eleven hours or even longer, waking around 7:00 A.M. The child is now able to put on his bathrobe and slippers if they have been laid out for him, can close the window, go to the bathroom, and then will usually play in his room until it is time to go into his parents' room. (Very young children may stay in bed not at all after they wake up. By Three, they *may* stay in bed until you tell them they may get up. By Four, many will wait until a certain hour [the clock says such-and-such] before getting out of bed.)

Though a few still really nap at this age, most have only play naps or no nap at all. Boys are more likely to go to sleep at naptime than are girls. Even if they do not sleep, here as just earlier even a play nap gives both parent and child a welcome change of pace, and a rest from each other.

The day's schedule, at Four, is often helped by the fact that many Four-year-olds enjoy the idea of a routine or schedule. They seem to like to know what comes next and to be able to count on it.

ELIMINATION

By Four years of age, things go pretty well with most. Most children are dry during the day and can manage this entire routine themselves, "Accidents," if any, tend to occur simply because the child does not want to interrupt his play and puts off going to the toilet until too late. If this happens repeatedly, a mother had best take some responsibility here. She can either see that the child comes in to go to the toilet at fairly regular intervals, or, if he resists this idea, she can tell him that she is going to blow a whistle when she thinks it is time for him to come in.

Many demand extreme privacy for their own bathroom functions now but show much curiosity about the activities of others. They are also very curious about strange bathrooms and may insist on seeing the bathroom, if visiting.

Out at play, especially if play is unsupervised, boys may like to urinate in front of other children, and there may be much silly talk about this function.

Perhaps the majority by now can stay dry all night if picked up around midnight. But it is not unusual for a child still to be wet at night. This, as a rule, should cause no concern. And if the midnight pickup does not ensure a dry night, it may be best to skip it altogether. Just pad the child up good and tight to save on laundry, and make very little comment about this immaturity.

(In fact, many quite normally developing boys and girls are Six years old or even older before it is easy for them to stay dry at night. So, it may be helpful for you to know that there are now available effective and reasonably in-expensive conditioning devices that in many instances can serve to dry up a child in a matter of weeks. Some that we have found most satisfactory are listed on page 122.)

Bowel movements in most are also usually rather well routinized, and this function, too, causes no problem in most. One movement a day, after either breakfast or lunch, is a common Four-year-old pattern, though some have more or fewer than one a day, or their functioning may occur irregularly.

As with urinating, most consider this an extremely pri-vate functioning and usually want the bathroom door to be closed or even locked.

Unfortunately, there are a few boys who are not up to standard in this department. There are some troublesome children, usually boys, who though they may be trained for dryness, seem to be making no progress whatever with regard to bowel functioning even as late as Four. They refuse to use the potty chair or toilet, and continue to defecate in their pants.

This refusal and continued immaturity of behavior tends to be related to severe mother-child battles. This is one way the boy who *must* control his mother finds it pos-sible to do so. Most mothers will interrupt almost any-thing they are doing if they feel that by doing so they can keep their son clean.

Some mothers have found that one way to solve the problem is to require the boy to wash out his own under-pants. In some, this cleans up matters in a very short time.

Perhaps a kinder approach is one that we have long recommended. After checking with your pediatrician to rule out any physical reason for this delay, we suggest per-mitting the child to play in the bathroom, with his pants off, at about the time of day when you expect him to function. (If his functioning has not yet settled down to any particular time of day, you will just have to admit that you still have a long way to go.)

Put a newspaper on the floor in a corner of the room,

and tell the child that when he is ready he may use the paper. Often he is able to get this far in just a few days— a few weeks at most. Once he has succeeded with this, it is often just a small step to get him to use a potty— best in saddle potty form or a potty chair. From there to the adult-size toilet is usually fairly easy.

BATH AND DRESSING

The bath is now an easy routine, the child often being capable of washing himself fairly well as long as his mother suggests part by part what should be washed. Otherwise he is apt to get marooned on some one part of his body and wash that over and over.

Most can now let the water out of the tub and can wash out the tub (after a fashion). And can dry themselves (after a fashion). Most can also make the necessary wrist-and-hand motions to do a reasonably good job of brushing their teeth, combing their hair, and washing and drying their hands and face. Many can now wash their faces without soaking shirt or blouse.

Time of bath may now be shifted to before supper, if the family schedule permits, since the child is less tired at this time and can do a better job of washing himself. And oh, how he loves to play in the tub with all his bathroom toys!

The child of this age often dresses and undresses himself without too much help, though clothes may need to be laid out for him, each garment correctly oriented, since a few may still have trouble distinguishing front from back. If any special garment gives trouble and makes the child angry, you can plan ahead for the future as to just how he can manage that particular garment more successfully. (Or, ask yourself, Why is the garment so difficult? Is it really appropriate or necessary?)

Special difficulty may occur in relation to buttoning, though most now unbutton with ease. Fortunately, with modern zippers, less buttoning is demanded than formerly.

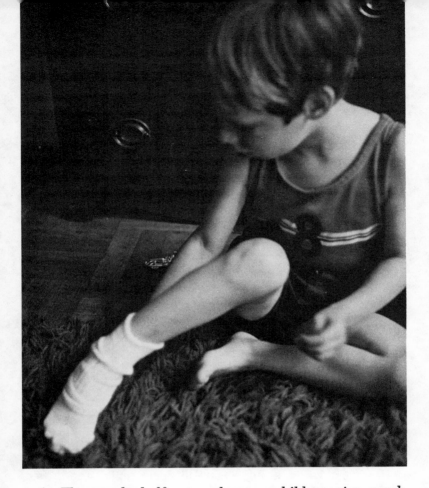

At Three-and-a-half, a good many children give much trouble about getting dressed. They resist and object. Four, as a rule, likes to dress himself, is proud of his increasing abilities, and may like to beat the clock or otherwise race to complete the process.

The majority can distinguish front from back, button some buttons, get shoes on the right feet and even lace them. (Some children consistently put their shoes on the wrong feet, and why this does not produce discomfort is hard to say.) Some can tie a knot in their shoestring but cannot yet manage a bow. Many boys, as well as girls, now *love* to dress up in adult clothes—hats, shoes, belts, scarves, skirts, pocketbooks—at playtime.

TENSIONAL OUTLETS

The Four-year-old seems much less tense than he was just earlier, at Three-and-a-half. There is less facial twitching, less stuttering, less blinking. There is even somewhat less thumb sucking, though many do still suck their thumbs, especially on going to sleep. Some have now given up their security blanket, though they likely still cling to their favorite stuffed toy. Some have replaced thumb sucking with nail biting and/or masturbating. Any of these behaviors may be expressed not only in private but even in public, as in nursery school at story time.

If tension is felt, it is more likely to be expressed in a large, gross-motor way, the child running, kicking, shouting. Tension may be experienced more in the genital region than in the facial region. Boys, in times of anxiety or excitement, may clutch their genitals.

Both boys and girls in social situations or at other times of excitement or strain are apt to have to go to the bathroom. This need is real and should, of course, be respected. Some may actually have toilet accidents in a demanding social situation if they do not get to the bathroom in time. A few may feel tension pains in their stomachs and may on occasion actually be sick to their stomachs with excitement.

However, when a Four-year-old feels tense and keyed up he may simply express this feeling in general over-activity, in running around and shouting or in talking too fast or behaving too wildly, rather than in the smaller and more specific ways (as thumb sucking or blanket fondling or nose or eye twitching) of just earlier.

Health in most is reasonably good, though a few seem to have one cold after another all winter. If these colds seem to be exaggerated by nursery school attendance, it may be best to keep the child at home for a while. At this age, if the child falls down (as he often does) he tends to fall on his face and may very possibly knock out a front tooth. (At later ages he seems more likely to break his collarbone or his arm when he falls.)

chapter seven
YOUR CHILD'S MIND, OR DON'T PUSH YOUR PRESCHOOLER

For all the talk we hear nowadays about the cognitive development, or the cognitive training, of preschoolers, it is most important that you not be self-conscious about all this. Without your doing very much about it, you will find that the normally endowed Four-year-old is a creature of tremendous curiosity, wild imagination, delightful creativity. You will want to answer his many "whys" and to encourage his imagination and creativity. But don't take too seriously the sometimes-proposed notion that it is all up to you to teach him to think.

Especially, *do not feel that you must teach your preschooler to read.* Hopefully you will read to him, and read to him some more. Hopefully he himself may enjoy looking at books. And if by chance he is somewhat advanced and is already asking what certain letters mean, or is trying to spell out words, give him the help and encouragement he seeks.

But do not push. It really doesn't make a bit of difference in the long run whether he begins reading at Three or Four or Five or Six or even Seven. If your child should show spontaneous interest in letters and numbers at an early age, fine for him but no special credit to him or to you. If, on his own, or through the stimulation of certain television programs, he should, fairly early, come to recite

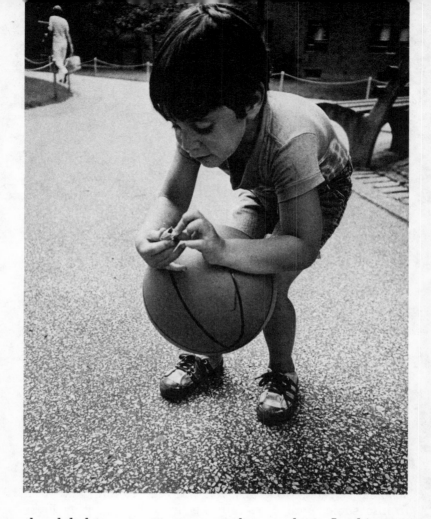

the alphabet or to say some numbers, so be it. Let him enjoy this activity, but don't take it as a sign that he is ready for early entrance to kindergarten.

In fact, try not to worry too much about your child's so-called cognitive development. It is almost, of recent years, as if psychologists and educators had discovered the child's mind. They rather give the impression that one must *teach* the child to think, and that it is necessary to provide all sorts of techniques and materials by means of which his mind will develop. It just isn't so!

So, try not to feel that you as a parent "ought" to be

doing something special about your child's intellectual life. Dr. Arnold Gesell commented long ago, "Mind manifests itself." The child's mind is not something separate from the rest of him. It manifests itself in almost everything he does, except perhaps through such purely reflex actions as swallowing or breathing. It manifests itself when he runs and jumps and climbs, when he shouts and laughs and sings, when he plays with his real friends or with his purely imaginary companions. A child who paints a picture or throws a ball is giving expression of his mind in action.

In fact, virtually everything the young child does is an example of his mind in action. It is not necessary for him to learn letters and numbers before he goes to kindergarten to show you, and others, that his mind is in good working order. If your boy or girl has good potential, and if you provide a reasonably rich and lively environment and give your love and attention, the mind should take care of itself.

Whatever his age, you do not have to be specially concerned about teaching your preschooler to think. If you provide a usual environment that contains a reasonable number of friendly, interested, sharing people, a reasonable number of books and toys and creative materials, a usual number of games and jaunts and pleasant excursions—the usual attributes of comfortable family living —he will learn as naturally as he grows and breathes. *Let us all relax!*

And here let us give you a specially important warning. Young Four-year-olds will, in the normal course of development, very shortly be turning Five, and you will be thinking about school for them. They will very soon be taking that important step of starting kindergarten.

And here is where all too many parents make that fatal mistake, which, for many children, stands in the way of school success and more or less guarantees failure, or at least academic difficulty, in all the years to come. They start their child too soon.

Regardless of what the law may permit in your particular state, we prefer to start children in school, and to promote them subsequently, on the basis of their behavior age rather than their age in years or their intellectual level.

It is the age at which a child is behaving, not his birthday age, that should ideally determine the time of school entrance. Thus, your child might be Six years of age come September and might have a decidedly high intelligence quotient, but if in his behavior (which can be determined by simple behavior tests[5]) he is only at a Five-year-old level, he will be best suited in kindergarten, with others who are behaving at this same level, rather than in first grade.

If your own school system does not offer prekindergarten screening and you have no way of finding out about your own particular child's behavior level, then you will more or less have to go by his chronological age.

In that case, we urge all parents to be very sure that that boy or girl is on the older side before he starts school. And since boys, as a rule, develop more slowly than girls, it would be best if your daughter is fully Five years of age before she starts kindergarten in September. Your son will do best if he is fully Five-and-a-half.

Teachers and administrators from all over the country tell us that it is the "fall babies"—children who have their fifth birthday in the fall after they begin kindergarten—who have the most trouble. They often have trouble not only in kindergarten but in all the years to come.

So, though we do not think that the notion of developing or improving your child's mind should be a matter of great concern for you, many parents are understandably interested in the way any child's thinking develops.

Here, then, are a few clues as to the ways that in general children's concepts of time, space, and number do develop in the usual child; a few clues as to the level of thinking often attained by the Four-year-old in such basic areas as sense of time, sense of space, sense of number, and sense

of humor. Here, also, is information as to what one may expect in the way of creativity in the child of Four.

SENSE OF TIME

Four may still seem young compared to what comes after, but the ordinary Four-year-old is actually a rather sophisticated person when it comes to his sense of time.

The child of this age seems almost equally at home, verbally, in past, present, and future, and use of tenses is usually accurate. Such a common time word as "day" is used in many different inflections: "today," "this day," "every day," "another day," "once a day," "day after today."

Generalizations include such somewhat sophisticated words and phrases as "for a month," "once a day," "usually."

"Time" is included in many compound words: "lunchtime," "dinnertime," "every time," "sometimes," "one time," "almost time," "meantime," "for a long time," "Our time is over," "Is it time?" Even such broad generalizations as "springtime," "summertime," "wintertime" are now used quite glibly.

Or the seasons can correctly be put in their context: "next summer," "last summer," "this winter" are used correctly.

And so far as "minute" goes, not only can the child say, and mean, "in a minute," but also "in five minutes," "this minute," "a minute ago," "just a few more minutes."

"Week" and "month," too, are used effectively, such as in "next week," "some other week," "next month," "for a month," "in a month." "Night" and "morning" are comfortably used in many expressions, such as "late at night," "early in the morning."

Children are beginning to grasp the sense of seasons and activities related to seasons.

Most seem to have a reasonably good understanding of when events of the day occur in relation to each other.

Four-year-olds can, as a rule, tell not only what we do

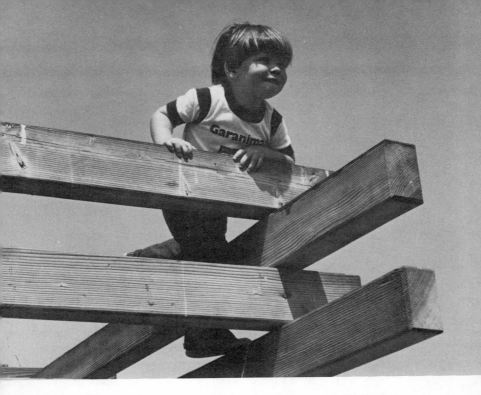

at Christmas and Easter but also what we do at Halloween, though Thanksgiving is still beyond most. Most Four-year-olds still cannot tell correctly what time they go to bed, have supper, get up, go to school.

Though most girls can tell their age correctly by Three-and-a-half, most boys are Four before they can give this response correctly, most often by showing four fingers. Four-year-olds cannot, as a rule, tell when their birthday comes.

SENSE OF SPACE

The space world of the Four-year-old, like so many aspects of his living, is definitely expanding. Outstanding at this age is the use of expansive space words character-istic of the out-of-bounds, expansive tendencies of the Four-year-old. Some of these words have been used before, but are especially noteworthy as a group at this age. Typical are "on top of," "far away," "out in," "down to," "way up," "way up there," "way far," "out," "way off," "way out," "out in."

"In," "on," "up in," "at," and "down" are space words perhaps most often used. As the child climbs on his Jungle Gym he is experiencing all these changes in space, and this may be why a Jungle Gym is such a favorite with Four-year-olds.

A new dimension is suggested in the frequent use of the word "behind." The Four-year-old tends to be much concerned with the backs of things. He wants a book to have a back as well as a front. And if his book has a house on the front cover, he anticipates that the back of the house will be on the back of the book.

He is especially interested in his own back and hopes he can view it with special mirrors. As two Four-year-olds, enamored of David Brinkley on television, watched him but saw only his front, one of them was heard to say,

"My daddy says David Brinkley has a back, just the way we do."

And, finally, most Fours can now tell both on what street they live and in what city they live. They can put put a ball *on, under, in front of*, and *in back of a chair*.

SENSE OF NUMBER

The ordinary Four-year-old can count, with correct pointing, three objects. Many are reported to count to ten, though they may start their counting with a number higher than one. Verbal counting, that is, rote counting, without objects, definitely exceeds counting of objects.

Stimulated by television, some children nowadays can count by rote even higher than ten, but this does not in most instances constitute any real understanding of numbers or an ability to count real objects.

Their hands provide at least ten units. Let them use their fingers as they wish. This is the way children learn naturally.

And, Fours love double numbers like 44 or 66 or 77. They also love games that include numbers, as beanbag throwing.

SENSE OF HUMOR

The typical Four-year-old is gloriously humorous. From a loud guffaw to a subtle, sly wink, he runs the gamut of humorous expression.

Nobody will ever appreciate your own humor more— so enjoy yourself while this full appreciation lasts. Enjoy the child's humor and enjoy his enjoyment of your own!

Four loves silly language. He loves the ridiculous. He loves the imaginative. He loves the very fact that *you* have a sense of humor and are making a joke, even when he may not fully understand what the joke is about.

He especially appreciates it when *you* appreciate *him*. Silly or funny books are among the things he appreciates most, and are among the things that you can enjoy together.

Four is not above the same kind of humorous appreciation one sees at Two and Three—anything that goes wrong: a shoe on the wrong foot, a sweater sleeve that sticks, a hat on backwards.

But he now has moved, also, into the somewhat subtler realms of humor. In his own spontaneous storytelling he demonstrates the kinds of things that seem funny to him. Thus, a Four-year-old child, in his stories, may think very funny something like:

A car went the wrong way. It broke the ceiling. He ate up her door and her whole house. He ate up hisself. He ate the whole world.

I had a silly dream about a talking tractor.

The mother clowns came. They made funny faces. Boy found anudder monkey and then the monkey did laugh.

By Four-and-a-half, most humor has not proceeded too much farther in the direction of subtlety. In typical stories, children of this age tell us:

David's mother pulled off my mother's nose. And then my mother pulled off David's mother's nose.

Rabbit, he ran. He got caught in a trap. He couldn't get out of the trap. Ha! Ha!

The girl shook when she took a look. And the tree shook. The whole world shook. A head shook.

The great thing about Four is that he can on occasion be really quite funny from the adult point of view, and even when he isn't, he so enjoys his own humor and is so ready and willing to share his enjoyment and his joke that his attempts at humor are amusing for you as well as for him.

DIFFICULT TO STOP THUMB SUCKING IN EARLY YEARS

Dear Doctors:

My Four-year-old daughter Donna constantly sucks her thumb. My dentist recommends that she stop this habit now. Is there any advice you can give me about this problem? Or, better yet, do you know of any device I may use to help my child correct this habit?

Some dentists do indeed take a very dim view of thumb sucking. But most today seem to believe that if sucking of an intense nature stops before the second teeth come in, probably little harm will be done if Nature has lined the teeth up straight to begin with.

Our own preference is not to make too much of the whole thing, certainly in the years before Six or so. Most children realize that their parents do not especially favor this behavior. Many by Five or Six are old enough to accept the rule that if they want to suck their thumb, they must go into their own room to do it.

Earlier, how much effort you make to stop the sucking can best be determined by the extensity and intensity of the behavior. If you have a child who sucks much of the day and most of the night, chances are your efforts to terminate the behavior will not be effective. And if you talk too much about it too soon, the child will become deaf to the sound of your voice later on when you might otherwise have had a chance.

Yes, there are devices, rather horrible-looking little wire devices, which can be fastened to the roof of the child's mouth and which then scratch the thumb as the child sucks. We have never recommended these, but your doctor might provide one if you wish.

Our own feeling is that if the child needs the comfort of his thumb, perhaps he's lucky that nature provided this handy device for consoling oneself. Most children no longer suck much in the daytime after they start school.

If sucking does persist on into the school years, then

the child may be old enough to plan with you for ways that will help him give up his habit. Four is not, in our opinion, a very good age to make an issue, but it can be an age when a child often restricts sucking to going to sleep. This suggests it is on its way out.

Many mothers now call thumb sucking a *tensional outlet* rather than a *bad habit,* and are not hostile to it. And there is now available a very comforting little book called *Danny and His Thumb,* by Kathryn Ernst, which actually goes so far as to assure young thumb suckers that their behavior is all right and urges them not to worry about it.

HOW TO TELL BOY ABOUT NEW BABY

Dear Doctors:

Our Four-year-old son Kenny has been the only one so far. Now we are expecting a baby. Though I am already six months pregnant, Kenny hasn't seemed to notice anything different about me. I am wondering when I should tell him about the coming addition to the family and what I should tell him.

How to tell him? In as unembarrassed and straightforward and matter-of-fact a way as you can manage.

What to tell him? Well, you know the facts. His own questions, once you have brought up the subject, will give you clues as to just what kind of information he is ready for. Some Four-year-olds are ready to believe that the baby grows inside their mother, but others cling to their earlier notion that it is purchased. Tell Kenneth the truth, but don't belabor the issue, and if he doesn't want to believe, don't insist.

When to tell him? You have done well, especially since he hasn't asked any questions, to delay telling him as long as you have. Four-year-olds have a quite different time sense from our own, and when a mother gives this information at the very beginning of her pregnancy, any preschooler grows very tired of waiting for the blessed event.

Any one of the many good books now on the market can help Kenny understand what it is you are talking about. If it's not too frank for you, we strongly recommend *Where Did I Come From?*, by Peter Mayle. If you want something more conservative, try *The Baby House*, by Norma Simon, *Before You Were a Baby*, by Paul and Kay Showers, or *Making Babies*, by Sara Bonnett Stein.

FOUR-YEAR-OLD MASTURBATES

Dear Doctors:

Our little boy, who is just Four years old, has been masturbating since the age of seven months. His only sibling is an Eleven-year-old sister with whom relations are exceptionally good. But otherwise he is a lonesome little fellow. We live in a third-floor apartment, with the people under us objecting to noise. And I can't allow him to play in the street with other children, who are invariably unattended.

Ours is a reasonably happy and well-adjusted home, and both our children are loved and wanted. The masturbating has increased lately, and there doesn't seem to be anything we can do to restrain him. We tried additional expressions of love, we tried to divert his attention, and we tried spanking and even a "serious talk." Nothing helps because, as he insists tearfully, "I have to do it so I'll feel better." We would greatly appreciate advice.

When a child masturbates during the first year of life, the course of this behavior may be a fairly long one.

You have tried all sorts of diverting techniques, but the problem continues. In general, Four and Six years of age are periods when boys, especially, have increased genital sensations and often do grasp their genitals. Your son's tension sensations may be more marked than they will later on.

In the same way you'd handle thumb sucking, you can at least request that he go into his room to indulge in this behavior and not do it in the presence of other people. Unquestionably, better outlets, such as a good play group, nursery school, or time outdoors with you (going for walks and excursions) would help considerably.

The very fact that he knows what he is doing makes us feel it is not just an automatic release. He sounds like a boy who a little later will really try to stop.

Few if any child specialists know how to stop this behavior, and many think it may be best not to step in at all. Except for the hygienic aspect, many feel that masturbation does not harm children unless they do it excessively. Your son's behavior does seem a little excessive, and hopefully more outside interests will make it unnecessary for him to rely on himself quite so much. So, for the present, try to work up good play interests for your boy, with more attention from both you and his father.

Eventually, if the problem continues into school age and interferes with school adjustment, you may need to take him to a local child guidance clinic for professional help. In the meantime, *must* you continue to live in a third-floor apartment? If there is any way to make your home environment more relaxed it might be of great help to your son.

SEX PLAY

Dear Doctors:

My Four-year-old Jennie and her friend David, who is Five, play together a good deal. About two years ago they began undressing and going to the bathroom outside. David's mother and I tried to stop this by explanations to the youngsters, and by watching them more closely. Last year, more tricks were added to this fascinating game. Again, I spoke to David's mother, and I personally kept them under closer supervision. David delights in a closed door or a secret hiding place. To be honest, Jennie also seems to enjoy this sort of thing.

Last week I returned home to find Jennie and David in her bedroom behind a closed door, again with their pants at half mast. My husband was at home but paid little attention to them as long as they were playing quietly. He feels I'm making too much of this. David's mother, too, seems quite satisfied to leave them to their own devices. Am I right to worry?

Your problem is a common one, and opinions differ. Some child specialists do not think sex play is particularly harmful at the younger ages, and believe that too much suppression and scolding might harm a child more than the actual play itself.

Most mothers don't like it and do prefer to prevent it. (Fathers are more unpredictable. They tend either to get very angry or to be quite indifferent.) So far as we know, adequate supervision is about the only way to prevent it. Talking, scolding, and punishing don't do much good. If the interest is there, and the opportunity presents itself, sex play does take place. If David and Jennie are going to play together, you will just have to supervise very closely.

Sometimes it is hard to supervise directly. But try to have them play in clear and open areas. Avoid closed doors and small, isolated places and bedrooms. Then, if the behavior still continues, the children may have to be separated for a few weeks. This may get the message across.

We're glad you recognize that, enthusiastic as David may be about all this, Jennie is also enthusiastic. Sometimes the greatest harm that comes from neighborhood sex play is that all the mothers of children involved become angry at each other and blame each others' children. It is important for all mothers to appreciate that this kind of play goes on in "good" neighborhoods as well as in "bad"; among "nice" children as well as among "naughty" ones.

Here are a few general comments on the subject:

Circumstances have a lot to do with it. There are some children who might skip it altogether if they never got a chance to play alone without supervision, or were always extremely busy at more productive activity. It is much worse in some children than in others; worse at some ages than at others.

Probably the two main things to do about it are: First, be calm and casual. Give the child the impression that you don't favor (or won't permit) this kind of thing. But avoid being shocked, horrified, or overly upset. The harm you might do a child by your attitude that sex activity is wrong and awful and shameful might do much greater damage than the actual sex play itself.

Second, try to keep your child out of situations that will lead to sex play. Some playmates may seem to arouse this more than others. There may be periods when you will avoid having him or her play with just those children. Or, there will be times when your child, in certain combinations, just can't seem to play unsupervised without getting into such activity.

A rather extreme but workable solution is to get one-piece underwear and also one-piece playsuits except for dress-up. Mere inaccessibility *can* provide an answer.

Who is to *blame* isn't the important thing. The boy next door may start it this year; next year it may be your own child who makes the initiating moves. We don't say that sex play is universal, but it seems to be nearly so. The absence of any sex interest or questions may be more indicative of later difficulties than a too great early interest.

BOY SUDDENLY AFRAID OF DYING

Dear Doctors:

Our Four-and-a-half-year-old son Robby has all of a sudden become terrified at the idea of dying. He had a pet dog die about a year ago, and we thought he had a general notion of the whole thing.

But now, all of a sudden, he is so frightened. My

wife assured him that nobody in this family was going to die. I thought that was wrong because she couldn't guarantee it. So I told him about God and that if he or any of us did die, we would go to be with God, so we would be all right.

Now he seems more frightened than ever because he says he doesn't *want* to go to be with God. What do we do now? His worry seems to be specifically about himself, and that he himself will die.

There are ages when the thought of God *can* bring children comfort in certain situations. The thought of God as a Father who takes care of you can sometimes allay the fears of a Four-year-old. But a child of this age has a lot of trouble with himself about what is real and what is not.

As reality takes a stronger hold, Robby may be able to accept the fact that people die mostly when they are old. But most Four-year-olds have only a very limited notion of what death means. You may be amazed at your son's callousness by the time he is Five. Many Five-year-olds in their discussions of death are like little lawyers, investigating the circumstances of death and the position of the body and just what will happen.

Some at Four, and many at Five, tend to think of death as reversible.

But Four-and-a-half-year-olds tend to be great worriers. Even without the impact of a specific experience, anxieties, and especially anxieties about death, do crop up. Some can be helped to an acceptance of the reality of death by the death of a pet. This didn't seem to help with Robby.

The notion of God does help some Four-year-olds, but Robby would probably have been helped more by the notion that God—if you wish to bring in this concept—is protecting him and looking out for him here on earth so that he won't die, rather than that if he went to Heaven he would be with God. Perhaps you can backtrack a little.

What Robby wants right now is a strong assurance that

he himself and, if possible, all members of his immediate family are going to be all right. Even though life is at best uncertain, we do think you would be reasonably safe to give him the assurance he seeks. However, word it a little loosely, so that you can get out of it if disaster should strike somebody near or dear.

HOW DO YOU TELL A FOUR-YEAR-OLD ABOUT DIVORCE?

Dear Doctors:

I am very much concerned about something that is happening in our family and don't know how to handle it. My husband and I are getting a divorce, and so far we haven't broken this news to our Four-year-old son Jimmy. How can I tell him? How will he take it? Do you think the effects of divorce are always disastrous to a young child?

My husband and I have known for some time that our marriage was not working out. At first we hoped we could manage to stay together for Jimmy's sake. Now we know that isn't possible. Help!

We think you are right *not* to stay together "for the sake of your son." Child specialists have long felt that it is the emotional divorce that precedes the legal divorce that harms most.

Jimmy, obviously, will not welcome this news. Even a young child generally would prefer that his family, even though an unhappy one, remain intact. However, a very young child often recovers from divorce, and adapts to a new way of living, more easily than an older one.

Jimmy will be most influenced, perhaps, by the way you and your husband conduct yourselves. If both of you remain calm, and at least superficially friendly, and you yourself don't act as if the end of the world had come, chances are that Jimmy, like thousands of other children of divorce, will survive emotionally.

So, make every effort to convey to your son that what

is happening is not dreadful. Assure him that his father is not leaving because of anything that he, Jimmy, has done or has not done. Assure him that his father will still be his father and that his father still loves him. Tell him specifically that he will continue to see his father.

Do your very best to refrain from saying hostile or ugly things about your husband. Try to give the explanation of why he is leaving in as calm and matter-of-fact a way as you can, explaining that when people marry they hope it will last forever but that sometimes it just doesn't work out that way. This does not mean that either person is bad, or that either does not love the child.

Be sure to emphasize to Jimmy that though his father will no longer be your husband he still will be Jimmy's father and will not be lost to him.

And, from a practical point of view, because even a Four-year-old does have practical questions, tell him what is going to happen to him. Thus, tell him, if this is the case, that he will go right on living in his own house and that he will have a chance to visit with his father on weekends. Parents need to determine the most desirable frequency of visits. Often, once every three or four weeks works out better than the more customary every weekend.

Be aware, too, that with the very young boy or girl you may need to give the same information more than once.

SHOULD YOU TREAT TWINS ALIKE?

Dear Doctors:

My husband and I have Four-year-old girl twins, Jane and Samantha. They are darling little girls, and we have had a reasonably easy time of it so far. Our problem now concerns school this fall. The twins are very close to each other and, though we certainly haven't pushed it, like to do things together. Some of our friends say they should be separated when they go to school. We're afraid that would be extremely upsetting to them both. Should we, or shouldn't we, urge the school to keep them together in kindergarten? And, can you recommend a good book on twinning?

People nowadays seem to feel rather strongly that twins should not be dressed alike, named alike, or kept always together. Most seem to feel that each twin should be treated as much like an individual as possible, even though it is a temptation to make a lot of their twinship.

Thus, it is generally felt that it's best to separate them in school. Then if they want to stick closely together in out-of-school hours, that's up to them. Kindergarten can be an exception. If your girls are the kind who find it hard to accept and adapt to new experiences, you may feel that school in itself will be enough of a problem without facing them with the problem of separating from each other.

If in your judgment they can make it, it would probably be desirable to start them in separate classrooms. If not, you might prefer to have them together in kindergarten and then start the separation with first grade. However, it can make a difference whether twins are identical or fraternal. We tend to allow identical twins to stay together until they are ready to separate. This may not be until third or fourth grade or even considerably later. But the sooner you separate fraternal twins, possibly the better.

The best, in fact just about the only book that talks about twins much past infancy, is Herbert Collier's *The Psychology of Twins: A Practical Handbook*. We think you'll find it helpful.

WILL BOY BE BORED IN KINDERGARTEN IF HE GOES TO NURSERY SCHOOL FIRST?

Dear Doctors:

I would like to send my oldest son, now Four, to nursery school. But people tell me that if he goes to nursery school now, he will be bored next year in kindergarten, and even more bored in first grade because by then he will be tired of school. Do you think this is true? And can you explain to me, clearly, the differences between kindergarten and nursery school?

Kindergarten and nursery school are not different by some arbitrary ruling. To some extent even the same materials might be used in the two situations.

Rather, they are different because of the different ages and abilities of the children enrolled, which make necessary quite different curriculums. In fact, the daily schedule and type of experience are actually quite different within the nursery school itself for the different age groups.

Thus, all groups might well play with drawing and painting materials, clay, and blocks, but Two-, Three-, Four-, and Five-year-old groups each play with these materials in an entirely different way. The skilled teacher not only recognizes the different needs of children using the same materials but would be prompted to change or modify materials when this is necessary.

The most important aspects of a school are the teacher and the children. Almost any appropriate materials, with skilled guidance, can enable the child to experience the satisfactions of his age level, and can stimulate him to growth toward the age he is to become. In addition, one important aspect of either nursery school or kindergarten is the satisfaction of being with children of one's own age.

As to the danger of being bored, it would be most unlikely for a rich nursery school experience to cause a child to be bored in a following year with a kindergarten experience that would in many ways be entirely different— different not only because the situation is set up differently, but mostly because the child himself is different. In any event, being bored in school seldom occurs because a child is too smart for his grade or because he has had too much earlier school experience. It usually occurs because a child is non-creative in using opportunities that are almost always available in a well-conceived school situation.

SHOULD DONALD START KINDERGARTEN BEFORE HE TURNS
FIVE?

Dear Doctors:

My problem is my oldest son, Donald, now Four. He
will be Five on November 13. The cut-off date in our
town is December 31, so Donnie is eligible to enter
kindergarten when school starts in September. Parents
are allowed to use their judgment about keeping a
child out of school.

My husband, having started school too early himself,
knows that school life can be miserable if you are not
physically and emotionally ready to accept it. Friends
and relatives, however, think we are being overconsci-
entious and that a problem exists only in our minds.

Both my husband and I would rather that Donnie
start next year, rather than start now, fail, and then
have to be held back. Another factor which contributes
to our confusion is that his two best friends will be sent
to school according to schedule. We fear that he would
be heartbroken, at first, if he were left behind.

Donnie seems to us like a very bright boy, but he is
small and seems immature. Both my husband and I
are thoroughly confused about this whole problem. It
seems that the more we read, the more we find conflicting opinions.

True, there are conflicting opinions. Our own is that it
is the very unusual November boy who is ready to start
kindergarten in the September *before* he has had his fifth
birthday. A December cut-off date is, in our eyes, inex-
cusable unless a young or Four-and-a-half-year-old kindergarten group is provided. The ideal cut-off date is September 1 or earlier.

You say that your husband knows from his own experience what a too-early start can do. He is right that it is
better to start late, rather than to start early and then
repeat.

True, Donnie may feel sad if his friends start school before he does. But it would be a very poor decision to put him into a situation where he may be unhappy and may do poorly for the next twelve years or more just to keep from hurting his feelings now.

EPILOGUE

Yes, Four is indeed wild and wonderful. We hope you will enjoy this age to its full because Five, if growth follows its usual course, is quite something else again.

Four is exuberant; Five is controlled. Four tests the limits; Five conforms. Four delights in seeing how far he can go; Five wants to do what you, his parents, want him to do.

When your boy or girl is only Four, visions of delinquency may dance before your eyes; when he is Five, you may wonder if he or she isn't perhaps a little *too* good.

The rhythm of growth seems at times almost as lawful as that of the tides. Equilibrium—disequilibrium. Expansion—contraction. If you can add respect for what is going on to your natural love and affection for your own preschooler, you will add immeasurably to *your* enjoyment of these early years as well as to his!

APPENDIXES
Good Toys
for Four-Year-Olds

Animals, toy
Balls
Baskets and boxes
Blocks
Boards and sawhorse for seesaw
Boards for balancing and sliding
Board games, simple
Books
Bouncing board
Brushes for painting
Camera (toy)
Cash register (toy)
Chest of drawers, cupboard, doll-size
Clay
Climbing apparatus, as Jungle Gym, Tower Gym, ladders, boxes
Cooking equipment (toy)
Costume box, including pocketbooks, hats, gloves, scarves, jewelry, curtains, shoes
Crayons, large-size
Dishes and cooking utensils

Doctor and nurse kit
Doll bed, carriage, high chair
Dollhouse
Doll clothing with large buttons and buttonholes
Dolls
Doorway gym
Drawing and coloring materials
Easel
Easel paper
Fingerpaints
Fit-together construction toys and Tinkertoys or Lego
Flannel-surfaced boards and pieces of flannel or felt in different shapes and colors
Flashlight
Garden tools, small
Hammer with short handle and heavy head
Hand puppets
Hollow blocks
Housekeeping toys, including broom, vacuum cleaner, dust mop

Jigsaw puzzles
Jump rope
Kegs
Kites
Logs
Magnets
Miniature people or animals
Musical instruments, such as wrist bells, drum, tambourine, castanets, triangle
Nature specimens, such as fish, turtles, salamanders, rabbits, guinea pigs, or plants. (These of course are not really toys.)
Nests of boxes or cans
Packing boxes large and sturdy enough for child to climb on
Paints and easel
Phonograph and records
Pipes for blowing bubbles
Playhouse
Pregummed dots, squares, triangles of colored paper
Punching bag
Ring toss
Rocking horse
Roller skates
Rope and string
Sailboats (toy)

Sand toys, including spoon, sugar scoop, pail, cans, sifter
Sandbox
Sawhorse
Scissors
Scooter
Scrapbook
Screwing toys
Seesaw
Sled
Slide
Small airplanes, automobiles, trucks, boats, trains
Small boards for building, hauling
Stove
Suitcase
Swing, adjustable
Table and chair, child-size
Toy telephone
Train, dump truck, steam shovel large enough for child to ride on
Tricycle
Wagon
Water-play materials
Wheels of all kinds: cars, dump truck, bulldozer, tractors, wheelbarrow
Workbench and vise

Books for
Four-Year-Olds

Allard, Harry. *The Tutti-Frutti Case.* Englewood Cliffs, N.J.: Prentice-Hall, 1975.

Benton, Robert. *Don't Ever Wish for a Seven-Foot Bear.* New York: Knopf, 1972.

Berger, Terry. *I Have Feelings.* New York: Behavioral Publications, 1971.

Boden, Alice, *The Field of Buttercups.* New York: Walck, 1974.

Bottner, Barbara. *Fun House.* Englewood Cliffs, N.J.: Prentice-Hall, 1975.

Brenner, Barbara. *Barto Takes the Subway.* New York: Knopf, 1961.

Brinckloe, Julie. *The Spider Web.* New York: Doubleday, 1975.

Brown, Margaret Wise. *The Indoor Noisy Book.* New York: Harper & Row, 1942.

———. *Shhh! Bang!* New York: Harper & Row, 1943.

———. *The Important Book.* New York: Harper & Row, 1949.

———. *Three Little Animals.* New York: Harper & Row, 1965.

Brownstone, Cecily. *All Kinds of Mothers.* New York: McKay, 1969.

Buckley, Helen. *Grandfather and I.* New York: Lothrop, Lee & Shepard, 1959.

———. *My Sister and I.* New York: Lothrop, Lee & Shepard, 1963.

———. *Grandmother and I.* New York: Lothrop, Lee & Shepard, 1965.

Clifton, Lucille. *Everett Anderson's Year.* New York: Holt, Rinehart, and Winston, 1974.

DePaolo, Tomie. *Michael Bird Boy.* Englewood Cliffs, N.J.: Prentice-Hall, 1975.

Duvoisin, Rogert. *The Rain Puddle.* New York: Lothrop, Lee & Shepard, 1965.

———. *Jasmine.* New York: Knopf, 1973.

———. *Our Veronica Goes to Petunia Farm.* New York: Knopf/Pantheon, 1973.

———. *The Crocodile in the Tree.* New York: Knopf, 1973.

Emberly, Ed. *Klippity Klop.* Boston: Little, Brown, 1974.

Ernst, Kathryn. *Danny and His Thumb.* Englewood Cliffs, N.J.: Prentice-Hall, 1972.

Ets, Marie Hall. *Gilberto and the Wind.* New York: Viking, 1963.

———. *Just Me.* New York: Viking, 1965.

Fassler, Joan. *My Grandpa Died Today.* New York: Behavioral Publications, 1970.

———. *Don't Worry Dear.* New York: Behavioral Publications, 1971.

French, Viona. *King Tree.* New York: Walck, 1973.

Ga'ag, Wanda. *Millions of Cats.* New York: Coward-McCann, 1928.

Galdone, Paul. *The Frog Prince.* New York: McGraw-Hill, 1975.

Garland, Sarah. *The Joss Bird.* New York: Scribner, 1975.

Geis, Darlene. *Dinny, Big Little Dinosaur.* New York: Wonder Books, 1959.

Grollman, Earl. *Talking about Death.* Boston: Beacon, 1970.

Hample, Stoo. *The Silly Book.* New York: Harper & Row, 1950.

Heide, Florence, and Van Clief, Sylvia. *That's What Friends Are For.* New York: Scholastic Book Services, 1968.

Hoban, Russell. *Bedtime for Frances.* New York: Harper & Row, 1960.

———. *Bread and Jam for Frances.* New York: Harper & Row, 1964.

———, and Selig, Sylvia. *Ten What: A Mystery Counting Book.* New York: Scribner, 1975.

Jewett, Nancy. *Cheer Up Pig.* New York: Harper & Row, 1975.

Johnson, Crockett. *Harold and the Purple Crayon.* New York: Harper & Row, 1955.

Joslin, Sesyle. *What Do You Say, Dear?* New York: Young, Scott, 1958.

Keats, Ezra Jack. *The Snowy Day* (and others in this series). New York: Viking, 1962.

———. *Peter's Chair.* New York: Harper & Row, 1967.

Kent, Jack. *The Egg Book.* New York: Macmillan, 1975.

Kessler, Ethel. *Do Baby Bears Sit on Chairs?* Garden City, N.Y.: Doubleday, 1961.

———. *The Day Daddy Stayed Home.* Garden City, N.Y.: Doubleday, 1971.

———, and Kessler, Leonard. *The Big Red Bus.* Garden City, N.Y.: Doubleday, 1964.

Klein, Leonore. *Silly Sam.* New York: Scholastic Book Services, 1971.

Kraus, Ruth. *The Backward Day.* New York: Harper & Row, 1950.

———. *A Hole Is to Dig.* New York: Harper & Row, 1952.

———. *I Want to Paint My Bathroom Blue.* New York: Harper & Row, 1956.

———. *Somebody Else's Nut Tree.* New York: Harper & Row, 1958.

Kuskin, Karla. *All Sizes of Noises.* New York: Harper & Row, 1962.

———. *Near the Window Tree.* New York: Harper & Row, 1975.

Langstaff, Nancy. *A Tiny Baby for You.* New York: Harcourt, Brace Jovanovich, 1955.

Leaf, Munro. *Ferdinand.* New York: Viking, 1962.

Levine, Joan Goldman. *A Bedtime Story.* New York: Dutton, 1975.

Lionni, Leo. *Swimmy.* New York: Pantheon, 1963.

———. *The Biggest House in the World.* New York: Knopf/ Pantheon, 1973.

———. *The Greentail Mouse.* New York: Pantheon, 1973.

———. *In the Rabbit Garden.* New York: Pantheon, 1975.

Lobel, Arnold. *A Zoo for Mister Muster.* New York: Harper & Row, 1962.

McGovern, Ann. *Too Much Noise.* Boston: Houghton Mifflin, 1967.

Mayle, Peter. *Where Did I Come From?* New York: Lyle Stuart, 1973.

Meredith, Judith C. *Now We Are a Family.* Boston: Beacon Press, 1971.

Merriam, Eve. *Boys and Girls: Girls and Boys*. New York: Holt, Rinehart and Winston, 1972.

Milne, A. A. *Now We Are Six*. New York: Dutton, 1961.

———. *When We Were Very Young*. New York: Dutton, 1964.

———. *The Christopher Robin Book of Verse*. New York: Dutton, 1967.

Minarik, Else. *Little Bear*. New York: Harper & Row, 1957.

Moffett, Martha. *A Flower Pot Is Not a Hat*. New York: Dutton, 1972.

Moore, Lilian. *Little Raccoon and the Outside World*. New York: McGraw-Hill, 1965.

Nôdset, Joan L. *Go Away Dog*. New York: Harper & Row, 1963.

———. *Who Took the Farmer's Hat?* New York: Harper & Row, 1963.

Parsons, Ellen. *Rainy Day Together*. New York: Harper, 1971.

Paterson, Diane. *Eat*. New York: Dial, 1975.

Petie, Harriet. *Billions of Bugs*. Englewood Cliffs, N.J.: Prentice-Hall, 1975.

Preston, Edna Mitchell. *The Temper Tantrum Book*. New York: Viking, 1969.

Ray, Wade. *A Train to Spain*. New York: Knopf, 1963.

Rey, H. A. *Curious George* (and others in this series). Boston: Houghton Mifflin, 1941.

Richelson, Geraldine. *What Is a Grownup?* New York: Crown, 1975.

Ringi, Kjell. *The Sun and the Cloud*. New York: Harper & Row, 1971.

Rodgers, Mary. *The Rotten Book*. New York: Harper & Row, 1969.

Schick, Eleanor. *A Surprise in the Forest*. New York: Harper & Row, 1964.

Schlein, Miriam. *Fast Is Not a Ladybug*. New York: William R. Scott, 1953.

———. *Heavy Is a Hippopotamus*. New York: William R. Scott, 1954.

Sendak, Maurice. *Where the Wild Things Are*. New York: Harper & Row, 1963.

Seuss, Dr. *The Cat in the Hat*. New York: Random House, 1957.

———. *Green Eggs and Ham*. New York: Random House, 1960.

———. *The Foot Book*. New York: Random House, 1968.

Showers, Paul. *Your Skin and Mine*. New York: Crowell, 1962.

——, and Sperry, Kay. *Before You Were a Baby* (New York: Crowell, 1968).

Silverstein, Shel. *The Giving Tree*. New York: Harper & Row, 1964.

Simon, Norma. *The Baby House*. New York: Lippincott, 1955.

Slepian, Jan, and Seidler, Ann. *Lester and the Sea Monster* (and others in this series). New York: Follett, 1964.

Stein, Sara Bonnett. *Making Babies*. New York: Walker, 1974.

——. *That New Baby*. New York: Walker, 1974.

Udry, Janice. *A Tree Is Nice*. New York: Harper & Row, 1956.

Ungerer, Tomi. *Crictor*. New York: Harper & Row, 1958.

——. *The Beast of Mr. Racine*. New York: Farrar, Straus & Giroux, 1971.

Watson, Jane, and others. *My Friend the Baby Sitter*. New York: Golden Press, 1971.

White, E. B. *Stuart Little*. New York: Harper & Row, 1945.

Williams, Babar. *Kevin's Grandma*. New York: Dutton, 1975.

Williams, Margery. *The Velveteen Rabbit*. Garden City, N.Y.: Doubleday, n.d.

Withers, Carl. *Painting the Moon*. New York: Dutton, 1970.

Wright, Ethel. *Saturday Walk*. New York: William R. Scott, 1954.

Zemach, Harve and Kathe. *The Princess and the Froggie*. New York: Farrar, Straus & Giroux, 1975.

Zindel, Paul. *I Love My Mother*. New York: Harper & Row, 1975.

Zion, Gene. *Harry the Dirty Dog*. New York: Harper & Row, 1954.

——. *No Roses for Harry*. New York: Harper & Row, 1958.

——. *The Plant Sitter*. New York: Harper & Row, 1959.

Zolotow, Charlotte. *Do You Know What I'll Do?* New York: Harper & Row, 1958.

——. *The Quarreling Book*. New York: Harper & Row, 1963.

——. *The Sky Was Blue*. New York: Harper & Row, 1963.

——. *Someday*. New York: Harper & Row, 1965.

——. *A Father Like That*. New York: Harper & Row, 1971.

——. *Hold My Hand*. New York: Harper & Row, 1973.

——. *William's Doll*. New York: Harper & Row, 1972.

——. *When the Wind Stops*. New York: Harper & Row, 1975.

Books for the Parents of Four-Year-Olds

Ames, Louise Bates. *Parents Ask.* A syndicated daily newspaper column. New Haven, Conn.: Gesell Institute, 1952–.

———. *Child Care and Development.* Philadelphia: Lippincott, 1970.

———, and Chase, Joan Ames. *Don't Push Your Preschooler.* New York: Harper & Row, 1974.

———, and Ilg, Frances L. *Your Two-Year-Old: Terrible or Tender.* New York: Delacorte, 1976.

———. *Your Three-Year-Old: Friend or Foe.* New York: Delacorte, 1976.

Braga, Laurie, and Braga, Joseph. *Learning and Growing: A Guide to Child Development.* Englewood Cliffs, N.J.: Prentice-Hall, 1975.

Brazelton, T. Berry. *Infants and Mothers.* New York: Delacorte, 1969.

———. *Toddlers and Parents.* New York: Delacorte, 1974.

Caplan, Frank, and Caplan, Theresa. *The Power of Play.* New York: Doubleday, 1973.

Cleveland, Anne. *Parents from Zero to Ten.* New York: Simon & Schuster, 1958.

Coffin, Patricia. *1, 2, 3, 4, 5, 6. How to Understand and Enjoy the Years That Count.* New York: Macmillan, 1972.

Colew, Colin. *How to Raise Your Child Without Threats or Violence.* New York: Exposition Press, 1975.

Collier, Herbert. *The Psychology of Twins: A Practical Handbook.* Phoenix, Ariz.: Twins, 4227 N. 32nd St., 1974.

144

Comer, James P., and Poussaint, Alvin F. *Black Child Care.* New York: Simon & Schuster, 1975.

Crook, William G. *Can Your Child Read? Is He Hyperactive?* Jackson, Tenn.: Pedicenter Press, 1975.

Dodson, Fitzhugh. *How to Parent.* Los Angeles: Nash, 1970.

———. *How to Father.* Los Angeles: Nash, 1974.

Feingold, Ben J. *Why Your Child Is Hyperactive.* New York: Random House, 1975.

Forer, Lucille K. *Birth Order and Life Roles.* Springfield, Ill.: C. C. Thomas, 1969.

Gardner, Richard A. *Understanding Children.* New York: Aronson, 1973.

Gesell, Arnold, et al. *The First Five Years of Life.* New York: Harper & Row, 1940.

Gesell, Arnold; Ilg, Frances L.; and Ames, Louise B. *Infant and Child in the Culture of Today.* New York: Harper & Row, rev. ed., 1974.

Grollman, Earl A. (Ed.) *Explaining Death to Children.* Boston: Beacon, 1967.

———. *Explaining Divorce to Children.* Boston: Beacon, 1969.

Harrison-Ross, Phyllis, and Wyden, Barbara. *The Black Child: A Parent's Guide.* New York: Peter Wyden, 1973.

Hartley, Ruth E., and Goldensen, Robert M. *The Complete Book of Children's Play.* New York: Crowell, 1970.

Holt, L. Emmett, Jr. *Good Housekeeping Book of Baby and Child Care.* New York: Appleton-Century-Crofts, 1957.

Ilg, Frances L., and Ames, Louise B. *Child Behavior.* New York: Harper & Row, 1957.

Ilg, Frances L.; Ames, Louise B.; Goodenough, Evelyn; and Andresen, Irene. *The Gesell Institute Party Book.* New York: Harper & Row, 1959.

Johnson, June. *Home Play for the Preschool Child.* New York: Harper & Row, 1957.

Kraskin, Robert A. *You Can Improve Your Vision.* New York: Doubleday, 1968.

LeShan, Eda. *How to Survive Parenthood.* New York: Random House, 1965.

Levinson, Boris M. *Pets and Human Development.* Springfield, Ill.: C. C. Thomas, 1972.

Liepmann, Lise. *Your Child's Sensory World.* New York: Dial, 1973.

McIntire, Roger W. *For Love of Children*. Del Mar, Calif.: CRM Books, 1970.

Maynard, Fredelle. *Guiding Your Child to a More Creative Life*. New York: Doubleday, 1973. (Contains excellent lists of books for parents on arts and crafts, drawing, painting, crayoning, clay, modeling, ceramics, fabrics and yarns, puppets, also children's records.)

Pitcher, Evelyn G., and Ames, Louise B. *The Guidance Nursery School*. New York: Harper & Row, rev. ed., 1975.

Sheldon, William H. *Varieties of Temperament*. New York: Hafner, 1970.

Slepian, Jan, and Seidler, Ann. *Mr. Sipple and the Naughty Princess, Magic Arthur and the Giant* (and others in this series). Chicago: Follett, 1964.

Smith, Lendon. *Improving Your Child's Behavior Chemistry*. Englewood Cliffs, N.J.: Prentice-Hall, 1976.

Toman, Walter. *Family Constellation: Its Effect on Personality and Social Behavior*. New York: Springer, 1969.

Wender, Paul H. *The Hyperactive Child: A Guide for Parents*. New York: Crown, 1973.

Wunderlich, Ray. *Allergy, Brains and Children Coping*. St. Petersburg, Fla.: Johnny Reads Press, 1973.

Young, Milton A. *Buttons Are to Push*. New York: Pitman, 1970.

NOTES

1. Information on visual behavior was furnished by Richard J. Apell, O.D., director of the Vision Department of the Gesell Institute of Child Development.
2. In order to make use of a controlled situation, our observations were made during the course of the Gesell Preschool Examination, as described in *The First Five Years of Life*, by Arnold Gesell et al. (New York: Harper & Row, 1940). This examination was given individually to boys and girls of each of the preschool ages.
3. Laurie Braga and Joseph Braga, *Learning and Growing: A Guide to Child Development* (Englewood Cliffs, N.J.: Prentice-Hall, 1975).
4. Among the physicians who have written helpful and informative books on the damaging effects that can come from a harmful diet are Drs. William Crook, Ben J. Feingold, Lendon Smith and Ray Wunderlich, whose books are listed on pages 144 to 146.
5. For a description of these tests see Frances L. Ilg and Louise B. Ames, *School Readiness* (New York: Harper & Row, 1965); and for a discussion of what they mean to the parent, see Louise B. Ames, *Is Your Child in the Wrong Grade?* (New York: Harper & Row, 1967).
6. Arnold Gesell, "Stability of Mental-Growth Careers," *Thirty-ninth Yearbook of the National Society for the Study of Education*, part 2 (Bloomington, Ind.: Public School Publishing Co., 1940).

147

INDEX

Photo Credits

CLARK BROADBENT, *pages* 11, 15, 16, 20, 26, 39, 43, 52, 68, 95, 99

MAURY ENGLANDER, *pages* 5, 45, 79, 82, 88

MARTIN IGER, *pages* 19, 40, 51, 71, 85

EARL SCOTT, *pages* 6, 87

Photos from "Playmates-Schoolmates," preschool children's television series, with permission by Group W (Westinghouse Broadcasting Company), *pages* 23, 55, 56

Tourism, Globalization and Development

Tourism, Globalization and Development

Responsible Tourism Planning

Donald G. Reid

Pluto Press

LONDON

First published 2003 by Pluto Press
345 Archway Road, London N6 5AA

www.plutobooks.com

British Library Cataloguing in Publication Data
A catalogue record for this book is available from
the British Library

ISBN 978 0 7453 1998 8 paperback

Library of Congress Cataloging in Publication Data
Reid, Donald G.
    Tourism, globalization and development : responsible tourism
planning / Donald G. Reid.
        p. cm.
Includes bibliographical references.
    ISBN 978-0-7453-1998-8 (pbk)
    1. Tourism. 2. Economic development. I. Title.

    G155.A1R4565 2003
    338.4'791—dc21

                                                    2003008498

10 9 8 7 6 5 4 3 2 1

Designed and produced for Pluto Press by
Chase Publishing Services, Sidmouth, EX10 9QG
Typeset from disk by Stanford DTP Services, Towcester
Printed and bound in Great Britain by
Marston Book Services Limited, Didcot

Contents

List of Tables and Figures

Acknowledgements

A book of this type does not get written without significant help and encouragement from a number of people. First and foremost, I want to thank my partner in life Patricia MacPherson for her patience and support during the writing of the manuscript. Additionally, Patricia assisted with the research that eventually became the Bermuda case study. Thank you to Judith Hall-Bean, Director of the Bermuda Tourism Department and Billy Griffith, President of the Hotel Association of Bermuda for their openness and interest in assisting with this project. Heather Mair and Jennifer Sumner reviewed earlier drafts of this manuscript and provided valuable advice along the way. My research team and colleagues Wanda George and Heather Mair have worked diligently on our research projects which allowed me to reflect on the state of tourism today and how it is tied to corporate globalization and, more importantly, its effect on many communities and people around the world. Many thanks to Victor Cumming, principle of the consulting firm Westcoast Economic Development Associates for involving me in the Golden impact assessment project which is included in this book as a case study. Thanks must also go to the people of Golden for their openness and interest in having their story told. Also, thank you to Isaac Sindiga (deceased) my Kenya research partner who would have coauthored the Kenya case study if he had survived. The cooperation of David Western and the Kenya Wildlife Service is also appreciated. Thanks also to Jim Taylor, colleague at the University of Guelph who has worked on many aspects of the research which provided background to this work. Also, a special thank you must go to Teus Kamphorst, Director of the World Leisure and Recreation Association's International Centre of Excellence (WICE), Wageningen, The Netherlands, where much of the manuscript was written while I was on sabbatical. The accommodations, office support and intellectual atmosphere provided by Teus and WICE was of great help. Lastly, a very special thank you must go to all of the communities and individuals involved in the many research projects which have led to the completion of this work. To them I am eternally grateful for their understanding and willingness to share their experience.

1 Introduction

TOURISM AND DEVELOPMENT

Tourism is a dynamic force homogenizing societies and commodifying cultures across the globe. It is promoted as a positive means of economic development for the many countries and communities who have lost their traditional industries, or for those who simply hope to improve their general economic condition. Historically, however, tourism has not been a positive experience for all parties engaged in the development process, or treated all stakeholders in the enterprise equally. While trans-national corporations and entrepreneurs benefit greatly from tourism development, local people often bear the cost of that development without adequate reward. In an attempt to expose these inadequacies and subsequently set out a different course, this book provides a critique of the tourism development process as it has developed historically. This critique is followed by a practical guide to the future development of the industry. It stresses the role of community as the foundation on which tourism development must be constructed if it is to achieve the results proponents suggest are important to society. Tourism is analyzed here from the point of view of holistic development, and the constraints placed on its sustainability by corporate globalization are examined.

After the dramatic attacks on the World Trade Center and the Pentagon on September 11, 2001, President George W. Bush announced that 'those responsible will be brought to justice, or justice will be brought to them'. At first blush this may seem to most US citizens like an appropriate response – particularly to those personally affected by the disaster, and their allies across the globe. However, it is recognized by many that this attitude will not deal with the root causes of the problem that provoked the incident in the first place, nor with what has been described as the worldwide rise of terrorism. Some scholars, including McMurtry (1999), argue that these types of event are incubated by what he calls the 'cancer stage of capitalism', and by the rise of trans-national corporate hegemony, leaving a single superpower dominating the world. Democracy is viewed from many parts of the world as skewed in favor of the rich and powerful. In his book *Jihad vs McWorld: Terrorism's Challenge to Democracy*, Benjamin Barber wrote:

> If democracy is to be the instrument by which the world avoids the stark choice between a sterile cultural monism (McWorld) and a raging cultural fundamentalism (Jihad), neither of which services diversity or civic liberty, then America, Britain, and their allies will have to open a crucial second civic and democratic front aimed not against terrorism per se but against the anarchism and social chaos – the economic reductionism and its commercializing homogeneity – that have created the climate of despair and hopelessness that terrorism has so effectively exploited. A second democratic front will be advanced not only in the name of retributive justice and secularist interests, but in the name of distributive justice ...
>
> (Barber, 1995: xiii)

This book is about the achievement of distributive justice through the development of tourism. However, at present tourism is a major force in the organization of 'McWorld', both symbolically and practically. It is a worldwide phenomenon dominated by transnational corporations, which both exports the culture of the West to developing countries, and – perhaps more importantly – drains the developing world of its resources, including capital. Tourism is a product of the hegemony of the West, and demonstrates both the rising difference in the conditions of material subsistence between wealthy and poor nations, and the growing Third World conditions found in many parts of the wealthy nations themselves. It is often the poorest people living in these already underprivileged circumstances who provide labor to the tourism industry across the globe. Employment in tourism provides a meager living to its workers, rarely allowing them to lift themselves beyond conditions of social marginalization and poverty. For distributive justice to be achieved, tourism will have to develop a new approach in both its planning and development processes, producing a project that would look very different to the one prevailing at present.

This book provides a critique of the principles on which tourism is structured at present, and presents an alternative prescription for tourism development, designed to address more directly the goal of distributive justice. The priorities of community planning and control are given greater importance in this new design, as opposed to the prerogatives of the trans-national corporation.

Economic globalization affects all countries and continents. Corporate globalization has been legitimized by the collapse of the Soviet Union and the supposed triumph of capitalism over socialism. Without a global counter-force, capital enjoys free rein to exploit labor and other resources in all corners of the globe. This exploitation is supported by the mantra of development, supposedly for the benefit of those who are left behind by the economic advances and increased standard of living created in the industrialized world. Tourism is advanced by businesses and governments alike as a development mechanism which can lift people out of poverty and make them equal partners in society. But regardless of how altruistic this claim may sound, it is doubtful whether those who are intended to benefit – at least according to the rhetoric – have gained nearly as much as those promoting tourism through corporate globalization. While no one can condone the carnage of the events of September 11, they must be viewed as a rejection of corporate globalization and the exploitation taking place across the globe, and not simply as the actions of a few deranged individuals, as some would have us believe. As Barber suggests, referring to public attitudes towards these events throughout the developing world, 'their quarrel is not with modernity but with the aggressive neo-liberal ideology that has been prosecuted in its name in pursuit of global market society more conducive to profits for some than to justice for all'. (Barber, 1995: xv)

The tourism sector is tied closely to the globalizing force which pursues profits over justice. In fact, tourism is one of the main products being globalized, while some even argue that it is one of the main forces driving globalization (Brown, 1998; George, 2002). While globalization is made possible by the drive of capitalism to expand and grow, and by the development and pervasiveness of new technologies, tourism is one of the important beneficiaries and vehicles of its expression. New technologies such as the internet and air travel have revolutionized the tourism industry; tourists are now able to travel almost anywhere in the world. Increased leisure time, combined with burgeoning disposable income for some, enables large numbers of people, especially from the developed world, to become dedicated worldwide travelers. The developed countries not only export travelers, but have also cultivated domestic tourism, providing interesting destinations within easy reach. In some cases this allows rural communities to survive after their primary industries have failed, and adds a new cultural dynamic to urban living. But these new conditions transform the social realm, moving life away from the imperatives of the manufacturing and extractive industries which provided the backbone of the industrial economy.

No matter how enticing the promise of tourism development may at first seem, all over the world – and especially in developing countries – tourism is characterized by uneven development, ensuring erratic returns and unequal incomes. This is particularly noticeable at the local level in both developed and less developed countries (LDCs). Local communities often form the front line in terms of service provision, but are last in line when it comes to benefiting from development. Local people are not only excluded from many of the benefits that result from tourism development; they are often neglected in the planning and decision-making process that generates it. The local community is all too often viewed by tourism developers either as a common resource to be exploited, or as an obstacle to be overcome in order to implement development strategies. With the exception of a few enlightened entrepreneurs who understand that it is in their long-term best interest to consider community values, developers almost never do so, unless forced to by the national government in whose jurisdiction their proposed development is targeted. As a result of the explosion of tourism attractions over the last few years, and their highly competitive nature, some entrepreneurs now understand that potential tourism sites are finite, and that the old conception of 'throw-away' tourism destinations no longer provides an appropriate strategy for the industry. 'Sustainability', then, takes on several meanings for the tourism planner: it not only refers to the community and its social and physical environment, but also to the competitiveness and longevity of the tourism enterprise itself. The sustainability of a tourism product must be considered from a holistic perspective, and not just measured in terms of one or only a few indicators.

Individuals living in communities that choose tourism as an economic generator become part of that destination's attraction, whether they want to be or not. What makes a tourism destination attractive in many cases is the unique culture and lifestyle of the people living in the area. In Canada, for example, the practices of many First Nations people or east coast fishers are of interest to visitors from around the world. Their unique way of life has been mythologized over the years, and many visitors are interested in observing it; the cultural practices of traditional societies are often fascinating to the tourist. The traditional life of rural communities is fast being extinguished by urbanization, and often caters to an appetite for the exotic on the part of many city dwellers. But when there are no restrictions on the observation of such societies, unwelcome intrusion often occurs, leaving individuals and communities feeling violated. Some First Nations communities in Canada's far north are viewed by many visitors as artificial constructions, the equivalent of Disney World – put in place simply for the benefit of tourists, rather than as private dwellings and living communities. The line between the observation of a commodity and the invasion of privacy becomes blurred. As a result, visitors have been known to take pictures through the front windows or open doorways of private homes, leaving the owner feeling violated. This negative interaction has been fostered by the dominance of the relationship between the servant and the served, where an emphasis on that between host and guest may have been more beneficial. While at first glance this distinction may appear small, it could in the long term enable some interesting improvements to the tourism system.

These inequities and intrusions are a consequence of commercialism and capitalism being taken to an extreme. McMurtry (1999) has gone as far as to refer to this stage of capitalism as constituting a cancer on the global social system. He argues, quite rightly, that the fundamental laws of the life code of value, which should provide the basis for social development, including universal health care, clean air and potable water, have been abandoned in favor of maximizing profit at all cost. In interpreting McMurtry, Sumner (2002: 147) suggests that 'two master principles of value-gain underlie the long economic war expressed by history. While these codes of value have often been confused, the future of civil and planetary life-organization depends on their distinction, especially given the present period of unregulated globalization'. For McMurtry (1998: 298), *life* means 'organic movement, sentience and feeling, and thought'. *Means of life* refers to 'what enables life to be preserved or to extend its vital range of these three planes of being alive'. This includes such entities as clean water, food and shelter in addition to affective interaction, environmental space and accessible learning conditions. I would also want to identify *leisure* as a human domain which belongs in the life code of value definition.

Contrasted with the life code of value is money code of value where 'money is the beginning and end of the sequence because money, not life' (Sumner 2002: 148), is the 'regulating objective of thought and action' (McMurtry, 1998: 299). Thus, money, according to Sumner, 'is not used for life, but life is used for money. From this code of value, it follows that more money is always better by definition', regardless of what happens to life circumstances in the process. (Summer, 2002: 148)

McMurtry (1999: 17) argues that scholars and social commentators must be open to examining the 'value structure' which has produced such a cancer, and not content themselves with lesser issues. As he puts it:

> This is why I have chosen the term '*value programme*' as a designator. A value system becomes a *programme* when its assumed structure of worth rules out all thought of alternative to it as 'nonsense'.
>
> When the Hindu does not think of a reality beyond caste dharma, and when the marketer cannot value beyond market price, we see examples of value programmes at work. A social value program is a jealous God. Consciousness and decision, preference and rejection are imprisoned within it. Whatever is against it is repelled as alien, evil, abnormal. The modalities of role and individuation, personal gratification and avoidance, become elaborations and differentiations of the programme internalized as the self. Lived alternative to the role-master is taboo. In the adolescence of the species, all members of the group see as the group sees. All experience as the group does. All affirm and repudiate as the group does. There is no reality beyond it save the Other.
>
> (McMurtry, 1999: 21)

Tourism is now a major force in the 'cancer stage of capitalism', which, according to McMurtry (1999), now exists throughout society. It is the fastest-growing foreign income earner worldwide, producing huge profits for such companies as Thomas Cook, Club Med, Carnival, Four Seasons, Marriott, Starwood, Hilton, and Canadian Pacific Hotels & Resorts, to name only a few (see Table 2.2 for a detailed financial analysis of these trans-national tourism corporations). As a consequence of its power, tourism must be analyzed in light of the value program that supports its growth and development. Because of its sheer size and power, an examination of tourism must also involve a critique of capitalism, and of the globalizing forces it has created, and which allow it to continue to grow unchecked worldwide.

As a result of the enormous pressure for increasing profits, and for the generation of national revenue to pay down foreign held debt, governments and the businesses that manage tourism destinations focus on the goal of profit maximization at the expense of the environment and social welfare. This exclusive focus on profit commodifies the host culture and devalues the potential interaction between the visitor and the local citizen. From social and environmental points of view, this is evidence of the poor planning and management of tourism destinations. The creation of sustainable tourism destinations requires a shift away from this commercial emphasis towards a locally and regionally based development strategy. This shift would entrust decision-making to those with the most to lose from unsustainable practices, and would necessitate the consideration of a multiplicity of factors in addition to the economic. Moreover, tourism in this context would redefine the experience of leisure from purely casual activity to serious leisure (Stebbins, 1997). This shift in perspective gives social and environmental development an importance at least equal to that of profit and economic growth. To accomplish this shift in attitude – and hence the creation of sustainable tourism – holistic planning is necessary; this in turn requires that environmental and social issues around the development of the host site provide the paramount organizing concept in the development process. No longer can social and environmental development be treated as an automatic outcome of business development, as the 'trickle down theory' beloved of orthodox economists would have us believe. Social and environmental development must be viewed as the concerns of a tourism project, not simply left to chance or viewed only as potential by-products. If a particular development is not socially and environmentally positive for the region and community in which it occurs – regardless of the benefits it may offer to the trans-national corporation or national government concerned – then at the very least it needs to be reconsidered.

Any comprehensive planning that does take place in relation to tourism destinations is generally at the behest of the corporation involved, and concerned exclusively with commercial and marketing issues. While individual businesses and entrepreneurs are very well placed to profit from tourism development, communities are often slow to organize themselves so as to benefit. More often than not, communities initially fail to understand the environmental value to the tourist of the area they live in, becoming aware of it only after an outside organization or company has profited handsomely from the exploitation of that same resource. A new approach is required to the planning of tourism within communities, organized according to a set of values outside the purely economic. 'Life code of value', as McMurtry has described it, is in the interests of those who live in communities organized around tourism. However, this holistic life-giving force as defined by McMurtry through his concept of the life code of value is rarely allowed to direct a tourism project, and the community is excluded from the early stages of the planning process, and only considered after a plan has been implemented. When a pattern of intrusion by visitors has been set, it is difficult to correct – although not impossible. When overuse and abuse occur, the inhabitants of the destination site feel degraded and exploited, and in some cases ready to participate in either passive or active resistance (see Butler, 1974). In a number of cases, community members have engaged in social action against tourism developments, causing disruption to everyday life for visitor and resident alike, as well as disrupting the affairs of tourism businesses. All partners in the system lose: businesses lose customers, and residents lose their tranquility. As a result, tourists lose the ultimate quality experience they seek.

Entrepreneurs engage in tourism development with marketing and profit maximization as their main objectives. Noticeably absent from the classical tourism development model is representation from other stakeholder groups – particularly from the communities most likely to be affected by development. Objectives relating to their well-being, including income generation and environmental sustainability, need to be made central to the tourism planning process. While entrepreneurs will always be integral to this process, their objectives must not be allowed to exclude other legitimate interests. Many authors (Mathieson and Wall, 1982; Mitchell, 1998) have written at length about the shortcomings of the tourism enterprise in the areas of environmental and cultural protection, so a lengthy reiteration of that discussion is not required here. A few summary comments on the subject will be made, however, in order to set the stage for later sections of the book dealing with issues of planning.

Discussions of the impacts of tourism generally focus on the social and environmental effects produced by tourism development. This book will attempt to provide strategies for assessing and monitoring such impacts (see Chapter 6). Since they are defined by individual perceptions, strategies which measure and analyze impacts of tourism are likely to be more beneficial to the discussion than a purely theoretical accounting of the impacts themselves. The impact evaluation strategies and methods outlined in Chapter 6 are not presented as absolutes, but rather as processes of negotiation grounded in the spirit of 'Limits to Acceptable Change' outlined by Stankey, McCool, Cark and Brown, (1999). This approach views impacts – environmental, social and economic – as forming a continuum, not as an absolute value, as is the case with other methods for describing carrying capacity. Instead of relating the absolute numbers of people that a particular environment or site may support, 'Limits to Acceptable Change' provides a description of a range of changes which are permissible for any given site. The changes produced by any development, in tourism or elsewhere, and the extent to which they are undesirable, are matters that should be decided by those most affected by the process. The process and outcome of change should be a negotiated conclusion as much as it is a quantitative measurement.

This book departs from the usual conception of tourism planning as a mechanistic activity divorced from community values and control, focusing instead on value-based planning and community-managed development of tourism. It is argued here that the sustainability of a tourism project, and of the community itself, can only be assured if the values of that community drive the tourism development process. This approach also demands that the process of development is given more importance than the product that is eventually developed. The primary focus of this process is on the building of community capacity, which will create long-lasting skills in the community allowing them to become more self-sufficient and less dependent on outside forces over the long-term. This focus, giving supremacy to the process over the product, has led me to refer to tourism development at the community level as the tourism 'project' rather than as the 'product'. While this may appear to be a merely semantic change, it must be seen as a major departure from the traditional way in which tourism planners have conceived of the relationship between the tourism industry and the community and the priorities given to the various parts of the tourism planning process.

The guarantee of community control is not an easy task in the face of the formidable power of trans-national corporations, which possess levels of capital sometimes exceeding those of national governments and international bodies such as the World Bank (WB), International Monetary Fund (IMF), and World Trade Organization (WTO), with whom governments are forced to deal, sometimes for their very fiscal survival. These international institutions lend or withhold needed capital on which many of the developing world governments depend for their daily transactions and to stave off economic collapse. It is they who hold the purse strings, providing much needed development loans to most LDCs. However, when communities are left out of the planning and decision-making process, conflict inevitably arises when the saturation point for tourist accommodation is exceeded, or community sensibilities are violated. It is only through negotiated tourism development, including ongoing monitoring involving all stakeholders in the process, that such problems can be avoided or quickly remedied. The focus of this book is on tourism planning processes emphasizing community involvement, rather than purely product development.

Much of the conflict described above can be avoided if communities are actively involved in whatever plans are developed for local areas, and if the benefits of development are shared by all stakeholders. Community participation in tourism development in poor rural areas has the potential capacity for increasing incomes and employment, developing skills and institutions, and thereby empowering local people (see Ashley and Garland, 1994). However, these benefits will not be realized if local people and national governments stand by and allow outside development forces to exploit local resources. While currently unfashionable, government intervention to ensure that local people are dealt with fairly, and that they benefit from tourism development, is necessary to ensure the long-term sustainability of both the tourism project itself and the environment in which it is located. Globalization and an over-reliance on capitalist ideology make it difficult for governments to regulate development – and tourism development is no exception. What is generally not understood is that improved tourism policies could help to fuel economic growth and provide for the equitable distribution of resources, thereby alleviating poverty, rather than concentrating wealth in the hands of a few and channeling profits to trans-national corporations and foreign countries. Above all, community participation can guarantee local support for conservation, and the sustainable use of natural resources more generally, thus ensuring a sustainable tourism product (see Ashley, 1995: 2). Only when communities are in control of the development agenda, and concerned with the built environment or the management of wildlife, can conflicts and competition over resources be resolved – if not to everyone's satisfaction, then at least adequately for all to live with the outcome. I argue here that community participation must be at the heart of the tourism development process, and not merely a condescending afterthought to appease those most negatively affected by a potentially inappropriate development. Issues other than that of corporate profit must be considered in the tourism plan; it must deal with the preservation of the culture and social values of the host community, as well as the conservation of the local environment; it must accomplish these goals while providing some economic benefit to the local people, as well as to outside investors. While conditions in the community will inevitably change because of tourism, there is a core set of community values which must guide change. Disruption or dislocation of this core set of values leads to alienation.

Human problems are too often defined from an exclusively economic perspective, and remedies to them are therefore thought also to be economic in nature. While the tourism literature provides many supposedly successful examples of tourism, the communities which host these enterprises are unlikely to have benefited to the same extent as their offshore owners. The tourism literature is filled with critiques of the overwhelming financial leakage associated with international tourism. It has been estimated that over 50 per cent of payments by travelers to tour companies for travel to the developing world never reach the host country (Mowforth and Munt, 1998). This is perhaps a conservative estimate, considering that most airlines are owned by companies from a few developed countries, and that most travelers book tours through agents in their home country. When money does reach the destination site, it quickly leaks back to the developed world to pay for such things as management wages, profits and supplies. The financial rewards of tourism fail to materialize on the scale envisioned by local communities. This can be depressing to a worker who, for example, has lost a lucrative, unionized forestry job and replaced it with a seasonal job in the outdoor adventure tourism sector, or who has opened up his or her private dwelling as a bed and breakfast enterprise. Similarly afflicted are the Maasai villagers watching busloads of European tourists stream past their village to view wildlife in the nearby national park, when they could engage in the same activity in the nature reserve of the Maasai village (or 'group ranch') itself, thereby contributing to the economic life of the community – as was the case in Kimana, the subject of one of the case studies presented in Chapter 7.

What has been lost in the discussion of tourism planning, and in the problem-solving process generally, is the plethora of everyday issues – such as social relations, local institutions, and the condition of the environment – that are central to the lives of individuals and communities. Discussions of tourism must consider these wider issues, rather than just analyzing development from an economic perspective. The critical areas of social development and global environmental change – which continues to plague the development process despite the promises made by those promoting tourism and other forms of development – are just as important to the discussion.

Entrepreneurs are primarily interested in maximizing short-term profits and in recovering their capital investment in the long term. This often leads to corners being cut in environmental protection, through inadequate treatment of human waste, and to the privatization of choice land and water resources essential to the survival of local people. Moreover, environmental safeguards are typically designed poorly in the tourism plan; or otherwise those constructed to protect the natural environment often fail to be implemented. It is often thought by government officials that safeguards are too expensive to implement, and that foreign capital will choose to go elsewhere rather than acquiesce to the social and cultural protection of local people or the environment. It is now beginning to be recognized by many of the stakeholders in the tourism development process that this mentality must change given the finite number of potential destination sites. Coral reefs, for example, are under threat around the world from overuse and widespread ignorance of their fragility. As the supply of once pristine destination sites becomes overexploited, or completely squandered, the demand for new sites increases, further limiting the supply and thus jeopardizing the expansion of the tourism industry itself. And understanding that there is a finite supply of potential destination sites makes planning of these destinations even more critical in the future, not only to local inhabitants but also to the tourism industry itself.

Cultural protection and conservation are rarely practiced by the tourism industry, while the exploitation of traditional culture through commodification is widespread. Little thought is given to the potential for cultural disruption, or to methods of enhancing and preserving traditional societies. Except when quaint displays of local culture in the form of traditional song and dance are of interest to the visitor, tourism businesses prefer the local population to remain invisible – particularly if that population is afflicted by poverty, creating an affront to the comparatively extravagant lifestyle of the tourist. Many hotels occupying prime beach front, wall off their properties in order to keep the tourist in, but – perhaps more importantly – to keep the locals out. Little attempt is made by either the hotelier or the guest to interact with the local population or genuinely experience their culture. At best, the tourist may see a contrived performance of local dance, performed in traditional costume, but reduced from a true form of cultural expression to become the level of mere spectacle. Perhaps even more important are the psychological changes that occur when people from traditional societies engage in tourism development – or, more precisely, have it thrust upon them. Helena Norberg-Hodge (1996: 34–5) presents a snapshot of those profound changes in Ladakh, Tibet, in a succinct section on tourism development in another volume exploring the potentials and perils of economic globalization. I present this vignette in its entirety to provide the reader with a flavor of the profound changes brought to a traditional culture by tourism.

> When tourism first began in Ladakh, it was as though people from another planet suddenly descended on the region. Looking at the modern world from something of a Ladakhi perspective, I became aware of how much more successful our culture looks from outside than we experience it on the inside.
>
> Each day many tourists would spend as much as $100 – an amount roughly equivalent to someone spending $50,000 per day in America. In the traditional subsistence economy, money played a minor role and was used primarily for luxuries – jewelry, silver, and gold. Basic needs – food, clothing, and shelter – were provided for without money. The labor one needed was free of charge, part of an intricate web of human relationships.
>
> Ladakhis did not realize that money meant something very different for the foreigners: that back home they needed it to survive; that food, clothing and shelter all cost money – a lot of money. Compared to these strangers, the Ladakhis suddenly felt poor.
>
> This new attitude contrasted dramatically with the Ladakhis' earlier self-confidence. In 1975, I was shown around the remote village of Hemis Shukpachan by a young Ladakhi named Tsewang. It seemed to me that all the houses we saw were especially large

and beautiful. I asked Tsewang to show me the houses where the poor people lived. Tsewang looked perplexed a moment, then responded. 'We don't have any poor people here'.

Eight years later I overheard Tsewang talking to some tourists. 'If you could only help us Ladakhis,' he was saying, 'we're so poor.'

Besides giving the illusion that all Westerners are multimillion-aires, tourism and Western media images also help perpetuate another myth about modern life – that we never work. It looks as though our technologies do the work for us. In industrial society today, we actually spend more hours working than people in rural, agrarian economies, but that is not how it looks to the Ladakhis. For them, work is physical work: ploughing, walking, carrying things. A person sitting behind the wheel of a car or pushing buttons on a typewriter doesn't appear to be working.

(Norberg-Hodge, 1996: 34–5)

These types of impact are not limited to LDCs. Tourism in Canada, as in most other developed countries, also produces negative impacts on everyday community life. The account below is a composite drawn from four well-developed tourism communities in central Canada, which formed part of a research project conducted by Reid, Mair, George and Taylor (2001). Like the anecdote above, it provides a snapshot of the difficulties experienced by people who live in communities dominated by tourism, although in this case the communities are situated in the developed world.

In this rural community, tourism has been developing quickly over the past few years and has generally been dominated by a few members of the business community. Initially, the residents and other members of the community were quite supportive and even a little excited about this quick growth and the increasing influx of visitors. New restaurants were being developed, people felt proud that tourists wanted to come and see their little town and some entrepreneurs were able to make ends meet by opening small bed and breakfast places and art galleries. However, as more and more people came into town on the weekend and more and more residents were unable to get out of their driveways or get downtown to buy their Saturday paper without an hour wait, tension started to build.

As more tourism businesses and developments sprung up and more tourists came to visit each summer, residents began to notice an increase in traffic congestion and pollution, a loss of access to amenities, an increase in the prices of basic necessities and real estate, and a general change in how the community looked and felt. Some members of the community started to wonder if tourism growth should continue without their say. Because tourism development had been generally unplanned, those who felt the need to voice their concerns were left feeling like there was no place to share their thoughts, to talk to the owners of the tourism businesses, or to be part of the decision-making process. A few residents started making plans to stay away from their community on the weekends altogether; others went to council to express their concerns or met with other residents to talk about how to stop any further tourism development. Some remained silent but grew increasingly frustrated about the way tourism was developing in their town. Divisions began to develop and soon it seemed like everyone was taking sides about the nature, scale and scope of tourism in their community.

(Reid et al., 2001: 4)

These two short vignettes provide us with a compelling description of how a planning process can be measured and judged. Tourism communities are subject to an array of impacts, some of which are positive and others negative; the trick, of course, is to maximize the positive and minimize the negative impacts. Pearce (1991) sets out the major impacts requiring attention in the tourism development process:

(a) Impact on population structure:
     size of population;
     age/sex composition;
     modification of family size;
     rural–urban transformation of population.
(b) Transformation of forms and types of occupation:
     impact on/of language and qualification levels;
     impact on occupational distribution by sector;
     demand for female labour;
     increase in seasonality of employment.
(c) Transition of values:
     political;
     social;
     religious;
     moral.

(d)   Influence on traditional way of life:
      on art, music and folklore;
      on habits, and customs;
      on daily living.

(e)   Modification of consumption patterns:
      qualitative alterations;
      quantitative alterations.

(f)   Benefits to tourists:
      relaxation, recuperation, recreation;
      change of environment;
      widening of horizons;
      social contact.

(Pearce, 1991: 218)

Most, if not all, of the impacts outlined by Pearce are found in the two scenarios presented above. It is inconceivable that in today's fast-paced and globally integrated world, a culture like that of the Ladakhis will not come into contact with the outside world. There are too many forces, both local and beyond the community which make protracted contact likely, and the impacts outlined by Pearce are sure to be encountered if not dealt with initially in the tourism project. The issue of greatest concern is how local contact with the tourist, and hence the outside world, can be made a positive experience for both the host and the guest. Likewise, those living in the composite community do not have to feel invaded by tourists; it is both poor planning and the lack of appropriate involvement mechanisms that have led to this antagonistic development. The recreational opportunities for people living in tourism communities can be just as pleasurable as those enjoyed by the tourists if the project is developed and managed properly. This book argues that this can only be achieved through a tourism planning process which places emphasis on the local culture and maintains the value system of the community, rather than focusing exclusively on maximizing profits to expatriate corporations and leading to the 'cancer stage of capitalism', as described by McMurtry (1999). While profit may be of concern to some in the process, it must be one of many goals of the tourism experience, and not the sole emphasis. The fact that local people live with the tourism project on a day-to-day basis demands that they have control of what gets developed. In fact, the community must be allowed to decide in the first instance whether or not any type of development is appropriate for them, and whether any strategy for economic development is to be pursued. The question of what constitutes sufficient development must also be part of the decision-making process undertaken by a community.

THE ORGANIZATION OF THIS BOOK

Chapter 2 takes on the task of identifying the essence of economic and corporate globalization, and its pervasive influence on local development, including that of tourism. Corporate globalization is not only seen as a mechanism for conducting business relationships, but also as a worldwide system of social organization, fast replacing the nation-state in the arena of policy development. Corporate globalization provides nations and communities with considerable challenges, and threatens to distort, if not control, daily life. How local communities can plan and control tourism in the face of such an all-pervasive force is the question confronting this text. To answer it, the forces driving corporate globalization, and the results of that system, need to be identified before planning strategies and theories can be brought to bear on tourism development projects. The concept of globalization from below is explored as an alternative to the corporate globalization that prevails today. This suggests that globalization in itself should not be viewed as negative, but that the locus of control within it determines whether the outcome is a force for 'the life code of value' described by McMurtry (1999), which includes issues of universal health care, clean air and potable water, or for reinforcing the money value system which mainly focuses on maximizing profit. Issues of sustainability, and what they mean for tourism development, are also explored in Chapter 2.

In order to provide a general picture of the political economy of tourism, the chapter gives a brief but important snapshot of the size of the tourism industry worldwide, and of the distribution of its receipts, in a section titled, The New Economy. This subtitle is used to denote a change in the focus of the world's economy from manufacturing and resource sector activities towards an emphasis on the service sector, touted as the area that will replace others to dominate economic relationships across the globe in the future.

The chapter ends with a section on reasserting the community's role in the new economy. This section is devoted to providing an alternative to the corporation as an influence over efforts towards globalization and social organization. Globalization from below is explored as a community-based, grass-roots alternative to the domination of corporations in the development process. Theoretical models that describe and, if implemented, can make this form of development possible, are presented.

This book examines tourism as an issue within development studies in a globalized world economy. To begin the discussion, Chapter 3 examines tourism development within the framework of development studies. The thesis of this discussion is that tourism must be examined in this larger context, not as an isolated development strategy separated from the larger picture. Here the concepts of general systems theory provide the framework for the discussion. The chapter deals with two important overarching issues. The first is the ideology of tourism, and the role this plays in development. It is often thought that tourism operates outside the more general conditions of society – particularly the socioeconomic trends. Many authors focus on the negative aspects of tourism, as if these were separate from the neo-liberal agendas of modernization and globalization. Brown (1998) suggests that this may not be the case, and that tourism development may simply reflect wider societal conditions. Chapter 3 reflects on this insight, and explores in detail how tourism is used as an instrument of structural adjustment in developing countries, and as a symbol of the new economy and restructuring in the developed world. The second area dealt with in the chapter is that of the myths and realities which give rise to the new economy, and the role of tourism in it. McMurtry's concept of the 'life-code of value' is explored in some detail. A discussion follows of whether or not tourism is truly an alternative to the more damaging extractive industries in rural areas. The expectations placed upon tourism as a vehicle for sustainable development are also discussed extensively in Chapter 3, which ends by exploring the implementation of general tourism development concepts at the grass-roots and community level.

Chapter 4 provides an analysis of how different disciplines define tourism, with the goal of developing a unified concept. This is no simple task, as there is no single definition to which all scholars and researchers of tourism agree – a lack of consensus that arguably constitutes one of the weaknesses of tourism studies as a discipline, although some may not see it as a shortcoming at all, but in fact a strength, demanding a multiple analysis of the subject rather than a single perspective. This book examines a multitude of definitions of the subject, including psychological, social, cultural, economic, community and environmental perspectives, approaching the subject from the perspective that there are many legitimate ways to define tourism, and that all are important for eventually understanding such a complex social subject. It is a central claim of this book that the weakness of tourism development is a result of a partial definition of tourism (usually economic) being employed by those organizing its development. The tourism planning methods presented later in the book therefore rely for their construction on all of the definitions outlined in Chapter 4.

Chapter 5 initiates a discussion of basic planning theory and its relationship to tourism planning. Unless planners understand the range of theoretical frameworks available to them, and the consequences of each, the planning of tourism development will retain the orthodox view, and the world will see more of the types of development that led to the two negative scenarios presented earlier. Chapter 5 describes the options available to the tourism planner and discusses the logical sequence of the planning process. It also instructs the tourism planner with regard to community organization – perhaps the most fundamental stage in the tourism planning process. While it may be thought that communities are naturally organized to control their own destiny, such has not been the experience of this author. Communities cannot be expected to jump straight into developing the nuts and bolts of a tourism plan without proper instruction and training, as well as the development of an organizational framework to maximize their efforts and assure the desired outcome. Chapter 5 deals with these issues in a practical way.

Chapter 6 provides the basic strategies and processes involved in planning a tourism project. A planning process to guide all aspects of tourism development is provided, along with the necessary discussion of the positivistic, interpretive and constructivist research paradigms (including an analysis of community needs) necessary to support the planning process. Techniques which bring tourism research to life are incorporated in the chapter. Methods devoted to analyzing the social, environmental, and economic impacts of tourism development are also provided. It is here that the place of communities in the monitoring process is outlined. The Community Development approach to tourism planning advocated in this book relies on planning theories, methods, and techniques that focus on rational as well as impressionistic data – that is, data which is interpretivistic and constructivist in nature rather than purely positivistic. The chapter stresses the need for the comprehensive collection of baseline data against which the impacts of tourism can be measured over time. It discusses the literature on the economic, social, cultural and environmental impact of tourism development. Identification of the theories from the contributing disciplines that are relevant to tourism development is discussed, and the research methods needed to support tourism planning are also outlined.

Chapter 7 provides three case studies of communities which have undertaken a recent tourism planning process. While none of these cases represents the ultimate achievement in tourism planning, each has done many things right, and they are offered as good examples of an appropriate planning process which attempts both to be sensitive to community needs and values and to maintain the sustainable use of the environment. Each case is evaluated individually and in combination with the others, to identify their strengths and weaknesses. This offers a basis on which to end the book with a review of the most appropriate principles and processes for future tourism planning and development.

Chapter 8 concludes this book with a discussion of the integration of tourism into the development process, in both LDCs and developed countries. The point is made that while there are some differences between LDCs and developed countries, we are in many ways grappling with the same issues of large-scale development; certainly, both types of country are affected by the pervasive forces of corporate globalization and the liberalization of the world economy. From this point of view, we all have much in common, and must work collectively rather than antagonistically, as has often been the case. Chapter 8 not only sums up the book, but presents principles, policies and processes which should provide a sound basis on which tourism development at the community level can proceed, and within which all partners in the process may be able to maximize their success and minimize their social, environmental and financial costs.

THE CONTEXT OF TOURISM PLANNING

The late twentieth and early twenty-first centuries have been confusing to both social analysts and citizens alike; the rules of social and economic engagement have changed dramatically. This has not been the result of a natural phenomenon but, rather, is driven by a pervasive force acting in society – the same force which champions the corporate globalization of the world's resources and governance. The changes produced by this force have benefited the capitalist class over other social groups, and traditionally marginalized populations have been left completely out of the planning and development process and continue to be neglected. The social agenda has been characterized as post-industrialism – variously termed post-Keynesianism or post-Fordism. However, Myles (1991) observes that

> ... the concept of post-industrialism ... is a negative one. It does not designate the kind of economy and society we are moving towards, but only the kind of economy and society we are leaving behind. It simply means that societies have moved beyond industrialism and are in the process of forging new types of social and economic arrangements, the parameters of which are still being created.

> (Myles, 1991: 352)

Those championing the corporate globalization project know exactly what kind of world we are moving towards. It is one where the wealthy have become wealthier, and the poor poorer; it is a world where the disenfranchised are left to serve the wealthy, without processes under their control which can assist them out of their condition. The tourism industry is not only a participant in that process, but perhaps a major contributor to it. This need not be the case, however. Tourism development can be a bottom-up activity, one that allows for control at the grass-roots level, and provides an improved standard of living to those engaged in it, particularly those at the community level.

Social commentators suggest that the post-industrial society will be dominated by the service sector of the economy – that many more of us will earn our livings in this sector of the economy in the future than previously. Most observers argue that tourism will constitute one of the largest sub-sectors of the service sector. Perhaps for this reason, it is an exciting time to study tourism planning and development; not only is the future configuration of the tourism industry at stake, so are the fundamental ways in which we organize society in general, and communities in particular. As was true of countries shaped by agriculture, fishing, and mining in the late 1800s and early 1900s, tourism will play a dramatic role in human and community development throughout the twenty-first century. For that reason, community tourism planning and development will provide the battleground upon which major social and cultural issues will undergo further transformation. One of these issues is the agenda of corporate globalization.

In his book *Spaces of Hope* (2000), David Harvey suggests that the phenomenon of globalization provides a powerful 'macro' tool with which to analyze contemporary society, just as is the body on a 'micro' level. Connecting these two phenomena as a lens for analysis provides a link between what is taking place on the world stage and its effects on the most personal of entities: one's own body. A large-scale environmental catastrophe in a far-off country can have directly observable, negative consequence to an individual's health. This has been described elsewhere as thinking globally and acting locally. Take, for example, the connection between the nuclear disaster at Chernobyl and the contamination of milk products in Western Europe, and its effect on individual health. To some extent, this book extends Harvey's connecting theme. While globalization is viewed in this volume as the 'macro' concept that Harvey proposes, this book takes the community as 'the body' (to extend the metaphor) of the social and political world. Even Harvey (2000: 120) admits that '... no body exists outside of its relations with other bodies and the exercise of powers and counterpowers among many bodies is a central con-stitutive aspect of social life'. While some may argue that the family unit is the smallest social unit, this book views the family in much the same way that Harvey considers DNA vital to life, but not the most important unit of analysis. The community is the smallest political unit which makes collective decisions on a day-to-day basis that affects the lives of all citizens, and therefore is instrumental in the analysis of tourism, the subject of this book.

When using community as the 'micro' unit of analysis, it is important to define what is meant by community, given that it is a contested concept. Communities are popularly viewed as geographic units. While this definition still holds true today, the term is also employed here to describe a group of people with a common interest but without any necessary physical contiguity. Communities of interest may transcend communities of location, particularly in these times of rapid electronic communication, including the internet. However, the word 'community' is usually, but not exclusively, used in this book in the geographic sense. Tourism communities are, for the most part, physical entities defined by political boundaries. In some communities, however, there may also be a tourism community inside the geographic unit; indeed, there may be said to exist a single tourism community of interest stretching across the globe. This type of community is considered to be a community of interest, and not defined solely by its geographic location.

Nevertheless, it must be remembered that any community, whether defined by geography or common interest will in practice consist of multiple identities. That is to say, a community will consist of multiple interests and differences; issues of race, gender, and class will always present themselves in differing points of view, in any type of community. This fact is one reason for analyzing tourism at this level. It is at the community level that multiple identities and voices are the clearest and, consequently, it is at this level that their incorporation in a tourism plan is most probable. Postmodernists are particularly sensitive to the issue of multiple identities. As Seidman instructs us:

> Our social narratives should be attentive to this concept of multiple identities; our stories should replace the flat, unidimensional language of domination and liberation with the multivocal notion of multiple, local heterogeneous struggles and a many-sided experience of empowerment and disempowerment.
>
> (Seidman, 1994: 133–4)

Some, including West (1994: 65–81), argue that the identities of gender, race and class must be further subdivided. Gender, for example, consists of women black, white, young, old and from differing cultures who view the world in many contrasting ways. These variations demand that the tourism planner understand the community in all its complexity, and not short-circuit the participation process by defining the community as a homogeneous unit. The inclusion of these multiple identities will become evident as this volume proceeds, particularly in the chapters dealing with community consultation and public participation.

A further factor must be recognized in relation to the idea of community: individuals are not exclusive to a single community; members of a geographic community may belong to multiple communities of interest. In fact, it is also possible that a person may be a member of more than one geographic community, as well as multiple communities of interest. This complex social reality can place an individual into several communities, each of which may have opposing positions on a proposed development. This possibility negates the tourism planner's concept of a homogeneous community which can be easily divided into discrete groups, with single and predictable positions on any issue. The implications of the foregoing are enormous for tourism planners attempting to engage citizens meaningfully in the planning process.

At times this book may appear to be simply a critique of tourism development – particularly as it is practiced today. On the contrary, tourism can play an important role, particularly in rural and remote communities in danger of disappearing because of the downturn in traditional economic activities. Tourism can also help a traditional society to preserve cultural practices which might otherwise be lost to subsequent generations; urban tourism has sometimes added flavor and vitality to what could otherwise be mundane living conditions. But for tourism to become the positive influence that this book hopes it will, tourism planning must be driven by a whole new set of priorities. Tourism will need to be constructed to serve the community and all its values, and not simply continue as the exploitative development that it so often is. To paraphrase the words of the great economist Karl Polanyi, in *The Great Transformation* (1957), tourism must serve the needs of humanity, and not use humans to serve the needs of the tourism corporation. While Polanyi was referring to the capitalist economy, the same can be said about tourism as a microcosm of the economy in general.

This book is about the commodification of tourism and its effects on community; it embraces the position of Meethan when he states that 'my main theme is to argue that tourism is part of the process of commodification (or commoditization) and consumption inherent in modern capitalism'. (Meethan, 2001: 4) He goes on to suggest that

> [a]ny book dealing with tourism as consumption must also address this issue of commodification as a central concern, that is, the ways in which material culture, people and places become objectified for the purpose of the global market. In general the debates surrounding this have been cast in negative terms ... I will argue that the processes of commodification, rather then [sic] being a side issue, are in fact central to the whole basis of tourism and, what is more, that tourism is one aspect of the global processes of commodification rather than a separate self-contained system.

> (Meethan, 2001: 5)

I agree that any analysis of tourism must examine the commodification of culture, but in my view that is not in itself sufficient. The analysis of development and the implementation of the commodified tourism system must also offer the instruments and techniques that are necessary for the management and control of the development project, and put those likely to be most affected in a position to control its creation. This can only be done by emphasizing process over product: only when a community has instituted the right process and constructed its relationship to the tourism industry in proper balance with other community life sustaining forces can the idea of sustainability begin to be reached. This will require the construction of a new relationship between communities, the tourism industry, and national governments eager to raise foreign capital in order to pay down foreign held debt.

This book attempts to provide a framework for that new relationship by offering one chapter on the theory of tourism development and another on the tourism planning process, including strategies and techniques for measuring the social, environmental and economic impacts of tourism on communities and the natural environment. An in-depth examination is also offered of three instances of tourism planning that have provided positive, cutting-edge approaches to tourism development. These case studies are diverse, in that one is situated in East Africa, the second in a small island state, and the third is Canadian. It is only through combining overarching theoretical insights with locally focused planning tools that the planner can hope to change the nature, and thus the impact, of tourism throughout the world.

2 Globalization and the Political Economy of Tourism Development

INTRODUCTION

This chapter examines the effects of late capitalism and corporate globalization on communities and society in general. While globalization negatively affects both urban and rural societies, and those in the developed as well as the developing world, it is also changing the basic structure of social relationships in general across the globe and for rural communities in particular. Agriculture and the extractive industries, once the main occupations of rural life, have been industrialized, and this has reduced the viability of the family farm, led to the depletion of fish stocks and mineral deposits, and marginalized rural people across the globe. Cities are growing rapidly, as large numbers of people pour into them from the countryside. Free trade and international agreements favoring trans-national corporations and business have negatively affected society by reducing state sovereignty in areas such as environmental regulation and the protection of fledgling industries. How citizens organize themselves and their communities to confront these forces and control development in the future is a social issue of great importance.

Tourism is widely viewed as an important instrument in this struggle. Some see it as a major force in the economic development of rural societies, and as an important area for growth in income and employment for urban communities. It is often viewed by the general public as environmentally friendly and initiated by the local community, but these impressions may be as much a myth as a reality. They give rise to the idea that tourism needs to be locally controlled and developed, and therefore provide an important issue for examination in this chapter.

A discussion of corporate globalization leads to a presentation of some principles of community participation as they relate to tourism development: Who should be involved? And how should their participation be organized? Finally, this chapter includes a discussion of the community's role in tourism development, and answers the question: Why bother going down the tourism development road at all? The vehicle of tourism development is used to introduce and support the concepts of social learning and social mobilization as mechanisms for establishing a healthy community – a topic examined in greater detail in Chapter 6.

CORPORATE GLOBALIZATION AND ITS EFFECTS ON SOCIETY

Tourism has traditionally been considered from a mainly economic perspective. Large companies and smaller entrepreneurs have provided the force for – and thus the main focus of – tourism development worldwide. In addition to conventional sector analysis, Brown (1998) argues that tourism must be seen in the larger context of the world economy. This demands a fundamental understanding and analysis of the world's economy – and particularly of corporate globalization. Just what are the consequences of turning the social organization of the world over to capital and the corporate sector?

The phenomenon of corporate globalization is receiving much attention from scholars and non-academics alike. In essence, the discussion – or perhaps more accurately the controversy – centers on whether it is a positive or negative force in society. The supposition that 'all boats will be lifted by a rising tide' – a metaphor to describe the intentions of corporate globalization – needs examination. Not everyone is affected equally by globalization: some benefit more than others because their position in society allows them to take greater advantage of its structures, while poverty is not alleviated through the worldwide expansion of uncontrolled business development. Many social commentators cite the increase in poverty in sub-Saharan Africa as a further example of the failure of corporate globalization in this area; some would even argue that it is exacerbating the problem. What is certain is that everyone in the world is touched, either directly or indirectly, by its pervasive influence – sometimes positively, but often negatively.

Tourism, like many other areas of economic activity, is shaped by the overall socioeconomic order. As a consequence, most tourism is currently organized by a few large trans-national companies, which exert great influence at the national, regional and local level. This may be truer for countries of the developing world because of their drastic need for economic development and their available natural resource base on which such a product can be developed. The opening up of the world to international travel has been made possible by the increased speed of transportation, and by communications technologies such as the internet. Today, tours can be planned, either by consumers or by their representative from a tour company, with great speed and precision. Moreover, tours can reach the remotest points on the globe thanks to more efficient transportation networks – particularly the airplane. No location is inaccessible, except for those parts of the world temporarily off limits because of war, natural disaster or some other exceptional circumstance. Temporarily, because many countries ravaged by war in the previous century, such as Vietnam, are now transforming their economies to include tourism. The fact that such countries are developing their tourist industries so rapidly suggests that they provide a viable mechanism for transforming formerly war-torn areas into attractive tourism destinations.

Globalization is not a new phenomenon, and it has occurred in many different guises throughout the last century. Its origins are debatable, and it has become a topic of wide-ranging discussion in recent years. Known earlier simply as international trade, it focused mainly on reducing obstructions to trade, such as tariff and non-tariff barriers. What is new about this round of internationalism is not only what it is called, but its pervasiveness throughout social life and its obstruction of the direct involvement of national governments in decision-making. Globalization now affects all aspects of trading and economic life, while governments are increasingly deprived of sovereignty in terms of the action they are able to take in areas such as labor and environmental legislation. This may, in fact, be the Achilles' heel of corporate globalization. An exclusive focus on trade and finance, with no balancing mechanisms for labor and the environment, will eventually see its legitimacy under threat – if indeed this has not begun to happen already. While jobs may be created by traditional tourism companies, as well as in other industries operating in many developing countries, they usually pay poverty wages, or worse. The long-held belief that any job is better than no job has come increasingly to be seen as a myth. Jobs at the lower end of the tourism industry require relatively few skills, and are often seasonal, leaving workers scraping out an existence at the margins of society.

New to this round of globalizing activity are its potential consequences for the nation-state. Trans-national corporations, with their size and pervasiveness, provide a formidable foe in the policy arena to an individual nation-state. As Beck suggests, 'globalization means one thing above all else: denationalization – that is, erosion of the nation-state, but also its possible transformation into a trans-national state'. (Beck, 2000: 14) Certainly, globalization challenges the basic precept of early capitalism and a more mixed economy: that is, the sovereignty of nation-states to create trade barriers, protect labor and subsidize fledgling industries. Global organizations like the World Bank (WB), the International Monetary Fund (IMF) and the World Trade Organization (WTO) have brought an end to that form of sovereignty. For Canada, this meant an end to meaningful trade agreements with the US like the auto pact, and to the long-standing support given by the Canadian government to regional industries through policy institutions such as the Department of Regional Economic Expansion (DREE), which attempted to encourage and stimulate development in Canada's less wealthy provinces.

In *What is Globalization?*, Beck summarizes the major features of globalization and its consequences:

(1) Transnational integration and national disintegration are simultaneous with each other...

(2) Transnational corporations have an interest in 'weak states'...

(3) The social welfare states of continental Europe are caught in a downward spiral...

(4) The replacement of labor by knowledge and capital.

(5) The twofold relativity of poverty. In these mutually reinforcing processes of inclusion and exclusion, the face of poverty has also been changing: it has risen dramatically, and it has fragmented in several ways ...the thread of social communication between (globalized) rich and (localized) poor is threatening to snap, since between the winners from globalization at the top and the losers from globalization at the bottom there are no longer any arenas in which greater equality and justice can be struggled for and enforced.

(6) Contradictions of self-organized glocal (*global and local*) life operate as criteria of exclusion. These 'failures' of intensified competition are regarded as 'weak', 'at risk' or 'handicapped', they are people with few or no recognized qualifications...

(7) Capitalism without work is matched by a Marxism without utopia. The neo-Marxist picture of the capitalist world-system no longer has any utopian energy, any systematic political hope or fantasy.

(Beck, 2000: 96–8; italics mine)

Economic globalization hands power to trans-national corporations by engaging countries in the self-destructive game of global competition. This new development encourages a race to the bottom, rather than a lifting of all economies to the level of the developed world, as orthodox economists suggested would be the case. While it is generally thought that competition between firms is healthy, in that it ensures efficiency, competition has in fact occurred between nation-states seeking the favors of trans-national corporations. As Sindiga (1999) notes, that prime land in the possession of indigenous people was often expropriated by colonial rulers, and eventually turned over to corporations in the rush to establish tourism and cash in on the abundant wildlife and other natural resources which had traditionally sustained local inhabitants. An example of this phenomenon is provided by Kenya's Amboseli National Park and reviewed in Chapter 7.

In order to attract businesses to their country nation-states are forced to engage in a bidding war. Forgivable loans, reduced taxes or complete tax holidays, and a failure to enforce environmental laws are maneuvers characteristic of this war. This process has simply engendered a race to the bottom among countries who engage in this unhealthy competition, rather than raising those economies to the standards enjoyed in developed countries, as its advocates argued would be the case during the debates held in many of the countries negotiating formal trade agreements such as the North American Free Trade Agreement (NAFTA) and the European Economic Union agreement recently achieved at Maastricht in the Netherlands.

Trans-national corporations pit one country against another in order to get the best possible deal, regardless of the consequences to the host country. This bidding war produces increased liabilities for participating countries, which also often suffer from corrupt politicians more interested in their own gain than the welfare of the country they serve. Proponents of globalization see it as a way to 'lift all boats', but critics (including Mander, 1996) now fear that it has ensured a race to the bottom of the socioeconomic ladder for many of the citizens of most countries. Tourism companies are especially complicit in this process, with new destinations created on this unsavory basis. However, as potential sites become ever fewer worldwide, the balance of power between the trans-national tourism company and the nation-state may change in favor of the latter. But at the moment, unfortunately, an unhealthy relationship exists between these two actors, producing high levels of exploitation of labor and substantial offshore leakage of receipts. This is particularly true for the tourism industry, as is demonstrated by the balance sheets of the largest trans-national tourism companies, presented later in this chapter.

While globalization might have been more comprehensive, incorporating social and environmental concerns, it has so far been driven mainly by the agenda of big business; some (see McMurtry, 1999) go so far as to argue that globalization has been hijacked by corporate interests alone, focusing exclusively on issues of trade and the movement of capital. It has affected social and political stability because of its demand for the removal of market impediments, regardless of the social and environmental costs. Globalization has in fact led to the disempowerment of people living in many communities across the globe because of the lack of policy options available to the nation-state for their protection from the depredations of trans-national tourism companies.

Those pushing the corporate globalization agenda see these changes to the nation-state as positive for society. Liberalizing trade, it is argued, will increase the wealth of all nations who participate. The World Travel and Tourism Council (de Croo, 1994: 69), for example, calls for continued liberalization of trade and the reduction of restrictions and regulations controlling the tourism business; an open skies policy which would deregulate the airline industry worldwide even further than it is already, is one example of this type of proposed liberalization. In support of this call, they argue that worldwide economic growth will eventually eradicate poverty and increase incomes generally. The metaphor often heard is, 'a rising tide will lift all boats'. This hypothesis has not been proved, and there is increasing evidence that globalization is not having the positive effect for many countries that was promised, and this is particularly true in the developing world. The *Maquiladoras* in Mexico, for example, have been the site of great economic transformation, with the development of many factories by the world's largest companies. This development has had mixed results for those attracted to work in the industries concerned. Migrant workers in search of prosperity who have relocated to work in such places are often little better off under these new conditions than those they have left behind. In fact, many would have fared better by remaining in the rural area they left, where they were supported by subsistence agriculture. Shanty towns have often sprung up in these new industrial areas, but without the necessary sanitation and other infrastructure necessary for a civilized existence. Tourism has displaced peasants in Mexico, for example, in order to create resort enclaves. Many once sustainable fishing villages throughout the world, including some in Mexico, have been transformed into resorts, owned and managed by transnational tour companies. These transformations drove the local fishers out of the area, while importing unskilled service workers from other parts of the country in order to minimize training costs. This practice does not adhere to anyone's notion of sound regional development practices, but reproduces the cycle of poverty that is so evident in the many texts dealing with the plight of migrant workers. This is done in the name of generating foreign currency, without any regional economic strategy to train and employ locals so that they could benefit from employment in the industry.

The pervasiveness of globalization is aided, if not driven, by the twin social phenomena of technology – which allows capital, goods and people to move around the globe at lightning speed – and the concentration of power and wealth through unrestrained acquisitions and mergers. Moreover, there is also a psychological component to the progress of globalization. The collapse of the Soviet Union provides supporters of the capitalist system with the self-confidence to throw off any restraints in declaring the victory of capitalism over socialism, in turn justifying US hegemony over the global social order. However, as Huntington notes:

What is universalism to the West is imperialism to the rest. The West is attempting and will continue to attempt to sustain its preeminent position and defend its interests by defining those interests as the interests of the 'world community'. That phrase has become the euphemistic collective noun (replacing 'the Free World') to give global legitimacy to actions reflecting the interests of the United States and other Western powers. The West is, for instance, attempting to integrate the economies of non-Western societies into a global economic system which dominates. Through the IMF and other international economic institutions, the West promotes its economic interests and imposes on other nations the economic policies it thinks appropriate. In any poll of non-Western peoples, however, the IMF undoubtedly would win the support of finance ministers and a few others but get an overwhelmingly unfavorable rating from almost everyone else ...

(Huntington: 1997: 184)

The welfare state, combined with the threat of socialism, managed to tame the extreme tendencies of unrestrained capital. The psychological victory for capital, however, has encouraged the exponential growth of the national and extra-national liberalization of trade, leading to trade agreements such as NAFTA and the creation of the recent economic pact in the European Union. These trading blocs now rival the power and sovereignty of the nation-state itself, particularly in domestic economic affairs. International trade agreements supervised by the WTO give supremacy to finance and trade, and by default dominate domestic social and labor policies. In this new world order, such agreements as outlined in Chapter 11 of the NAFTA treaty, allow private corporations to sue governments who enact environmental or social policies that limit their ability to make profits, regardless of the consequences for the citizens or environment of the country concerned. Unlike other forms of international trade, the regime inaugurated by this new form of globalization intrudes into all aspects of social and political life, as Ulrich Beck articulates so well:

> Institutions of industrial society which seemed shut tight can be 'cracked' and opened up to political intervention. The premises of the welfare state and pension system, of income support, local government and infrastructure policies, the power of organized labor, industry-wide free collective bargaining, state expenditure, the fiscal system and 'fair taxation' – all this melts under the withering sun of globalization and becomes susceptible to (demands for) political moulding.
>
> (Beck, 2000: 1)

One of the chief hallmarks of globalization is capital's focus on reducing production costs in order to maximize profit. A relentless struggle to increase profits continues without limit, often at the expense of the environment and labor. Globalization, with its drive to reduce the role of labor through the increased use of technology in the production process, could provide advantages for both workers and the tourism industry if structures were in place to distribute the benefits more equally (Reid, 1995). At the beginning of the era of industrial manufacturing, Henry Ford soon came to understand workers would need to earn a sufficient wage to enable them to purchase the products they were manufacturing. Consequently, auto workers were paid wages that allowed for such a level of individual expenditure. Modern society needs to re-learn this lesson. If the majority is to participate fully in the global economy, specifically in tourism and other leisure pursuits, then wages and social conditions must be created that will allow for this full participation to happen. Those promoting tourism must come to realize that their businesses depend on the discretionary spending of a large section of society, and that most wage earners throughout the world are not paid well enough to accumulate sufficient savings for this type of spending.

During this time of renewed globalization, trans-national corporations, including those wholly or partly involved in tourism, have increased their profits dramatically while national governments have been forced in some cases to reduce, or at least not increase, their social welfare spending. And during periodic episodes of market correction, when the business cycle causes profits to fall or even become negative for short periods, there are increased calls for reducing the size of the workforce and taxation, in association with increased pressure to decrease government spending on social welfare, in the name of maintaining corporate health. Such measures, it is said, will prevent the otherwise inevitable movement of companies to other countries, where the business climate is claimed to be more favorable. This is the mechanism of the 'race to the bottom' mentioned above. More recently, this type of behavior has continued even in good times, under the imperative of providing larger returns to the shareholder.

While governments are asked to cut back on spending for social programs, the profits of trans-national corporations have grown exponentially. While declaring a fiscal crisis for the nation-state, and sworn to fight budget deficits and government debt, business has been jubilant about a substantial increase in profits, even while corporate debt has risen dramatically. In Canada, globalization has brought reduced taxes for corporations while increasing taxation for individuals; consumption taxes have replaced manufacturing taxes, in the name of making the country more competitive in the global marketplace. Provincial governments like Ontario and British Columbia have been elected on the strength of this mantra. Ontario now boasts of having one of the lowest corporate tax rates in North America, while the education system – particularly its infrastructure – is in a perilous condition, and the publicly sponsored universal healthcare system is in danger of becoming second-rate. What is short-sighted about this trend in policy – for the tourism sector as well as for other industries – is its negative impact on the workforce.

Tourism is a labor-intensive industry that relies on a semi-skilled workforce. Where training is truncated, the industry is weakened, while diseases such as HIV/AIDS particularly in many parts of the developing world increase the turnover in the workforce, further compromising the industry.

This assault on public enterprise is also having a deleterious effect on local municipalities, by transferring services to the community government level without ensuring the necessary flow of funding. With more homeless people on the streets of cities like Toronto, it is becoming difficult to venture out to many of the city's tourism attractions without being panhandled, even after panhandling was made illegal by the provincial government in order to hide the consequences of their failed ideological policies. There is likely to be a corresponding deterioration in the tourism industry as inner cities, where much of the tourist infrastructure exists, start to decline. Cities like Toronto are attractive to tourists because of their reputation as clean and relatively free of crime. But as government at all levels cuts funding to public services, and cities become more inhospitable, their attractiveness as tourism destinations will also decrease.

Capitalism and globalization have affected rural communities first of all by increasing efficiency in agriculture and the extractive industries, through mechanization and the increased use of technology. The technological revolution in rural industries has been so successful that in some sectors, such as the fishing industry, stocks – notably cod – are now threatened with collapse. Factory fishing fleets have severely depleted the world's oceans within a half century. Machinery has replaced thousands of loggers in the forests around the world, increasing the efficiency of the logging industry but reducing forests to levels which may have detrimental effects both on the air we breath and on the levels of rainfall necessary to maintain the world's fresh water reserves, to say nothing of the consequences for forestry itself. Technology has opened up to tourism areas that would otherwise have remained inaccessible, or at least hard to reach; the mass population visit locations formerly only accessible to the elites. While this may seem to represent greater equitability, it has placed great stress on many parts of the countryside as it attempts to cope with an overwhelming influx of visitors. The urbanization of both developed countries and LDCs has also changed the demography of the countryside. Young people are leaving rural areas in ever greater numbers, making the average age of rural communities decidedly higher than it was 25 years ago. As a consequence of these changes, these communities are seeking new ways to revitalize the rural economy, and tourism is one of the prominent industries in that effort. Rural areas are attractive to city dwellers as their environments continue to deteriorate, physically and socially, and tourism is quick to capitalize on that attraction. The rural environment becomes the playground of the urbanite, providing such activities as holiday cottaging, as well as hiking, skiing and other outdoor activities. Moreover, rural areas provide the opportunity for city dwellers to come into contact with their historical traditions. Particularly in North America, the re-enactment of past forms of human life and settlement is a major force in rural tourism development. Many urban people seem to be attracted to historical societies and early pioneering life, perhaps as part of an effort to escape the complexity and bustle of modern city life.

Not only have rural areas been affected by globalization; cities have also changed in its wake. Labor-intensive industries have moved from developed countries to LDCs, where labor is cheaper and environmental laws less strict. Where old manufacturing jobs have been replaced at all, they have given way to the sophisticated technology of knowledge industries. While there is certainly a wider separation between the wealthy and the poor worldwide, there is more discretionary income in the hands of larger numbers of people today than there was in the past. Part of this newfound wealth has been created by the redistribution of income from those at the bottom of the income ladder to those at the top – a result of misguided incomes policies on the part of governments eager to establish what they see as a positive climate for business. The shift in taxation from the corporate sector to the individual is one example of this transfer. The ability of the wealthy to hide their wealth from the tax man through such devices as pension accounts (RSPs in Canada's case) is a second example. This corporate bias in tax policy has led to a greater separation today between the wealthy and the poor than ever before, leading to sharper divisions between groups of people in society. This concentration of wealth has produced a robust service sector, with those at the top receiving personal service from those at the bottom. Tourism – a prominent player in the service sector in urban areas – initially benefited by this newly created wealth and renewed urban vitality. It is now being jeopardized, however, by the neglect of the social infrastructure and the disintegration of the built environment that were necessary to accomplish wealth creation.

While urban and rural areas have both been affected by globalization, they have been affected in different ways. Cities have been challenged to accommodate immigration. In English-speaking countries, language training for new arrivals who do not speak English has been problematic, while the tendency for ghettos to spring up also leads to mistrust and issues of racism. For their part, rural areas have had to grapple with demographic changes produced by the flight of the young, and to adapt to a new economy that has moved away from agriculture and the extractive industries. Rural areas are being rapidly depopulated. The latest Government of Canada statistics suggest that there has been a 4 per cent reduction in the rural population since the previous census period of ten years ago. This trend is not exclusive to Canada alone but is being experienced in most countries across the globe. Industries such as tourism will be relied upon in the future to increase economic activity and attract people back to the countryside. The positive side of tourism is that it can provide much-needed jobs in rural areas. In both rural and urban areas tourism is playing an even larger role in development, as service industries come to dominate in place of manufacturing.

Globalization has become a pervasive instrument in the reorganization of the world. Many (Brown, 1998; George, 2002) argue that tourism is a force in this major transformation. At the global scale, Cox (1992) identifies globalization with six large-scale changes. These may be summarized as follows:

1. The internationalization of production, in which companies make components in various places around the world and bring them together for final assembly in the country where they are to be sold.
2. The internationalization of the state, in which nation-states have lost sovereignty and are now directed by extra-national institutions such as the WTO.
3. A new pattern of uneven development, in which some formerly third-world countries have benefited through specialization within certain production niches while others have sunk even deeper into poverty. Many African countries are examples of the latter case.
4. The internationalization of the debt of the US, which allows its population to achieve a standard of living not justified by its productive capacity.

5. A global migration from South to North, evident in the worldwide increases in both illegal migration and the movement of refugees.
6. The peripheralization of the core. Although 'periphery' was originally a geographic description, it now connotes a socioeconomic group of people living among the affluent. In a sense, the core is now the periphery because of the increased separation between the rich and the poor.

These changes in the social organization of the world's population have given rise to what scholars and social commentators have termed the 'new economy', in which tourism is seen as a major player. Will tourism development address some of the issues outlined by Cox, especially in the marginalized areas of both the developed and developing countries? Or will business continue as usual? This is the question that confronts both the tourism industry and communities all over the world as we move into the twenty-first century. The issues of globalization and sustainable development will take on increasing importance as the world runs out of the natural resources on which twentieth-century industries relied so heavily.

GLOBALIZATION, SUSTAINABILITY AND SUSTAINABLE DEVELOPMENT

Corporate globalization has produced a specialized way of looking at the world. As Ralston Saul points out, 'highly professional, indeed experienced understanding has been used repeatedly to justify destructive behavior. The tendency is to break reality down into a multitude of factors and then to make decisions on the basis of one or two of these factors at a time, without asking the basic questions about the whole'. (Ralston Saul, 2001: 45) In addition to breaking down the whole into parts and then acting on only a few of those parts, corporate globalization has viewed the world only in financial terms, to the exclusion of considering labor and the environment, as already discussed. However, Ralston Saul also states:

> ... the more commerce the better, so long as it is within the desired political and social context. ... No sensible, intelligent person would imagine that our desire to buy and sell as effectively as possible should eliminate other considerations. And of course trade and economics do not stand alone. Without us, they don't exist.

And being subsidiary activities, if allowed to lead the way, they will deform every aspect of our society.

(Ralston Saul, 2001: 53)

Ralston Saul's assertion that by all means commerce, but not commerce by any means is critical to the development of tourism. Butler (1980) has presented a variation of the 'product life-cycle' model to the development and management of tourism destinations. This model traces the trajectory of the tourism product from initial exploration of development possibilities to its eventual decline. The model is contingent on the overexploitation of the product, without due concern being given to the other factors to which Ralston Saul alludes. The market economy, which may indeed prove beneficial for tourism development, should not be allowed to override social and environmental considerations in the formulation of social policy – either in tourism or other industries.

While issues surrounding the economy and free trade have dominated the political discourse over the last three decades or more, the subject of environmental sustainability has continually loomed in the background. The Rio Earth Summit in 1992 crystallized the problem for the world, and since that time the impending crisis in the global environment has become an accepted reality for most observers. Governments and citizens alike have been made aware that the ecosystem is severely affected by the unrestrained pursuit of economic growth, at the expense of the quality of both the air we breathe and the water we drink, among other issues. While there is no agreement on how severe these problems are, there is recognition by all interested parties they are real, and that if left unattended they will only become worse, and thus more difficult to rectify in the future. One problem is that not all parties are in agreement over what constitutes sustainability, in both environmental and economic terms. A debate continues to rage, for example, on the contribution of carbon dioxide and other greenhouse gases to global warming. While no one disputes that greenhouse gases damage the environment – except perhaps for a few fossil fuel producers – the disagreement centers on how best to predict their long-term effects, and how to eliminate the problem without severely impairing our standard of living.

Corporate globalization, with its unrestrained pursuit of profits worldwide, is certainly a major contributor to environmental deterioration. Tourism plays its part in this process; the burning of jet fuel alone causes significant environmental damage. It can also be argued, however, that tourism has the potential to be environmentally friendly, if developed as an alternative to factory agriculture and the other resource-based industries, themselves typically practiced in an unsustainable manner. The difficulty is that what constitutes sustainable development remains undefined, at least at a level which could provide concrete guidelines for development on the ground.

For the time being, sustainable development will be characterized by compromise. This was clear in 1987, when the World Commission on Environment and Development's report, *Our Common Future*, warned that present generations should not jeopardize the natural resources that will be needed by future generations. The World Commission went on to recommend that the LDCs would need to grow at an annual rate of 5 per cent in order for countries around the world to become stable, and that such a growth rate would remain within the overall general conception of sustainability. It also recommended that there would need to be a 25 per cent redistribution of wealth from the developed to the developing world. Clearly, little has been done to address the redistribution problem over the last two decades. At the same time, the recommendations by the World Commission are so vague that their realization may be very difficult to achieve, if not impossible.

In essence, there are two opposing positions in this debate. There are those who recommend that growth be minimized, if not flattened out completely, and that humanity must reduce waste and conserve natural resources as much as possible. To accomplish this goal, international tourism would need to be eliminated altogether. Others argue that this austere approach would further impoverish those who are already poor, and that accelerated economic development is not only inevitable but desirable. This position also implies that a less than perfectly clean environment is preferable to the consequences of stagnant growth and the resulting poverty that would promote. They would leave all decisions regarding the environment and wealth distribution to the market mechanism. The majority take a position somewhere between those two extremes. As Overton and Scheyvens point out, 'sustainable development also presents a long-term strategic goal rather than a short-term policy agenda'. (Overton and Scheyvens, 1999: 3) However, many would argue that, in the absence of serious efforts to address such issues, humanity will not have a long-term future in which to achieve the goal of sustainability. Time is running out, and action is what is needed if the worst effects of processes such as global warming are to be avoided. As a result, tourism planners must place issues of sustainability at the forefront of their practice; the tourism industry must be part of the solution rather than part of the problem. The fact is that, with little hardship, the tourism and hospitality industry could place itself on the leading edge of progressive change in this area. By its nature, tourism has the potential to provide a clean and sustainable way for both developed and less developed countries to earn significant levels of foreign currency, as well as providing employment for many otherwise jobless citizens.

The issue of sustainability relates not only to the environment, however; it is also an issue for those concerned about other economic and social issues. Sustainable practices are relevant to communities as well as businesses. Inefficiency at the business and community level has negative consequences for the environment. Poor farmers commonly cut down forests for fire wood, as well as overexploiting their land, leading to the depletion of nutrients, and providing the leading cause of soil erosion; but they have little choice other than to behave this way, or risk starvation. Tourism can provide an alternative to these negative practices by focusing attention on local business, and on ways of living that are less dependent on destroying or overusing the natural resource base. The issue is not whether or not to engage in tourism development, but on what basis that development should proceed.

There are two main areas of environmental concern that need to be addressed by the tourism planner. Large-scale issues include concerns over energy consumption and pollution caused by the transport of tourists over long distances. Fossil fuel combustion and consumption are major contributors to environmental damage, contributing to global warming and constituting large-scale issues for the tourism industry to solve. Such changes in practice as arranging for tourists to stay longer, and thus reducing the average number of trips per year, is one small example of a measure that might address this issue. There may be additional solutions to this problem which are not yet apparent, demanding increased research efforts in this area.

Small-scale issues include concerns about the use of natural areas for recreational purposes. For the most part, nature is used by tourists in a non-consumptive way – at least, as far as this is possible for any human activity. However, there are always problems of waste disposal and intrusion into sensitive ecological areas by the tourist, as well as of the compaction of soil through overuse of specific areas, leading to increased erosion and problems with soil aeration. The issue of waste disposal is particularly acute in LDCs, where sophisticated treatment technology may not be accessible, or is otherwise too expensive to install and maintain. Many coral reefs around the world suffer from human waste pollution. In some parts of South-East Asia, the construction and greening of golf courses has changed the hydrological patterns of entire regions. These are some of the sustainability problems to which the tourism industry will need to find solutions in the short and long term. If left unattended, not only will the conditions of entire countries be affected, but resorts depending on these types of natural resources will also find it difficult to survive.

Chapter 6 outlines a process for monitoring the environment which provides a basis upon which the tourism industry might deal with problems around sustainability. Once a monitoring program has been implemented, tourism managers can employ management techniques which will provide partial or comprehensive solutions to some of these problems, particularly at the small-scale, local level. Management practices such as the resting and rotation of areas used, and the dispersion of use over a wider area, are examples of these techniques. However, there is no uniform solution to all environmental problems created by tourism, and considerable inventiveness on the part of the tourism industry is required if these problems are to be remedied. Additional policies and management practices presently available to the tourism planner, and to the industry as a whole, will be introduced and described in greater detail in later parts of this book.

Environmental issues related to transport are more difficult to deal with effectively. International tourism does require people to travel long distances. However, during economic recessions and downturns in the business cycle international travel has tended to be replaced by higher levels of domestic tourism, which has had less negative impact on the environment. Greater concentration on public transportation systems such as rail as an alternative to the exclusive use of the automobile is certainly a critical part of the solution to this problem. The tourism industry will need to be concerned not only with moving people to destinations around the world, but also with providing less consumptive and polluting methods of transportation in the future, to deal with the problems of environmental sustainability that are inherent in the industry. Moreover, individual site audits must be undertaken to determine the most environmentally efficient methods of operation. Hoteliers and entrepreneurs are accustomed to undertaking operational audits for financial reasons, but in the future they will also be required to consider the ecological efficiency of their infrastructure and programs – particularly as new tourism sites become limited, and the rejuvenation of established facilities becomes more important to protecting the bottom line, perhaps even the survival, of the industry. These practices are not followed today by tourism companies under the spell of corporate globalization, with their exclusive concern for profit maximization. As the consequences of this form of development become even more apparent, thinking people will look for improved practices. Given the poor state of many popular tourism sites around the world, that time may be upon us.

The agenda of corporate globalization, with its overwhelming focus on commerce, including tourism, has taken hold of everyday life in a pervasive fashion. There is an urgent need to return to a public agenda which is comprehensive in its outlook and objectives. As Ralston Saul suggests,

> ... a sensible society is therefore very careful when it comes to market fashions parading as intellectual truths. And it never lets such a perpetually virginal domain as economics get control of the public agenda. Not that there is anything wrong with having juvenile enthusiasms in the marketplace. These strong emotions are necessary. They drive capitalism onward. But when it comes to society's well-being, they are best kept in a subsidiary position.

(Ralston Saul, 2001: 55)

Governments need to become more involved in protecting the natural and human-made sites that often serve as focal attractions around which the tourism industry constructs accommodation facilities. Increasing government involvement in tourism development has not been the recent trend, and the drift towards declining public involvement in this sector must be reversed.

THE NEW ECONOMY

Much has been written about the new economy brought about by globalization. Van den Bor, Bryden and Fuller (1997) describe the new economy as an advanced stage of capitalism with a heightened sense of competition and increased speed of the movement of capital around the world. They understand that the new economy is built on the premise that capital can locate 'wherever the costs of production are the lowest and where social and environmental restrictions are fewest'. (van den Bor et al.: 3) In addition, the new economy is characterized by the growth of the service sector in comparison to the primary and tertiary sectors of the economy. The World Tourism Organization reported in 1997 that 'in 1996 tourism receipts represented one-third of the value of world trade in the service sector' (World Tourism Organization 1997: 3). Peter Sutherland, the Director General of GATT, suggested in the World Travel and Tourism Council trade journal *Viewpoint* (1994: 19) that 'trade in services is likely to surpass trade in goods by 2005', and further, that 'tourism, which is currently one third of service trade, is expected to double by 2000'. Tourism is a major player in the new economy, in both urban and rural areas, and in developed countries and LDCs alike. The World Travel and Tourism Council estimated that by the year 2005 employment in the tourism industry would account for 11.8 per cent of total world employment (one in nine workers, 167 million direct and 181 million indirect workers, totaling 348 million); 11.4 per cent of world GDP; 11.8 per cent ($1.6 trillion) of capital investment; 11.6 per cent ($1,410 billion) of taxes; 11.7 per cent ($3.9 trillion) of personal consumption; and 6.8 per cent of government expenditure worldwide. (WTTC/WEFA, 1994: 67; Golub, 1994: 12) They went on to suggest that it was 'the largest industry, at $3 trillion and one tenth of world employment at the outset of 1995, and will more than double its output – to $7 trillion – in a decade and add 93 million new jobs'. (WTTC/WEFA, 1994: 67) The third-largest fully integrated tourism company in the world is Thomas Cook, which provides an example of just how large individual firms can become in the tourism industry. In a news release dated March 7, 2002, the Thomas Cook company reported entertaining 14 million tourists worldwide each year, annual sales of 8 billion euros, 30 tour operator brands, approximately 3,600 travel agents selling their products worldwide, 73,000 beds under their control, a fleet of 85 aircraft, and a workforce numbering some 28,000 employees. The company is represented in the sales markets of Germany, Great Britain, Ireland, France, Belgium, the Netherlands, Austria, Hungary, Poland, Slovakia, Slovenia, Egypt, India and Canada. Around one-half of Thomas Cook AG's group earnings are generated in the sales markets of Great Britain and those of Western and Eastern Europe. As an integrated leisure group, it works right across the travel value chain, encompassing airlines, hotels, tour operators, travel and incoming agencies. By any standard, Thomas Cook is a major trans-national corporation operating on the world scene. Such a high level of integration demonstrates the problem of leakage, or more accurately, the money spent for the individual travel purchase remains in the home country of the travel corporation, and does not reach the destination community where the tourism activity takes place. This causes problems for many LDCs in their attempt to earn foreign currency and pay down foreign-held debt, let alone increase savings and investment at home. All monies are paid up-front in the country of origin, with considerably less expenditure required at the host site. Certainly, payments will be made in the host country in the form of wages to service workers, as well as in the purchase of produce and payments for building and maintaining the infrastructure of the site, but most of the money does not reach the destination site. Integration thus has its downside to the host community, while providing an upside to the country or countries where a trans-national firm is based. Despite this, Sindiga (1999: 5) provides additional evidence of how tourism has increased in importance for most countries over the last decade (see Table 2.1).

In spite of the problems caused for many host countries by highly integrated travel firms dominating the tourism landscape, tourism continues to provide considerable revenues to participant countries. In recent years, tourism has grown steeply worldwide, as shown in Table 2.1. With the exceptions of 1991 and 1997, all other years in that period experienced substantial, if not extraordinary growth. This period corresponds to the advent of the latest interpretation of the corporate globalization of the economy, and it was when the NAFTA treaty and the European Economic Union agreement created at Maastricht were conceived, if not fully implemented (the single currency did not come into full effect until 2002). All regions of the world increased their tourism receipts substantially. Tourism in Africa and the Middle East grew the least, and this slower growth may be attributed to the political turmoil found in many parts of those regions. Even in Africa's case, the elimination of apartheid in South Africa had a dramatic effect on increasing Africa's tourism growth rate. While the Middle East has long suffered from periodic outbursts of violence, which act as a deterrent to tourism, the strong pull of religious pilgrimage sites helps to compensate for this weakness.

A particularly dismal year in comparison to most of the others in the decade was 1991. This was the year of a protracted worldwide

Table 2.1 International Tourism Receipts (Excluding International Transport), Percentage Share by Region and Percentage Change, 1988–97

Region	1988	1989	1990	1991	1992	1993	1994	1995	1996	1997
World (US$ bn.)	204	221	268	277	313	321	353	401	434	443
% share	100.0	100.0	100.0	100.0	100.0	100.0	100.0	100.0	100.0	100.0
% annual growth	15.6	8.3	21.5	3.2	13.3	2.4	9.8	13.8	8.2	2.2
Africa (US$ bn.)	5	5	5	5	6	6	7	7	8	9
% share	2.5	2.3	1.9	1.8	1.9	1.9	2.0	1.7	1.8	2.0
% annual growth	20.1	-1.7	18.0	-6.3	23.7	2.0	8.5	6.4	15.0	3.1
Americas (US$ bn.)	51	60	70	78	85	91	95	103	113	120
% share	25.0	27.1	26.1	28.2	27.2	28.3	26.9	25.7	26.0	27.0
% annual growth	19.3	17.3	16.5	11.1	9.8	6.7	4.6	7.9	9.7	6.8
East Asia/Pacif. (US$ bn.)	30	34	39	40	47	53	63	74	81	83
% share	14.7	15.4	14.6	14.4	15.0	16.5	17.8	18.5	18.7	18.7
% annual growth	32.6	12.3	14.4	3.2	17.2	11.0	19.5	17.6	10.1	2.2
Europe (US$ bn.)	111	115	147	148	167	163	178	207	220	218
% share	54.4	52.0	54.9	53.4	53.4	50.8	50.4	51.6	50.7	49.2
% annual growth	11.1	3.7	27.7	0.06	13.1	-2.4	9.6	15.8	6.4	-0.8
Middle East (US$ bn.)	4	4	4	4	5	5	6	7	8	9
% share	2.0	1.8	1.5	1.4	1.6	1.6	1.7	1.7	1.8	2.0
% annual growth	-4.7	3.5	-2.4	-14.4	33.4	12.2	12.0	17.1	18.8	14.7
South Asia (US$ bn.)	2	2	2	2	3	3	3	3	4	4
% share	1.0	0.9	0.7	0.7	1.0	0.9	0.8	0.7	1.1	0.9
% annual growth	1.6	6.3	2.4	14.9	19.0	-3.3	14.4	13.8	13.1	5.9

Source: Sindiga, 1999: 5.

recession, which had a dramatic effect on tourism growth rates, as well as other economic activity, in all regions of the world. The tourism industry is particularly sensitive to economic downturns and recessions.

There is an obvious discrepancy between the 1995 receipts of $401 billion and the revenue of $3.9 trillion forecast by the WTTC/WEFA. On closer examination, it is clear that Table 2.1 provides estimates excluding costs of transportation and, perhaps more importantly, domestically generated tourism receipts. One can assume that the difference between the two figures just cited corresponds to airline revenues and the costs of domestic travel. However, it must be remembered that, with the exception of a few companies, most airlines are based in Europe and North America, and that the domestic tourism industry is strongest in developed countries, where consumers have considerably greater levels of disposable income than those in LDCs. The huge amounts of money spent by tourists on transport does not find its way into most of the destination countries on which tourism depends; nor does it go to support employment in the airline industries of those countries. The repatriation of receipts to the developed world is another example of the leakage of tourism dollars from the host countries and partners in the tourism enterprise. In this case the funds do not in fact leak from the host country, since they probably did not arrive there in the first place. Domestic tourism requires that society support a substantial middle class, which often does not exist in LDCs. If the challenges of creating domestic tourism industries in LDCs and of distributing all tourism revenues more equitably can be met, then tourism may be able to play an even greater role in sustainable development, particularly in the developing world. If these issues are not resolved, then tourism will not play the positive role in development that it can and should.

Between 1997 and 2001, tourism receipts worldwide maintained their torrid upward spiral. This growth came crashing back to earth after the events of September 11, 2001, when terrorists flew hijacked airplanes into the World Trade Center in New York and the Pentagon in Washington, DC. At the time of writing, it is not known if tourism will be permanently affected by these events or whether it will recover its former levels of growth. But early indications are that it will not suffer permanent damage in the long term. The tourism industry, through its trade journal *Viewpoint* (World Travel and Tourism Council, 1994), predicts worldwide growth of tourism of up to 9.3 per cent annually. Already the WTTC (2002) reports a turnaround since the September 11 attacks, and the dramatic events in New York, as outlined below:

> For most of 2002, output has been running slower than in 2001 as demand has been hit first by worries over travelling as a result of September 11, 2001 and, second, by spending cutbacks associated with the global economic downturn. However, fourth quarter output is running well above that seen in the immediate aftermath of September 11, so the end-of-year estimates are looking more positive than they were in March of this year. In fact, the relative strength of consumer spending in many countries compared with expectations earlier in the year has helped maintain personal Travel & Tourism spending, and we now see industry output in 2002 as flat rather than the declining levels we were expecting in the spring. In our forecasts prepared in March 2002, we had foreseen record growth in 2003. These forecasts have been dampened by the bombing in Bali, continuing risks from terrorism evident in several countries, possible military action against Iraq and a more fragile world economic recovery.

> Source: <http://www.wttc.org/mediaCentre/
> WTTCForecastsStrongForthQuarter0812002.htm>

While the tourism industry has been severely affected worldwide by the events of September 11, 2001, the president of the WTTC sees growth returning to normal soon, although not as strongly as originally forecast immediately following those tragic events. A recent WTTC (2002) press release indicates a modest increase in tourism growth worldwide.

> The World Travel & Tourism Council (WTTC) released a series of new economic reports today with research produced by Oxford Economic Forecasting (OEF) that shows a modest increase in Travel & Tourism activity for 2002 compared to forecasts released in March of this year, and solid expectations for growth in Travel & Tourism in 2003. ... [T]he updated WTTC/OEF forecast for 2003 shows a solid 4.1 per cent real growth for the year.

> Source: <http://www.wttc.org/mediaCentre/
> WTTCForecastsStrongForthQuarter0812002.htm>

Like other industries, tourism is consolidating and being heavily influenced by large trans-national corporations. Some would argue that this movement towards oligopoly is unhealthy for the industry, and particularly to tourism communities. The statistics in Table 2.2 demonstrate that seven of the largest trans-national tourism companies in the world have enormous influence within the industry, and upon many of the countries in which they operate. They provide a glimpse into the performance of a handful of the trans-national tourism companies operating worldwide. There is nothing special about these companies except that they are broadly representative of the large companies involved in the business throughout the world.

What is evident from Table 2.2 is that revenues and shareholder equity has increased substantially over the three-year period reported. Perhaps more important in this discussion is the financial size, and hence the influence, of the industry worldwide. The table reports only seven of the largest companies operating in the travel and tourism sector worldwide, and these seven, while critically important to the industry, are certainly not the only players in the system. In the year 2000 these seven corporations earned revenues of US$37.7 billion between them. Under any circumstances this represents a huge business operation, but it only partially accounts for the size of the industry. Comparing the data for 1997 in Table 2.1 with that reported by the seven companies in 1998 (Table 2.2), it can be calculated that these hospitality companies accounted for approximately 6.5 per cent of the tourism receipts generated by the industry worldwide – only a small amount in comparison to what the airlines generate.

Statistics Canada (2000) reported tourism receipts for Canada for the year 2000 to be $15,898 billion (Canadian). This amount represents approximately 5 per cent of the receipts in the total Canadian economy. The seven hotel and resort chains in Table 2.2 reported over twice the revenue of the entire tourism industry of Canada – a sophisticated Western country which is home to a large, mature tourism industry. Revenues for these seven corporations represented the equivalent of 10 per cent of the gross domestic product in the Canadian economy. This would obviously give them an overwhelming dominance in many LDCs.

As long as the economy continues to grow and development continues, tourism will play a vital role in that development process worldwide. People are naturally curious and want to visit the major

Table 2.2   Financial Analysis of Seven of the Largest Trans-National Tourism and Travel Corporations

(US$ million, except per share amounts)

	2000	1999	1998
Hilton Hotel Chain			
Revenue	3,451	2,150	1,769
EBITDA	1,271	695	596
Operating Income	830	495	464
Cash earnings per share	1.32	0.81	
Marriot			
Revenue	19,781	17,684	16,000
EBITDA	1,052	860	
Operating Profit	922	830	736
Cash earnings per share	1.89	1.51	1.46
Four Seasons Hotels and Resorts			
Revenue	2,821	2,370	2,271
EBITDA	139.4	97.5	88
Net Earnings	103.1	86.5	69.7
Cash earnings per share	2.98	2.52	2.06
Carnival Corporation			
Revenue	3,779	3,497	3,009
EBITDA			
Net Income	965	1,027	836
Cash earnings per share	1.6	1.66	1.4
Club Mediterranean			
Revenue	1,889	1,477	1,278
EBITDA			
Operating Income	103	71	59
Cash earnings per share			
Starwood			
Revenue	4,345	3,829	3,281
EBITDA	1,573	1,352	1,111
Net Income	403	303	1,302
Cash earnings per share	1.96	1.54	1.05
Canadian Pacific Hotels and Resorts (Can $ have been converted to US$ for comparative purposes)			
Revenue	2,467 (1628)	1,790 (1181)	1,215 (802)
EBITDA	299 (197)	256 (169)	174 (115)
Net Income	143 (94)	116 (77)	83
Cash earnings per share			
Total Revenue	37,693.7	32,188.7	28,409.7

Note: All data in this table were taken from the 2000 annual reports of each of the corporations listed. Empty cells represent data not provided in the annual reports.

tourist destinations across the globe. Whether the ecosystem will be able to sustain these levels of tourism development is an open question. Environmental degradation is a concern not only for those who make their living from tourism, but also for the inhabitants of destination sites.

Tourism can play a positive role in the efforts to achieve sustainability but not as it is approached at present. In rural areas which depend on the natural environment for a number of human activities, including tourism, the environment will certainly need protection and conservation. The world is running out of new, unspoiled tourism destinations, and many of the large airlines realize that sites cannot continue to be spoiled and then replaced with completely new developments further down the coast, or in a neighboring country. The supply of new sites that this type of development requires is simply drying up. Moreover, designated destination sites always form part of a wider ecosystem, and can easily be affected adversely by activities occurring miles away; air and water currents transport any pollution to ecologically sensitive areas. Dumping waste some distance from where tourists congregate provides no guarantee that it will not affect resorts and recreation activities. As tourists visit a particular area in greater numbers, producing more human waste, this problem becomes more evident in the areas where recreation activities take place. This type of pollution easily offends otherwise happy tourists.

The tourism industry has the potential to give leadership to the recycling and conservation movements – not out of philanthropic impulses but because it is in its long-term interest to do so. The conservation ethic will also be enhanced if local communities take charge of their environment and demand a voice in, if not control over, their surroundings and the tourism development that takes place in them. In some cases this may necessitate conflict between global institutions and the locals themselves. This type of confrontation has occurred in a number of highly developed tourist sites, particularly in the developed world. Citizens have blocked buses from entering main streets in tourism communities as a form of protest of overcrowding and vehicle exhaust pollution. If cooler heads prevail, and both parties make efforts to respect the other's needs and point of view, each will realize that it is in everyone's best interest to cooperate and develop the community tourism project jointly, in a spirit of truly equal partnership. The sustainability of tourism and of tourism communities demands compromise among the many competing needs and views expressed by the totality of interests that present themselves in the planning process.

In order for such partnership to materialize, communities must organize themselves so that they can participate substantively in tourism development projects. Certainly, the tourism corporations will bring business acumen to a partnership, but that is not the only expertise needed to develop a successful and satisfying tourism project for the many stakeholders in the process at the local level. As is suggested throughout this book, tourism must not be conceived in isolation from other aspects of community living, but must be understood as one part of a greater whole. As research suggests (Reid, Mair and Taylor, 2000), if members of a community are in open opposition to the tourism development taking place in their midst, business will also suffer. The mood of a host community is extremely important in ensuring visitor satisfaction, as tourists can quickly sense any tensions that may exist within it. As a result of such a negative mood, the return visits that the tourism industry relies on so heavily will be reduced; this effect will, in turn, damage word-of-mouth advertising, and the formerly positive image of a particular destination may take many years to recover.

Of critical importance to the new economy, and to tourism development specifically, is the creation of adequate income and the discretionary time to engage in leisure pursuits. As Drache and Gertler (1992: 21) suggest, 'the proposal for a comprehensive income security package may sound utopian today, but it stands a good chance of becoming tomorrow's reality'. They make this assertion because of the growing crisis produced by the widening gap between rich and poor throughout the world. David Harvey (2000: 43) points out that in 1991, 85 per cent of the world's population received 15 per cent of its income. Even though very few people control a vast majority of the world's wealth a large section of those outside the top category should not necessarily be thought to be in dire poverty. But it clearly demonstrates the continuing and increasing separation between rich and poorer people throughout the world. As Harvey points out, '[t]his polarization is astounding, rendering hollow the World Bank's extraordinary claim that international integration coupled with free-market liberalism and low levels of government interference is the best way to deliver growth and to raise living standards for workers'. (Harvey, 2000: 43)

As the gulf between rich and poor continues to increase, and unrest – including terrorism – also grows, the privileged members of society must do more than retreat into walled-off communities in order to avoid these problems. New institutions and policies designed to ensure that all sections of society benefit from the new economy must be created. Institutions like the World Trade Organization will need to broaden their mandates to include environmental and social issues, including labor standards. Until now, corporate globalization has focused exclusively on trade laws and the improvement in the business climate, including the elimination of restrictions on the free flow of trade and capital, but not on the movement of labor. If the new global economy is to be successful, these issues must be treated in the same way as those relating to capital and trade.

In the developed countries, there has been a revolution in the workplace, which has embraced technology and reduced the value of labor in the production process. In this new economy, labor is no longer as instrumental in productivity gains as it was. This has led some authors (Reid, 1995: Rifkin, 1995) to conclude that the new economy will be a workless one. In a more recent work, Beck outlines the consequences to work of corporate globalization and the maturation of the capitalist system:

Capitalism is doing away with work. Unemployment is no longer a marginal fate: it affects everyone potentially, as well as the democratic way of life. But abrogating responsibility for global capitalism undermines its own legitimacy. Before a new Marx shakes up the West, some long-overdue ideas and models for a different social contract will need to be taken up again. The future of democracy beyond the work society must be given a new foundation. ... Three myths screen public debate from the reality of the situation: first, everything is much too complicated anyway (the unfathomability myth); second, the coming upturn in the service sector will save the work society (the services myth); and third, we have only to drive down wage-costs and the problem of unemployment will vanish (the costs myth).

(Beck, 2000: 58–9)

While the effects on human society of corporate globalization may not yet be fully understood, it is conceivable that work will not play the dominant role in recreating the human condition and in providing the personal satisfaction that it once did. To continue to force the survival of this most sacred of human traditions into the future will be to reject the potential of the new economy. It is clear that human society can produce more using less labor than at any other time in human history; it may be more important for society to own the fruits of production than the means of that production. This approach represents a subtle but profound shift in the Marxian tradition: as the new economy matures, humanity may perhaps come to see the benefits of a more leisure-oriented society, in which tourism would obviously play a major role. This transition takes on new significance in defining life for many people; if it were indeed to occur, domestic tourism would become even more significant in the new economy than it is already expected to be.

There are scholars and social thinkers who are challenging the very premise on which the new economy is being constructed. While corporate globalization has embraced individual freedom and the maximization of self-interest as its defining principle, scholars such as McMurtry are suggesting a different course for development, built on an alternative code of ethics. McMurtry suggests that a life-code of ethics which emphasizes such issues as health care, clean air and potable water which is accessible to all, needs to replace the money code which focuses solely on profits for the few, which now exists throughout corporate globalization. He goes on to explain that:

> just as the life-ground of value is expressed in 'the life-code and sequence,' so what we call 'the civil commons' is the instituted bearer of this life-code. The nature of the civil commons can be explained as follows: it is society's organized and community-funded capacity of universally accessible resources to provide for the life preservation and growth of society's members and their environmental life-host. The civil commons is, in other words, what people ensure together as a society to protect and further life, as distinct from money aggregates.
>
> (McMurtry, 1998: 20)

The community tourism project, conceived as a system, would be enhanced by McMurtry's suggested reorganization of the premise on which it is presently constructed. While money remains the medium through which transactions are conducted, the life-code of ethics provides a philosophy according to which the system might be built and managed. This would ensure that community members would drive and control the tourism development process, rather than being subordinated to mechanisms which maximize the individual entrepreneur's self-interest. What is best for individual self-interest rarely equates to what is best for the collective, or to use McMurtry's term, the civil commons. From this perspective, tourism development should be viewed as a system of relationships, rather than in terms of its individual parts.

TOURISM AS A SYSTEM

Conceptualizing tourism as a system in itself and part of a larger system rather than as an independent entity accepts the premise that the whole is greater than the sum of its parts, and that the relationship between the parts has an equal importance to the parts themselves in the eventual success of the tourism project. Systems theory was a reaction to Cartesian science, which was reductionist in the sense that it attempted to reduce all matter to its most elementary parts in order to understand it thoroughly. Systems theory asserted the need for understanding the organization of a phenomenon, rather than just its substance (Macy, 1991). It is modeled on nature, in contrast to the mechanistic view that is the foundation of enlightenment science. It is therefore understandable that systems theory is embraced in the study of biology. Macy sums up systems theory as follows:

> The organized whole found in nature, then, is not only a system but an open system. It maintains and organizes itself by exchanging matter, energy, and information with its environment. These flow through the system and are transformed by it. These exchanges and transformations are the system's life and continuity, for no component of the system is permanent. The way they happen, that is, the principles by which a pattern of perpetually changing substance both retains its shape or identity and evolves its order, have been a central focus of systems enquiry.

(Macy, 1991: 73)

Macy provides the overarching concept of the tourism system as conceived in this book. The problems faced by the tourism industry in the past are a result of a failure to conceptualize tourism as a naturally occurring system. Tourism has been traditionally analyzed in a reductionist manner – as purely a function of supply and demand, for example. There have been few attempts to view tourism's development as an exchange of matter, energy, and information; let alone as a dynamic system perpetually changing its shape and subjected to a myriad of forces not necessarily directly related to the tourism product itself. The case studies presented in Chapter 7 treat tourist developments, and the communities in which they take place, as open systems, and their organizational characteristics are seen as key elements in their sustainability and success both as tourism destinations and as communities.

Macy suggests that a system is in continual stress because of the inflow and outflow of energy, matter and information. The tourism system in any community acts no differently. This seeking of a 'steady state' by a system is claimed to give rise to the stages in Butler's product life-cycle model, discussed briefly in Chapters 2 and 6. Practitioners and tourism planners do not act as if the tourism system is dynamic, but view it as static. This behavior ignores the inflow and outflow process described by Macy. As a result, tourism destinations are notoriously open to decline and eventual collapse, as seen, for example, in such events as the demise of the seaside resort in Britain during the middle of the twentieth century. Such a result is not inevitable, however, if the tourism destination is seen as an open, natural system; that is, as a structure with relationships to the social and environmental subsystems in which it is embedded.

A critical feature of an open system is the feedback it receives from its own changing dynamics. Adjustments are made to the system based on this feedback, which is another reason why the whole is greater than the sum of its parts. Feedback in the tourism system has typically been truncated, given that many of the subsystems of which it is comprised have been overlooked in the course of development. When the needs of the capitalist are the overwhelming concern in the monitoring program, and the social and environmental impacts are given secondary status or ignored altogether, the system is sure to break down. As McMurtry suggests,

> We know a life-organization is breaking down when it excludes or does not respond to the feedback that reveals its disorder, even though this failure may be exposing it to systematic destruction. On the social level of life-organization, for example, there may be evidence of contradiction between the *representations* of the value programme as 'free' or 'God's will' and the *reality* of progressive destructions of social or environmental life following from its

imposition. In the social life-organizing that is breaking down, the conflict between representation and feedback does not enter its accounts. Rather, *the problem is relocated in those who assert it exists.* Its displacement is effected by the standard mechanism of stigmatization, which is always as an enemy of the values that the given order falsely imagines it embodies. This discourages dissent, and so the feedback pathways remain closed.

(McMurtry, 1999: 24)

This critique should not be interpreted to mean that economic analysis should be played down or removed from the monitoring system altogether; on the contrary, economic analysis should remain strong. What is being recommended, however, is that economic analysis must form one part of the total analysis, along with environmental and more broadly-based social impact assessments. The basis on which economic analysis proceeds should also be altered. Economic analysis in the tourism system must embrace those forces which protect life, as well as the traditional supply–demand equation which focuses on maximizing profit to the shareholder. For example, the techniques and methods of the resource economist, some of which are presented in Chapter 6 of this volume, must receive equal status in the planning and development of tourism to the traditional economic analysis which has historically dominated the economics discipline. Embracing this holistic philosophy recognizes that all people living in tourism communities are part of the project, whether they want to be or not, simply by virtue of living within it. To quote McMurtry again:

From the standpoint of the civil commons, the standard disjunction between individual rights on the one hand and community rights on the other hand is a shallow and false opposition. The individual's right to the resources of life – health-care, learning, clean air and water, and so on – is grounded in the community's ability to provide them. ... As the life-ground that gives us our shared air, sunshine, water, plant life, and earth is privatized, polluted, or depleted to 'keep the economy going,' the civil commons is ever more needed to preserve and enable life, not to 'save costs' for market commodity transactions.

(McMurtry, 1998: 25–6)

REASSERTING THE COMMUNITY'S ROLE IN THE NEW ECONOMY

While globalization and the new economy have changed the balance of power throughout the world, the pendulum will inevitably swing back towards local communities from the position which gives exclusive authority to capital. This is what some authors (Brecher et al., 1993; Sumner, 2002; Falk, 1993) have termed 'globalization from below'. Globalization, like tourism, is in itself not a bad thing; who is in charge of it, and the basis on which it proceeds are the critical issues. Falk defines the notion of globalization from below as 'an array of trans-national social forces animated by environmental concerns, human rights, hostility to patriarchy and a vision of human community based on the unity of diverse cultures seeking an end to poverty, oppression, humiliation, and collective violence'. (Falk, 1993: 39) The late 1990s and early years of the twenty-first century witnessed the unsophisticated beginnings of this movement in demonstrations against the World Trade Organization in Seattle, the Organization of American States in Quebec City, and during a G7 meeting in Genoa. Most, if not all, of these events were reactions against corporate globalization and its effects on the poor regions of the world. Events of this type are likely to be even more positive and orderly in the future. Emphasis could very well be placed increasingly on education and less on disruption. Equally important, work in this area will need to be done at the community level, through coalition building in and between communities, which are the smallest political unit and the place where most of us spend the greatest part of our lives. Coalition building is likely to occur through the leadership of community interest groups with compatible goals. Tourism development may become a focus for much of this coalition building. As tourism becomes more community-controlled, opportunities for individual involvement will present themselves. This involvement could very well lead to social learning and coalition building, given the inevitable contact that will take place between the various parties involved in the project.

Some of the prerequisites for making globalization from below a reality have been outlined in the previous section, and are further elaborated in Chapter 6, but the means by which community members can play a greater role in the development of their community must be articulated here. But is globalization from below just a utopian ideal, or can it be made a reality? Cox not only thinks it is an important ideal, but lays out the ground on which such a reform could be achieved:

> The condition for a restructuring of society and polity in this sense would be to build a new historic block capable of sustaining a long war of position until it is strong enough to become an alternative basis of polity. This effort would have to be grounded in the popular strata. The activities that comprise it will not likely be directed to the state because of the degree of depoliticization and alienation from the state among these strata. They will more likely be directed to local authorities and to collective self-help. They will in many cases be local responses to global problems – to problems of the environment, of organizing production, of providing welfare, of migration. If they are ultimately to result in new forms of state, these forms will arise from the practice of non-state popular collective action rather than from extensions of existing types of administrative control.
>
> (Cox, 1991: 349)

Sherry Arnstein (1969) has identified and articulated a theory of citizen involvement which views citizen participation as a spectrum of various approaches, and not as a single concept or method. In other words, citizen participation is defined differently by different actors in the system. Arnstein's continuum places professional manipulation of the public (the engineering of popular support for elite decision-makers) at one end of the continuum, and citizen control (citizens taking power over decision-making) at the other. In between these polar opposites, the other points in the spectrum are: therapy (experts treating citizens as if they need help to make the right decisions); informing (the one-way flow of information from expert to citizen); consultation (the invitation of opinions from citizens); placation (the treatment of citizens as token representatives – for example, placing a few of the poor on advisory boards); partnership (the redistribution of power equally between citizens and power-brokers); and delegated power (citizens being given power over certain decisions by the elite). As Arnstein suggests, the continuum ranges from empty ritual at one end to real citizen empowerment at the other, with gradations in between. She describes the lower two stages of her model as forms of non-participation, and the middle three as degrees of tokenism, while the last three stages provide substantial degrees of citizen power. Any of these processes may be at work at any one time in the course of a tourism development project. Each may be legitimate in specific circumstances, but the upper end of the continuum is generally considered to be citizen-focused, while the lower end is dominated by practitioners or corporate power. What is critical in this model is that all participants in the process understand the limitations of each stage and therefore the chosen strategy is acceptable to those involved in the process. Moreover, approaches to citizen participation in any community tourism project must also be consistent with other planning strategies being implemented in that development (for a further explanation, see Figure 5.1).

Rocha (1997) transforms and modernizes Arnstein's theory of citizen participation in an article in the *Journal of Planning Education and Research*, titled 'A Ladder of Empowerment'. The major transformation in thinking, as the title of the article suggests, is the movement from participation to empowerment. Moreover, Rocha's idea combines some of the elements contained in the models of Arnstein and Arai. She views empowerment as a continuum, much as Arnstein does, and also connects individual and community empowerment in the same way as Arai. Arai views empowerment as a cumulative process dependent on education and involvement. She provides a diagrammatic interpretation of Habermas and Freire's concepts in her model of the process of personal empowerment in connecting individual and community empowerment as envisioned by Rocha (see Figure 2.1).

In the first stage – awareness – individuals become concerned with an issue or problem that confronts them. Through discourse they come to see a long-term problem from a new point of view or perspective. In Habermasian terms, the individual becomes aware of the oppression under which they live. Freire would define this stage as conscientization. The second stage – connecting and learning – is the process of beginning to deal with the problem which is causing the oppression. People who share the problem come together and, through discourse (Habermas' notion of 'communicative action') identify and analyze the problem in detail. The third stage – mobilization – involves creating an organizational network and the political skills necessary to act. Finally – in the contribution stage – the actor is ready, in collaboration with others, to use the skills learned to address the problem.

Rocha outlines several positions between individual and community empowerment: atomistic individual empowerment, in which the locus for power is with the individual; embedded

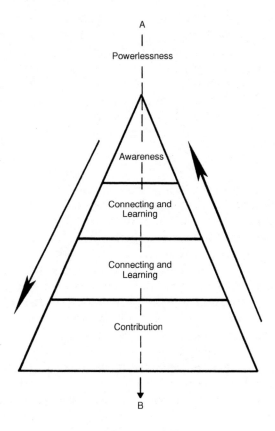

Figure 2.1   Arai's Process of Personal Empowerment

Source: Arai, 1996: 37

individual empowerment, where the locus of power is still with the
individual, but recognizes the context of the environment; mediated
empowerment, in which power is mediated through a professional
or expert; socio-political empowerment, where the focus is on change
within the community or environment; and political empowerment,
in which a network of individuals acts in the political environment.
The benefits of this model are summed up by Rocha as follows:

> This typology serves a dual purpose. First, it provides a coherent
> way of looking at empowerment theories that allows for

complexity and variation and that clarifies their differences and similarities. Second, the typology can be used by practitioners to clarify their own goals and strategies concerning empowerment; by community organizations to gain a clear conceptual view of how empowerment can be realized; and by local government to evaluate methods and strategies used by community organizations (especially relevant for planners concerned with the allocation of block grant funds or the distribution of other federal funds).

(Rocha, 1997: 31)

In the final analysis, this transfer of power from the boardroom to the community center will only be successful if citizens are highly skilled in organization, communication, and community development. It will not happen without direct intervention and a firm sense of direction. Before concrete planning or negotiations can begin between the partners in this process, extensive community capacity building activities including communication, networks, empowerment of the citizenry and so on, may be necessary, to be directed towards creating equal partnerships between professionals in the tourism sector – including entrepreneurs – and the community.

Perhaps the first tasks in community capacity building are raising awareness and enabling empowerment (see Friedmann, 1995). Habermas and the Frankfurt School discuss empowerment as a concept within Critical Theory which is an emancipating force 'giving new life to ideals of reason and freedom by revealing their false embodiment in scientism, capitalism, the "culture industry," and bourgeois Western political institutions'. (White, 1995: 4) Habermas uses 'communicative action' to denote truth and reality, which in turn depend for their expression upon equal dialogue among all actors in the system, rather than domination by one of the partners in the dialogue. Critical theory depends on individual awareness or what Freire terms 'conscientization', which means that the individual enters or creates his or her own understanding of the factual and moral aspects of the world, rather than being subjected to a hegemonic view.

The strategy for implementing fundamental change through communicative action is set out succinctly by Sumner, who quotes the work of the Transformative Learning Centre (2001), defining transactive learning as:

... a deep, structural shift in basic premises of thought, feelings, and actions. It is a shift of consciousness that dramatically and permanently alters our way of being in the world. Such a shift involves our understanding of ourselves and our self-locations; our relationships with other humans and with the natural world; our understanding of relations of power in interlocking structures of class, race and gender; our body awareness; our visions of alternative approaches to living; and our sense of possibilities for social justice and peace and personal joy.

(Sumner, 2002: 301)

Transformative learning suggests a process not an end point (as when learning is associated with strategic action) which is dedicated to the Habermasian notion of communicative action and the Freirian concept of conscientization. The community's reality is created from within, but in dialogue with outside forces with an interest in it – perhaps from the point of view of a tourism enterprise. This process is very different from one suggested by the assertion that there is only a single economic alternative available to society, usually dominated by the priorities of big business, and that the community had better get on board with that emphasis or be left behind in the great global race. This type of rhetoric has outlived its usefulness, and it is now time to take seriously the Habermasian concept of communicative action. The 'system world' is characterized by the interpretation of reality from the point of view of capital and the state, while the 'life world' is determined by the individuals in society acting in their own interests, through discourse and communicative rationality. Communicative action as envisioned by Habermas is basically juxtaposed with the system world's (reality created by state and capital hegemony) reliance on positivism and the scientific explanation of the world. The other important distinction in Habermas's framework is between 'system world' and 'life world'. Moreover – and related to the 'system world' and 'life world' concepts – Habermas insists that both the 'technical' interest in control and the 'practical' interest in understanding are properly subordinated to an 'emancipatory' interest in 'liberation'. (Dryzek, 1995: 99) When discussing critical theory as social science, Dryzeck writes:

In this light, the task for the social scientist is first to understand the ideologically distorted subjective situation of some individual or group, second to explore the forces that have caused the situation, and third to show that these forces can be overcome through awareness of them on the part of the oppressed individual or group in question. Thus a critical social science theory is verified not by experimental test or by interpretive plausibility, but rather by action on the part of its audience who decide that, upon reflexion, the theory gave a good account of the causes of their sufferings and effectively pointed to their relief.

(ibid.: 99)

Raymond Guess expands on these ideas, suggesting that 'critical theories aim at emancipation and enlightenment, at making agents aware of hidden coercion, thereby freeing them from that coercion and putting them in a position to determine where their true interests lie'. (Guess, 1987: 55)

Tourism planning must incorporate the philosophy of critical theory into its practices. If planning for tourism is truly to be developed from bottom up, people must become aware of the corporate power confronting them, and the effect of that power on their life-style and value system. 'Critical theories, are claimed to be "reflective", or "self-referential": critical theory is itself always a part of the object-domain which it describes; critical theories are always in part about themselves'. (Guess, 1987: 55) In bottom-up tourism planning, citizens learn about themselves and their values. They can determine what is in their long-term interest and not be swayed by short-term needs articulated by large international corporations who have a self-serving agenda. This idea does not exclude the recognition of 'enlightened self-interest', but it includes much more of what McMurtry (1998) calls life-code ethics or values. Guess (1987: 55–6) concludes his list of criteria for critical theories by suggesting that 'critical theories are cognitively acceptable only if they survive a more complicated process of evaluation, the central part of which is a demonstration that they are "reflectively acceptable"'. Critical theories involve a high degree of citizen participation not only in the formative stages of tourism development, but also in the ongoing monitoring and evaluation phase. This necessitates the incorporation of transformative learning principles into the tourism project, as outlined earlier in this chapter, as well as of Friedmann's notion of social learning, outlined in some detail in Chapter 6.

In the final analysis, critical theory anticipates that, through discourse, communities will determine what inhibits their development as a human community. Further, it will provide a forum for creating and implementing actions which ameliorate those conditions. Such communities will not be willing to be controlled and directed from the outside, although they will certainly see outside groups as partners in their development process. They will develop values consistent with the 'life world' as posited by Habermas as opposed to the hegemonic 'system world'. This shift in conceptual orientation has considerable implications for not only tourism planning, but also for the more equal distribution of benefits emanating from the tourism project.

Communicative action is intended to give rise to emancipation through the transformative learning process, which can provide a framework for development in community tourism planning, particularly in rural and remote areas, and in LDCs where holistic development is particularly essential. In this way, tourism development can become not only a tool for economic development, but also a vehicle for community development and capacity building.

In order for transformative learning to be effective, community-based forces must establish a well planned program of action in advance of considering implementation. To wait until a community was in crisis before initiating this process would be to condemn it to failure. There are historical examples of successful social actions developed through the transformative learning process. One of the features leading to the success of the Coady Institute, described in Chapter 3, was that it was a cumulative, ongoing adult education program, rather than a one-off crisis-driven project. While it was not focused exclusively on teaching academic subjects, it did educate the fishers of the east coast of Canada about their plight, and the measures available to them to rectify their situation, as well as providing them with some basic literacy skills. It counted as community development in the sense that its participants defined their own problems and decided on the solutions to them, rather than being directed by an outside agent.

The establishment of a transformative learning process ensures that necessary time is devoted to sufficient dialogue which is focused on encouraging communities to develop an understanding of their own situation, rather than being instructed from outside. Acceptance of the orthodox view of the world portrayed by the corporate and political elite – often the modus operandi of tourism planners – produces sterile tourism destinations at best, and community discontent at worst. Allowing sufficient time for the definition of both problems and solutions by the community concerned is an aspect of community development which has often become lost in the world of tourism planning, where quick solutions to immediate problems are required. The approach advocated here requires the community to view tourism as one component of a holistic community development strategy, and to eschew the compartmentalization of development into sectors. Some of the possible methods and techniques for raising the awareness of communities, as well as the transformative learning practices required to make it sustainable within a tourism community, will be further discussed in Chapter 6.

3 Tourism as a Function of Development Studies

INTRODUCTION

This chapter deals with two important overarching issues. The first is the ideology of tourism and the role it plays in development. It is often thought that tourism operates outside the more general conditions of society, particularly socioeconomic trends. Many authors and scholars focus on the negative aspects of tourism as if they had no connection to the neo-liberal agendas of modernization and globalization. Brown (1998) suggests that this may not be the case, and that tourism development may simply reflect larger-scale conditions of society. This chapter reflects on that suggestion, exploring in detail how tourism is employed as an instrument of structural adjustment in the developing countries and as a symbol of modernization and the new economy in the developed world, thus situating tourism planning and development within the domain of development studies.

Also addressed in this chapter are the myths and realities that bolster the new economy, and the role of tourism in it. A central exploration is the role of community development in tourism planning. The question is explored of whether or not tourism truly provides an alternative in rural areas to the environmentally damaging extractive industries, while the alleged promise of tourism as a vehicle for sustainable development also forms a major area of discussion.

THE CONTEXT FOR TOURISM DEVELOPMENT

Tourism has become the development sector of choice for many LDCs as they strive for economic growth and prosperity. This book, like most others, deploys a distinction between developed and less developed countries (LDCs) when examining tourism development. While this is a convenient way of understanding the world, it is probably more accurate to distinguish between peoples and societies which are more or less developed, rather than between countries. Martinussen even suggests that 'there is disagreement on just how large a part of the world development research can or should cover

– and in connection with this, to what extent it still makes sense to talk about a Third World, or about developing countries as a special category of countries'. (Martinussen, 1997: 3) Even a country like my own – Canada, generally thought of as a developed country – has social and geographical areas which are more characteristic of the developing rather than the developed world. Many First Nations communities, and remote areas of this vast country – particularly in the far north – possess such developmentally disadvantaged characteristics. Certainly, people living in these areas have access to a social safety net not available in LDCs – albeit more of a legislative than a practical reality for many. Many First Nations and remote villages in Canada have seen this safety net break down, and whole communities have become dysfunctional as a result. In less developed countries, and in the underdeveloped sections of developed countries like Canada, tourism thus takes on a more critical role in income generation and general development – or at least, that is the conventional wisdom. Hopkins suggests that '[p]ost-industrial restructuring has compelled [communities] to exploit and promote local tourism attractions, especially natural amenities, in an attempt to minimize, halt or reverse decline induced by collapse or contraction in more conventional, resource extraction or manufacture-based sectors'. (Hopkins, 1998: 66) Agricultural tourism is cultivated by many national and provincial governments as an instrument for the economic development of the countryside. The artificial and natural resources of the countryside are thus exploited to satisfy the economic needs of rural residents as well as some urbanite entrepreneurs and the tourism needs of city dwellers. Many main streets in rural areas are no longer there to serve the needs of local residents, but are now simply tourist enclaves catering exclusively to the needs of visitors. Agricultural income alone is usually not sufficient to support a farm – unless it is a corporate, factory farm – and agricultural tourism therefore supports farm incomes, in many cases saving the family farm ideal. This is particularly the case in the countryside which lies on the periphery of the more urbanized cities in developed countries.

Dealing with the developed and developing parts of the world in the same book is a risky business. Critics of this approach may argue that it is Eurocentric in that it is usually Western academics who develop and interpret theories that are applied to the developing world, and therefore may result in an overdependence on theoretical models designed for conditions in Western Europe and North

America. As Martinussen (1997) suggests, 'there is a widespread tendency to assume a kind of universal applicability and validity, again especially within economics'. Views such as these appear Eurocentric because, '... they a priori give precedence to methods and theories which are developed with empirical foundations in Western societies and culture'. (Martinussen, 1997: 4) This trap should of course be avoided. However, we do live in a new world, where many parts of the developed world face similar problems to those commonly encountered in the developing world. Certainly, the trend towards trade liberalization has implications for developed countries and LDCs alike. One could argue that the distinction between developed and developing countries no longer holds in a world that is being re-colonized – except that this time the colonization is being carried out not by one national government dominating others, but by global corporations no longer restricted by geography and barriers of time, and increasingly less hindered by country-specific regulations. The new rules are designed by capital, without regard for any barriers or limitations, and capital is relatively unrestricted by local regulations because of international trade agreements negotiated by the very people who govern the corporations. This reality provides a challenge for all countries. But it should be acknowledged that the developed world still consumes the majority of world's natural resources, while those living in LDCs exist on a fraction of the consumption of those in developed countries. At the same time, of course, consumption is the driving force of tourism.

Travel – and thus, in the modern world, tourism – appears to be endemic to human society. Prehistoric humans searched for new areas, presumably to satisfy the quest for survival, but perhaps also to search for the unknown, out of pure curiosity. While the conventional wisdom is that hunter-gatherer societies spent the majority of their waking hours scratching out a living, this notion has turned out to be spurious. Speaking about the Kung people of the Kalahari desert, the distinguished anthropologists Richard Leakey and Roger Lewin suggest that 'working life begins at fifteen years at the earliest, and finishes at sixty, with an average of about two and a half hours labor each day in between'. (Leakey & Lewin, 1978: 96) Apparently the Kung traveled substantial distances for social reasons, not only compelled by scarcity, as had been originally thought. While this will have to remain a matter for speculation, modern humans seem to be psychologically driven to personally discover and experience new things, including other lands and people, whether for religious or purely recreational purposes. Curiosity appears to fuel the human need to travel, especially to new areas of the world. Anthropologists have documented a large number of peoples throughout history and prehistory who have lived a nomadic and semi-nomadic existence, expanding their territories to secure food supplies and to dominate territory, and apparently for social reasons as well. This need for travel, which has taken different forms throughout history, is expressed today in the vast quantities of movement undertaken by individuals, especially those from affluent countries. A more cynical perspective might suggest that what appears to be a psychological need to travel for purposes of recreation may in fact be created by slick Madison Avenue advertising firms in support of the expansion of the capitalist system. Regardless of the locus of motivation, whether innate or driven by external forces, travel and tourism have been constant occupations of humanity throughout time.

The selection of tourism as an engine of growth by many LDCs may be a result of a lack of alternatives, rather than a matter of preference. For many developing countries, tourism represents an industry that can utilize their abundant natural and cultural resources, which are easily exploited without the need for massive amounts of domestic capital. In other words, it appears to be a cheap alternative for the governments of many developing countries, which have limited financial resources but an abundance of potentially attractive recreation destinations. There are many developed countries that posses the capital and organizational infrastructure necessary to exploit such resources, but not the resources themselves. There is thus often a good match for partnership in tourism development between developed countries and LDCs. Many such alliances are entered into by LDCs under pressure from such organizations as the IMF and World Bank – pressure which may not be overt but rather subtle. Many of these heavily indebted countries are forced by their lenders to reduce debt by opening their borders to foreign businesses and capital, with little consideration given to the long-term implications of that arrangement. What is often neglected in such decisions is the impact on the local people, who will be subjected to the voyeuristic gaze of the large numbers of visitors to their environment without reaping any substantial financial benefit. Tourists often see themselves as central to the tourism process, and appear to have little regard for the cultures and traditions of the host culture. Many of the inhabitants of Kenya's eastern seaboard – in Lamu and Mombassa, for example – are Muslims, and therefore subject to certain codes of dress and religious practices. Visitors to the area often view such mores as picturesque relics, but pay little heed to their seriousness. Western women, for example, do not follow the practices of Muslim women, who cover their bodies and faces completely, but dress in scanty swimsuits that offend the values of the host society. Young Muslim men and women are lured away from their religious backgrounds and values to work in the tourism industry, which often involves alcohol – a clear taboo in Islamic society – and even sometimes resorting to prostitution, which is in direct confrontation with the practices and values of the faith. On the positive side, however, the Islamic architecture is being preserved in Lamu through a visitation tax, whose proceeds are used both for preserving historic buildings and for constructing new, architecturally sympathetic buildings. Without tourists and their money, this type of program would probably not exist, and the local population would have to subsist in more meager circumstances.

While the nature of tourism development in the developed world may be different, its motivations may be similar. While tourism development in LDCs is often influenced by expatriate pressure, rural tourism in many towns within developed countries is also influenced by outside forces – although generally not outside the country or cultural tradition. While the difference in culture between the tourist and the host community may not be as great in developed countries as in LDCs, many other issues, such as crowding and control of product development, may be similar. Tourism is in many ways just as intrusive for the residents of communities in developed countries as it is in LDCs.

THE CONTEXT OF DEVELOPMENT STUDIES

The pervasive globalization of economic activity and trade governance has had an extensive impact on institutional relationships worldwide. Sovereign states, both developed and developing, are subject to increasingly intensive external corporate forces, and enjoy less autonomy today than before globalization, in its contemporary form, emerged as a dominating force. In spite of this omnipresent force for change, Frances Brown in her 1998 book, *Tourism Reassessed: Blight or Blessing* makes the important point that tourism researchers and scholars have continued to compartmentalize their studies, failing to adjust their focus to accommodate the global perspective. She points out that we continue to examine the impacts of tourism as if they formed a locally controlled, isolated set of phenomena, independent of the large number of worldwide pressures and influences exerted from without. One possible explanation for this neglect, suggested by Brown, is the separation of the field of tourism studies into distinct parts – particularly the separation of politics from economics. As a result there is a need to bring such disciplines as sociology, economics, and politics together into a single inter-disciplinary field. Brown points out that 'while tourism has certainly aided the spread of globalization, it has done this more by reflecting the characteristics of the external system of which it is a part, rather than by itself creating globalizing processes', (Brown, 1998: 20) suggesting that the changing shape of tourism is greatly dependent on globalizing forces. She suggests that scholars interested in tourism need to

> investigate how the impacts of tourism are conditioned by its place in the global system; how far any of the other activities that make up this system could provide a valid economic alternative or substitute for its more harmful effects; and how far significant change for the better is produced by that system.
>
> (Ibid.: 6)

Brown's point is well taken. In spite of the criticism of tourism in this book, as elsewhere, tourism may be a more benign form of development than the best of alternatives. That said, improvements in its implementation will only occur as a result of critiques of this type, and by improved practices on the part of tourism planners and the industry.

Tourism experts and planners are essentially subject-specific specialists. That is, they are trained in a specific discipline and tend to conceive all issues in tourism from the point of view of their specialization, with its set of familiar and accepted instruments. Joanna Macy (1991: 71) observes that 'as specialists, from geologists to neurologists, learned more and more about less and less, their disciplines became virtually air-tight – the specificity of their topics and terminology hindering communication with the uninitiates out-side their narrow domains'. Many of the professionals guiding tourism development come from hospitality or business disciplines. Due to the repertoire of courses and expertise found in those areas, tourism development problems are commonly conceived from a business point of view, rather than from a multi-disciplinary perspective. The fact is that biologists, as well as many other types of expert, may be just as important to the sustainability of a tourism project as the hospitality specialist. Later chapters in this book adopt and implement concepts from many disciplines, including biology, and present a systems view of tourism planning concerned with the relationships between the parts involved, as much as – or perhaps more than – the individual parts themselves. As Macy goes on to say,

> [g]eneral systems theory arose first in the science where the need to transcend an atomistic approach was the most obvious – biology. Here, in the work of von Bertalanffy, attention was directed not to parts, but to wholes and the way they function, not to substance but to organization. ... Von Bertalanffy found that wholes, be they animal or vegetable, cell, organ, or organism could best be described as a system. A system is less a thing than a pattern. It is a pattern of events, its existence and character deriving less from the nature of its components than from their organization.

> (Macy, 1991: 72)

Tourism development has suffered from an exclusive focus on parts, as opposed to an examination of the whole system. This has generally been due to the entrepreneurial nature of tourism, in which individual businesses are privately owned. The Disney Corporation, for example, while focusing entirely on its own operation, has a profound effect on adjacent communities and other businesses associated with it. A multi-layered subsystem has developed around this huge enterprise. This concentrated focus leads quite naturally to an internal focus on the dominant part of the system, rather than on the system as a whole, and its relationships to the individual parts. Many African hotels were established inside national parks and reserves without consideration of the ecological consequences and infrastructure needs which came with that development. Sustainability suffered, and now many of those parks and reserves are threatened, not only from an ecological point of view but also from the perspective of local, human needs. Both cases illustrate that any development which is only considered from a single perspective will fail to take account of the strains inflicted on other areas of the system of which it forms a part.

Tourism is not a single entity, but a pattern of facilities and activities which includes the reaction of one part to the others.

Animals, for example, react to an influx of tourists and their vehicles. In Africa, many of the large animals have reduced their rate of breeding because of the harassment that tourism has brought. Moreover, human settlements and the livelihoods of their inhabitants have also been negatively affected. Tourism encourages the growth of certain types of animals, like elephants, and this in turn has added to the competition for water and grazing land required by cattle. Macy observes that entities 'function and evolve within a larger system – in regard to whose character it is both dependent and indispensable'. (Macy, 1991: 72) Tourism must be made to fit into this larger system, and not be seen as separate from other systems in the environment. This is the essence of Brown's call for tourism to be considered from the globalizing point of view. A new approach that views development as the subject and tourism as the vehicle of development can bring a fresh perspective to the examination of the subject matter. At present, too many scholars and entrepreneurs regard tourism as the subject of their activity, with development as an inevitable spin-off. Unfortunately, they fail to ensure that this development actually produces benefit to those who are most intimately affected by virtue of their residence. In many cases it does not benefit those people directly – particularly for those living in the host country, and in the local area where the tourism occurs. Most benefits accrue to the off shore companies who invest in facilities and program. Communities must determine what development means to them, rather than relying on the definitions provided by orthodox economic theory and its advocates.

It can be argued that the present trajectory of tourism development is a direct consequence of capitalist expansion. Those of us who are unhappy about the changes to the developing world brought about by tourism development should be critical of the particular form of capitalism that has created it. Tourism, as Brown suggests, is a product of the system and not its creator. She makes the point that tourism may not be the cause of the degradation often ascribed to it, but a consequence of the dominance of capitalism which is growing worldwide. At the very least, tourism may be considered an accomplice to the crime, but not its perpetrator.

In responding to the critique outlined above, tourism studies must view itself as a subset of development studies, and not as a self-contained discipline. In fact, tourism is a multi-disciplinary field which utilizes various academic perspectives, theories and methods. Tourism is concerned with geographical issues, such as spatial and environmental analyses of destination sites; sociology contributes a focus on social class and leisure analysis; psychology throws light on individual behavior; economics is concerned with issues of supply and demand, and the equilibrium of tourism markets; and hospitality studies concerns itself with product development, particularly in the areas of hospitality and management. Planning – the specific focus of this volume – concerns itself with processes of deliberate intervention in the human, social and environmental system. As a result, planners are inter-disciplinary by nature and draw on many of the theories and methods from the disciplines outlined above, as well as from theoretical understanding developed specifically in the planning field.

While all of the fields outlined above, including planning, provide the theoretical framework for the analysis and implementation of tourism developments on the ground, development studies provides an overarching framework for understanding the larger context in which tourism must be viewed. Most tourism texts analyze tourism from a single disciplinary perspective (usually the economic perspective), which concerns itself only with issues of direct relevance. But tourism must be seen as one sector among the many available for achieving the higher-order development goals of society. As a result, it must fit into the overall development needs and strategies of developing countries and underdeveloped regions in developed countries, and not be seen in isolation from the society in which it is being implemented. Many writers on this subject confuse their critique of tourism with their concerns for growth in general. Brown makes a plea for the holistic study of tourism on the grounds that 'the phenomenon is conditioned by the political and economic organization of what is now the global system, and by the attitudes and social relations that result from this organization'. (Brown, 1998: 111–12) In response to this analysis, the framework of development studies provides this volume with a means for evaluating the contribution of tourism to development in both the developing and developed world. By doing so, it examines the conditions shaped by globalization which allow or encourage certain forms of tourism to emerge.

DEVELOPMENT STUDIES

As in any other area of enquiry, ideas within development studies are subject to constant fluctuation and reformulation. There are, however, some fundamental concepts which have enjoyed long-standing centrality within the discipline. In Hettne's words, 'development studies, as I understand it, can be conceived of as a problem-oriented, applied, and interdisciplinary field, analyzing social change in a world context, but with due consideration to the specificity of different societies in terms of history, ecology, culture, etc'. (Hettne, 1995: 16) Development studies began as a European discipline, so many of its underlying structures and principles are based on Western thought, leading to an understanding of alien cultures as representing 'otherness'. It is essentially based on the pursuit of an external created image of reality, and is criticized because of that perspective. That is, Western based observers create the image of the traditional culture which is then sold to potential tourists who originate from outside the host culture.

In its early years development studies viewed development on a comparative basis – in terms of a trajectory of evolution from traditional to modern. Modernization is based on the supposed development of all societies from a traditional to an industrialized economy, simply by means of time and effort. The paradigm is summarized by Hettne as follows:

- Development is a spontaneous, irreversible process inherent in every single society.
- Development implies structural differentiation and functional specialization.
- The process of development can be divided into distinct stages showing the level of development achieved by each society.
- Development can be stimulated by external competition or military threat and by internal measures that support modern sectors and modernize traditional sectors.

(Hettne, 1995: 50–1)

Tourism is an industry which follows this pattern of development. Tourism is part of industrialized society, as a service industry developed from, and dependent on, the more fundamental industries of manufacturing and commerce. Modern tourism and its infrastructure are usually imported by people from other areas of the world, bringing with them the practices and culture of that industry as they exist in the originating country. The concept of leisure on which tourism rests was a creation of the industrial revolution's division of social time into working and leisure periods. Most traditional societies do not view the day in such a fragmented manner and, as a result, do not usually possess a word equivalent to 'leisure' in their native language. In many traditional societies, tourism is not a commercial enterprise. Many Inuit, in the far north of Canada, for example, have no conception in their traditional culture of what the service industry and tourism are all about, yet they are asked to work in this industry and cater to the needs of foreigners in the manner in which the visitors are accustomed in their own culture. The Inuit, like many other traditional societies, integrate work and leisure into the same activities, making them almost indistinguishable. However, one of the important early theories on which development studies rests is that of modernization which divides social life into fragmented categories.

The concept of modernization is one that derives from economic liberalism. As Martinussen suggests, 'central to classical modernization theories is a contrasting of tradition and modernity ... The modernization theories are concerned primarily with how traditional values, attitudes, practices and social structures break down and are replaced with more modern ones.' (Martinussen, 1997: 56) This is in contrast with the mores of most traditional societies, whose economies and world-view rest on values of cooperation and community. It is often said that Western society is founded on the philosophical premise that 'I think, therefore I am', while Bantu philosophy views the organization of life from a perspective summed up in the sentence, 'We are, therefore, I am'. This Bantu philosophy exists in many variants throughout the world. This subtle, yet profound, distinction describes the enormous differences between the modern, Western-based cultures responsible for the concept of modernization – in this case represented by tourism – and the traditional societies which inhabit the areas so attractive to tourists. It is not the adaptation of technical materialism to a non-technical and non-material culture that is called for, but a comprehensive cultural reorganization of the society in which the development is taking place. Tourism has become one of the primary means of encouraging this interface and transition. Unlike many products shipped to various parts of the world, tourism imports people to the host community, whose environment is equivalent to the export product. In the case of tourism, then, the importation of people acts like an export, which creates a direct interface between the parties in the transaction. When the interacting cultures are relatively distant from one another, considerable bewilderment can result from a conflict of values. In order for these differences to be worked out, education of the tourist to these differences and their potential consequences to the host community needs to be a consideration of the tour company, but little effort is made in such a direction by tourism corporations. In fact, the notion of the tour company as educator – particularly in the area of explaining cultures – is a totally foreign concept within the industry. It is also potentially fraught with danger in that it may become an extension of the marketing process rather than the intent described here. However, some effort in this area needs to be considered by tour companies and then monitored by appropriate outside institutions.

When speaking of modernization Martinussen (1999: 56) asks the question, 'What conditions promote and impede such a transformation and modernization process?' The answer to that has taken different approaches in the history of development studies. Most of the responses to Martinussen's question have taken either an economic or structuralist flavor. Rosenstein-Rodan (1943) and Nurske (1953), for example, focus on capital investment and balanced growth in several sectors, rather than concentration on just one sector, as the key to modernization. Hirschman (1958) sees a lack of entrepreneurial spirit and management capability as the critical factors limiting development. The importance of growth poles as a necessary ingredient to development also became an important factor in modernization theory. Growth poles are a collection of industries clustered together and strategically located to promote modernization. On the other hand, Rostow (1960) sees modernization as a series of stages through which all modernizing countries or societies would be propelled. Rostow's model calls for the traditional society to establish the 'preconditions for take-off', 'take-off' and 'drive to maturity'. Preconditions for take-off included increased savings and investment, and the creation of a social and political environment conducive to utilizing this investment.

Most, if not all, of these theories attempt to drive aggregate demand and increase production and supply. It is thought that this can be achieved through the injection of capital and by transferring labor from less productive to more productive industries. In a developed economy, growth depends on increasing productivity, usually through the introduction of technology to the production process. It is assumed that new jobs, and hence income, will be created by new technology, at a magnitude sufficient to replace those lost jobs. This is a theory which has yet to be verified, however. It is further assumed that technology (innovation) will be transferred (diffusion) to LDCs. In a developing economy, the process of restructuring made the theories of innovation and diffusion important as a support to many of the modernization theories. However, a general lack of capital, in the form of savings and income, was a critical shortcoming constraining the modernization of traditional economies and inhibiting the concept of innovation and diffusion.

Equally, it is unclear whether tourism is able to propel development along the lines envisioned by the modernization model of development. Most analysis in modernization theory concentrates on the agricultural and industrial sectors of the economy. More specifically, the concentration is on the transfer of the unemployed or underemployed from the agriculture sector to large manufacturing industries, and from rural to urban areas in the hopes of employing their labor or in making a better living. While tourism creates economic activity in many traditional societies, it is subject to a high degree of economic leakage, because of extensive foreign ownership of enterprises. It is also debatable whether a service industry such as tourism can play a significant role in creating sufficient capital to induce other development, or whether – given the low-income nature of service jobs in the tourism industry – it can lead to the development of an entrepreneurial class, as Hirschman (1958) suggests is critical. If resorts and other parts of the hospitality industry were to commit themselves to establishing local suppliers for their operational needs, and to undertake the training and development of employees, then tourism may meet the criteria of modernization theory. More recently, classical economists have identified a lack of foreign exchange as a constraint on development from the modernization perspective. Tourism has the potential to contribute to a nation's foreign currency balance if it can reduce the high rate of leakage that is so prevalent in the sector. Again, this problem can be addressed by focusing on establishing stronger forward and backward linkages in the economy, particularly within the tourism and associated sectors.

Modernization theory requires a fragmentation of labor in order to achieve development, rather than a holistic existence built on a cyclical rhythm to life. To many traditional societies and peoples, this change can be soul-destroying, but it is necessary to the concepts of many of the economic activities of modernization such as tourism. Traditional societies are those with a unique culture, adhering to an economic system based on direct commodity exchange and not on currency exchange. Such societies are often considered by observers not to be modern, in the sense of basing their economy on manufacturing or modern technological development. Traditional societies are normally based around agriculture, or hunting and gathering. In an absolute sense, few if any traditional societies exist today, due to the pervasiveness of modern communications technology and travel patterns. However, some societies, such as the Maasai in Kenya and Tanzania, can be said to be traditional even though some of their younger members are receiving a modern education. The core group, however, still maintains traditional social systems based on kinship practices, or a variant of them. In spite of their adherence to these basic traditional practices, tourism is viewed by many national governments and businesses as a legitimate activity for these societies. Tourism acts to move these groups away from a traditional way of life towards a more modern model of society.

Many of these traditional societies are being inundated by modernizing pressures. In the north of Canada, for example, modernization through tourism requires societies like the Inuit – whose economy has traditionally been tied directly to the land through hunting and gathering – to abandon their lifestyle and adopt a monetized economic system. While this may not be a bad thing in itself, it does require the abandonment of one set of cultural practices for another, which in the short-term, at least, is considerably disruptive and confusing for those living through the change. For the Inuit, this has meant that some become tourist guides, taking visitors out onto the land, a practice which is compatible with their traditional lifestyle, and thus apparently not too disruptive. However, the work of the large majority is more menial than for the select few, and devoted to providing services (in many cases menial and unskilled) to foreign guests. The relationship of such people to the land, and hence to their traditional culture, is slowly disappearing, which leads to anomie and eventual social breakdown. Many other societies throughout the world are being asked to make the same type of change to their way of life. In Africa for example, the Maasai are being encouraged to abandon their semi-nomadic cattle-herding lifestyle in favor of the money-based tourism industry. Again, it can be argued that, in the long term, this change will have positive effects, even though it may drastically change a culture along the way. After all, who would not want to give up cataracts at 40 years of age for a more healthy and, perhaps, prosperous future? It would be foolhardy to argue for the rigid maintenance and preservation of a historical culture. Culture is not static, but constantly changing and adapting to new conditions. A culture which is not changing is a dead culture, and does not deserve to be protected or to survive. Modernization and change is not the issue of major concern, but who is in control, and how change in social structures is motivated. It appears to be mainly driven and controlled by exogenous influences. As Hettne suggests in his discussion of the fundamental characteristics of modernization theory, 'modernization appeared as a guided process rather than as natural history'. (Hettne, 1995: 56)

Some would argue, with the proponents of modernization theory, that while it might be disruptive in the short-term, the long-term implications of increased materialism, resulting in extended life expectancy and various technological conveniences is preferable to the persistence of poverty and disease. Advocates of tourism suggest that many of these societies can maintain the integral parts of their culture through tourism, because that is what the visitor wants to see and experience. While this may appear to be an advantage on the surface, this practice tends to the commodification of those parts of the culture being preserved, while abandoning other practices and ways of thinking that were once and may continue to be important to those practicing it, although not necessarily to visitors. This constitutes an externally motivated preservation and not one from the center, an issue which modernization theorists have not yet resolved satisfactorily.

This is a critical issue, and will be dealt with in more detail in a later chapter. A short but important example, however, may be quickly set out here. The focus of cultural tourism needs to be considered from the 'inside out' rather than from the 'outside in'. For example, North American aboriginal communities participate in many cultural events not primarily as tourist exhibitions, but as cultural celebrations in their own right, and primarily for aboriginal people. Outsiders are invited to view and participate, but not as the main purpose of the event. In this way authenticity is guaranteed and the components of the event – song, dance, crafts and food – are not contrived solely for outside consumption. This method of organizing celebration prevents the complete commodification of the event, which would turn it into an inauthentic spectacle, at risk of alienating people from the practicing culture.

As you might guess, 'modernization theory' has its critics. Most of the criticism centers on the political goals inherent in the concept, and their colonizing tendencies. The central issue is that modernization theory is Eurocentric, favoring the Western notion of development at the expense of other versions. Linked to this critique is the idea of the indigenization of development, which suggests that development and the theories on which it relies must be driven from within, utilizing their own resources. The movement formed from within the society is fundamentally a liberation movement tied directly to the realm of political economy, rather than a strategy supported by the orthodox economic position (Martinussen, 1997; Hettne, 1995). This struggle of competing views has serious consequences for the tourism industry, since tourism development has to date been exploitative rather than empowering, and top-down rather than bottom-up in its approach. The development paradigm most prominent today stresses relations and agreements between international capital and national governments, with little, if any, involvement by other stakeholders. Leaving local communities out of the planning process will surely guarantee that local needs will not be met, or even considered, by the development process.

The next stage of development theory moved away from a normative account of how development might take place, and took the form of a critique. While modernization theory examined development from an economic perspective, and such issues as employment and unemployment were seen as critical factors, theories which embraced structuralism were concerned with identifying the underlying causes which seemed to keep underdeveloped countries poor. Development was then viewed as a problem of social and political structures, and positive development was considered dependent on changing those structures.

Dependency theory suggests that Western approaches to LDC development are a sham, and that it is really a movement of resources from the periphery to the center. (Frank, 1967; Prebisch, 1984) More specifically, it views development as a movement of resources from the LDCs to the developed world. The structuralist school relied heavily on Marxist and neo-Marxist thought, and took root in Latin America. It is best exemplified by Dos Santos (1970) who thought that Latin America, and perhaps all underdeveloped countries, were subjected to domination by the economies of the developed countries and, for that reason, would never rise above their traditional level through market competition alone. In relation to tourism, this would play itself out in travelers visiting LDCs, consuming both physical and cultural resources, while leaving little of benefit behind. It should be noted that most of the expenses of a tourist trip are consumed by transportation and hotel firms, which are usually located in the countries of departure and not in the destination country. Moreover, most tourism in LDCs is subject to a high degree of monetary leakage, since profits are repatriated, and many of the higher-paying managerial jobs are held by expatriates rather than locals. The Caribbean represents a particular example of this dilemma, addressed eloquently by Wilkinson (1997).

As a consequence of the shift in analysis towards a tone of critique, social scientists focused on five areas of crisis, namely: legitimacy, identity, participation, penetration and distribution (Martinussen, 1997). The legitimacy of the business arrangement which produces the destination or project giving rise to the tourism activity must be vetted by local parties. Offshore organizations with interests in the development must be forced to give final control of development to the host country or society. Without local control and support for any project, legitimacy will not be sufficient to justify the development in the short or long term. The identity of the local social system must be preserved as development is considered and implemented. While societies inevitably change over time, it is in the interests of projects and local communities for certain aspects of local cultures to be preserved. There are many examples in the history of tourism where social identity has been forced to change at the expense of the indigenous culture, leading to the irritation and exploitation of the tourist as well as local residents. Respect for the tourist is highly unlikely to persist if the host culture and society feels itself to be altered by outside forces completely. Lack of respect for the tourist will have a profound effect on return rates, and unofficial word-of-mouth publicity. Any tourism project must entail participation by those who will be affected by the development. Those who do not feel they have a stake in the project will not respect the development. All too often, entrepreneurs do not realize that the supposed benefits to the community of their product are not transparent, and that residents have legitimate concerns, in fundamentally altering economics, which must be addressed. Primacy must be given to protecting community and social values; the penetration of foreign culture into the local tradition must be minimized. Tourism and tourists are intrusive to communities and cultures, and a balance must be sought and maintained in order to preserve both the community and the tourism project. Finally, the benefits of tourism must be shared equally between host communities – those most directly affected by development – investors, and national governments eager to extract profits and raise foreign currency. If any of these conditions are not met during tourism development, then a point of crisis may be reached in the area affected, and in the LDC of which it is a part. Experience with tourism development suggests that these crises have been very common in many destinations throughout the world, due to exploitative and otherwise inadequate planning practices. In many cases these crises, often characterized by unrest among the local population, are simply ignored or explained away by those wishing to maintain the status quo. The five crises of legitimacy, identity, participation, penetration and distribution, provide a framework for analyzing the construction of a development project, and the progress of tourism development generally, and therefore provide a general thematic framework for this volume.

The structuralist school argues for an increase in wages in order to establish and maintain a domestic market. Without a domestic market, they suggest that any advance in production will only service export consumption, without the benefits of savings and reinvestment so much discussed by the modernization school. The citizens of LDCs have witnessed for some time the attention paid to export markets with no meaningful advance in their standard of living. There was little prospect for the development of a domestic pool of capitalists and entrepreneurs without wage rates high enough to encourage saving and investment. Henry Ford understood the value of wage rates generous enough to allow discretionary spending by the mass of workers in his employ. It was Ford's workers who bought many of the automobiles that came off his assembly line in the early 1900s. The failing of many of the developing countries in this regard has been their inability to create a middle class, which was what made modernization in the developed world possible. The structuralists focused on wage rates in order to create a domestic industrial complex and markets which, they felt, would eventually lead to the construction of a middle class. This middle class would be developed partly through industries focusing on import substitution, and tourism was an industry in which import substitution could play a dynamic role, along with the development of associated industries to service everyday operations. Although only constituting one aspect of structuralist theory, Martinussen (1999: 82) observes this model to include the basic consideration that:

industrialization is a precondition for aggregate growth and economic development of backward societies. These theories further assert that industrial development under the given international economic conditions has to focus chiefly on import substitution, starting with light consumer goods and thereafter moving on to durable consumer goods, basic intermediaries and, finally, production equipment.

(Martinussen, 1997: 82)

The structuralists also saw a larger role for government than did the modernization school. The capitalist class that existed appeared too weak to compete with capitalists from the industrialized countries. Without protecting fledgling industries, LDCs could not expect to develop a competitive, domestically-owned industrial sector. Even if governments in the developing world wished to engage in protectionist practices, the institutions of the global economy, such as the International Monetary Fund and the World Trade Organization, would not allow that to happen today, making LDCs more vulnerable to the overwhelming influence of trans-national corporations.

In spite of many of the principles enunciated above being relevant to both LDCs and developed countries alike, recent patterns in the developed world have taken a slightly different path. Most recently, the liberalization of trade and the introduction of instruments to make the labor market more flexible have formed the centerpieces of development. This has caused the focus of community development to shift subtly, but profoundly, over the last decade or two.

International agencies such as the World Bank and the International Monetary Fund have provided loans to LDCs in order to assist them with development. For many of these countries, borrowing was initially intended to create a domestic industry by means of 'import substitution' which, it was hoped, would create forward and backward linkages in the economy. After a period of protection, the theory had it that these companies would then be able to compete internationally without protection. This did not turn out to be the case, and many of the countries concerned wound up with little industrial activity, but with huge government debt as a result. The loans have consequently increased the dependency of the LDCs so much that many are now afflicted by excessive indebtedness, without much prospect of extricating themselves from it even in the long term. In fact, many NGOs and social commentators now realize that these loans must be forgiven if the LDCs suffering from this burden are ever to re-establish themselves on a sound fiscal and monetary footing. The accumulation of such large levels of debt in LDCs has simply led to the strengthening of interest in the center and periphery that structuralists were initially so focused on. Martinussen's analysis of Frank's theory suggests that,

> according to Frank, empirical evidence showed that the economic surplus generated in Latin America was drained away. Instead of being used for investment in the countries of origin, most of the surplus was transferred to the affluent capitalist countries, especially the US. Frank's basic point was that satellites would be developed only to the extent and in the respects which were compatible with the interests of their metropoles.

> (Martinussen, 1997: 89)

This transfer of money out of the developing world – the destination of many tourists – is commonplace, most of the money that initially makes it into poor countries leaks back out quickly to pay for such things as supplies, labor and profits. The vast majority of money spent by tourists does not remain in the host country. Certainly, Frank's criticisms of the shortcomings of the center–periphery model of development hold true for the international tourism industry, especially when the destination is a developing country. In an ideal world the surplus value generated by tourism development in the LDC would be invested in the country in which it was generated, but occurs only rarely. Much of the surplus value created by tourism in LDCs leaves the country in which it was earned to pay foreign-owned airlines, expatriate staff, equipment and supplies, and for profits.

In spite of these setbacks, the structuralists have not abandoned their fundamental notion of development from within. They have maintained this fundamental principle of development from within in their writings but have modified their broader ideas about what is realistic. Establishing an entrepreneurial class is still a priority, but on a smaller scale and without the concentration of government support which was originally demanded. In fact, tourism may be one of the few sectors which is compatible with this revised view. With support from the larger tourism enterprises, local businesses can flourish in a manner similar to that envisaged by advocates of import substitution. But such local tourism enterprises will be established on a much smaller scale than was originally envisaged. Moreover, many of these small, locally-owned enterprises could cater to a growing domestic market, in which they could compete quite capably with larger, offshore businesses. It is the domestic tourism market which will provide real local economic development in most LDCs.

Development theory has a strong history of attempting to explain the failure of many LDCs to benefit from the pervasive rising standards of living in the developed world in recent decades. Some theorists have laid the problem of underdevelopment at the door of the affluent countries, who, it is alleged, have exploited their neighbors in order to develop and maintain their own high standard of living. It has been suggested that the West – particularly the US – has simply exported its debt to foreign countries in order to continue to raise its own standards of living at home. Modernization theory attempts to describe a mechanism by which underdevelopment might be addressed. That said, there are many countries throughout the world – particularly in Africa – which find themselves further behind today than decades ago. This lack of development is occurring at a time when capitalism is in control of the world's economic system. However, the problem results from a lack of economic surplus, and hence of disposable income, producing a resulting lack of internal investment in most LDCs.

If there has been a struggle for control of the world's social organization strategy, capital has had a clear advantage, and forces for social democracy and progressive politics have been required to rethink their position. While 'structural adjustment' programs emphasizing debt reduction and trade over subsistence agriculture have been imposed on LDCs, in order to implement this new world order, 'economic restructuring', including the demand for labor flexibility and international trade agreements favoring business over government, has been imposed on the developed countries. In a sense, this has given new primacy to business and reduced the role of the state in both developed and underdeveloped countries alike. As we enter the twenty-first century and look back over the second half of the twentieth, the victory of business and the private sector over control of political and economic life is very apparent. This organizational structure has influenced the approach to development on the ground, in both the developing and developed world. While the development theories discussed above have provided a framework for large-scale analysis, other theories have been employed to analyze grass-roots processes on a day-to-day basis. These theories have been implemented in both developed and developing countries throughout the world. The next section focuses on one of the most important of these theories – community development – and its relationship to tourism development.

GRASS-ROOTS IMPLEMENTATION IN DEVELOPED AND LESS DEVELOPED COUNTRIES

While modernization, dependency, and alternative development theories, including neo-Marxist theories, have been dominating the discussion of social organization and political formation in the developing world, capitalist theories and the ideology of the liberal welfare state have dominated that of developed countries. Texts dealing with each of these areas are numerous, and no attempt will be made here to provide a comprehensive examination of them. What will be addressed, however, is the manner in which practitioners and academics concerned with planning and development interpret and implement these overall approaches to social development and organization. Clearly, the manner in which community development is conceptualized depends on the prevailing ideology of the period during which it is being implemented.

The ideas of classical economics, entailing the supposed perfection of market forces in the supply and demand of consumer goods, are well known. However, many developed countries have historically been uncomfortable with leaving issues of development strictly to market forces. There have been many attempts at blending the qualities of the market approach with collective intervention, so as to smooth out the imbalances the market produces if left unchecked. Non-governmental organizations (NGOs) have played a similar, if more limited, role in LDCs, in an attempt to compensate for the inability of governments to undertake many such initiatives.

Since the end of the Second World War, the theoretical approach to development in the developed world can be divided into three separate eras. Points of demarcation between these periods are somewhat arbitrary and, as in all schemes which attempt to divide human movements into discrete periods, are subject to numerous exceptions. However, for the purposes of this discussion the stages of capitalist development, the introduction, maturation and decline of the liberal welfare state, and perhaps even the decline of the nation-state itself, will provide the focus for the examination. Perhaps even more important in this discussion are the schools of thought which developed around each of these stages, and by which they were given practical shape.

Rising from the ashes of the Second World War was the neo-conservative work dominant society. This era focused on a community and country building approach to development. This can be described as early capitalist society, and particularly in North America the US was one of its most successful architects. Countries like Canada, while creating an early capitalist society, attempted to soften the harsh effects of this model by introducing what became known as the 'mixed economy'. This entailed blending the market distribution of consumer goods with state control and collectivist provision of such services as healthcare. For most societies of the developed world, the focus during this period fell on physical nation-building – particularly in Europe, which had been devastated by the Second World War, and in North America simply because it too had turned its energy to supplying the war machine with both soldiers and equipment, and therefore neglecting its internal development. Tourism in this period was characteristically domestic, with families traveling to the lake or sea shore, depending on the geographic location of the tourist. Only the wealthy were able to travel abroad for vacations, through the grand tour, while the less wealthy North Americans and Europeans confined themselves to their own continent or the colonies.

It was during this period, however, that the idea of the collective, universal provision of fundamental social services to all citizens began to take root in all societies except perhaps in the USA. The debate centered on whether there should be a floor beneath which no citizen should fall in order to enjoy a reasonable quality of life, or whether, by contrast, the state should be the provider of services only as a last resort, and at a very meager level. Most countries in Western Europe opted for the former option, while the US chose the latter; while Canada, which is often the case, adopted features of both philosophies. The focus of this debate was political, and it was fought out in houses of parliament around the world. The geographic scope of tourism expanded for the middle class and elites during this period. Tourism thus became a more substantial enterprise in both the developing and developed world. It became a junior partner to the smokestack manufacturing industries as a generator of foreign currency.

Tourism development was mainly the domain of the entrepreneur. However governments provided infrastructure such as motorways, airports, museums, waste and water treatment systems, among other facilities which enabled tourism businesses to become established. Tourism, albeit domestic, was made possible by the generation of discretionary spending by the middle classes. A substantial middle class had emerged in the developed world, and its members were increasingly interested in leisure activities. The period gave birth to the classic seaside resort in Britain, Europe and in North America. Urry's description of the rise and fall of the seaside resort is a classic account of tourism during the period. (Urry, 1990) Tourism was one method for the emerging middle classes to display their new-found affluence, and for a fledgling tourism industry to establish itself.

Once the debate was settled by each state individually in favor of the introduction of some form of social welfare no matter how menial, the discussion turned to how it might be implemented. In Canada, as in most other developed countries, implementation attempted to deal with the whole person and the community in which they lived, and not just with income maintenance. In addition to providing service to the individual the Community Development (CD) approach also stressed social development and community capacity building. This approach was seen as an educational tool, just as much as a matter of product development. Reid and van Dreunen summarize the concept as follows:

> Community development is broadly defined here as a process for empowerment and transformation. The focus on community development is to identify and resolve problems of a social, physical, or political nature that exist in a community in such a way that these conditions are changed or improved from the perspective of the community members. The goals of community development are self-help, community capacity building, and integration.
>
> (Reid and van Dreunen,1996: 49)

The academic literature on community development is considerable (Biddle and Biddle, 1965; Cary, 1970; Roberts, 1979). While there are many definitions, there are common elements to most of them. These elements can be synthesized generally to include a focus on change, indigenous problem identification, participation of all concerned community members in the activities and processes of the community, the notion of self-help, and community control of the process and outcome. Perhaps the most overarching concept of community development is that which stresses process over product. As Ross (1967: 15) points out when speaking of community development, 'development of a specific project (such as an industry or school) is less important than development of the capacity of people to establish that project'.

Additionally, Sanders (1970) suggests four basic ways of viewing community development: as a process, as a method, as a program, and as a movement. Practitioners usually approach their work from one of these orientations and rarely do they combine approaches.

Community development during this period was more than just the creation of a physical product. It was first and foremost a movement, and a process. As a movement, it was expected to lead to the empowerment of those involved in the process as well as collectively achieving identified tangible goals. Arai, in a study which examined the Healthy Community's movement in Ontario, suggested that 'the benefits described by the citizen participants in the WHCI [Woolwich Healthy Communities Initiative] correspond to many characteristics that define personal empowerment'. (Arai, 1996: 36) She went on to outline the 'process of personal empowerment' that results from such development. People involved in the community development process move through the stages of powerlessness, awareness, connecting and learning, motivation, and finally to a position from which they are able to make a contribution. (Arai, 1996: 37) This outcome takes the scope of community development beyond product-creation and into individual and social capacity-building. The outcome of the community development process suggests that a 'contribution was expressed through the carryover of learning into other aspects of the individual's life' (Arai, 1996: 39), which motivated the continued intellectual and emotional development of the person and the community. Tourism presents such an opportunity if it is organized and planned at the community level, and not left solely to the vagaries of the market and the prerogatives of the corporation.

The most notable instances of this type of development leading to empowerment were initiated by the Coady Institute, an NGO located on the east coast of Canada, in the late 1960s and programs initiated in the early 1970s by the Canadian federal government, such as a program called 'The Company of Young Canadians'. As its name implies, this group was a cadre of young Canadians who were hired by the federal government to work with communities, when opportunities presented themselves, with the goal of assisting them to organize for action on all types of issues. Eventually, the looseness of this mandate caused the demise of the program. In some cases, elected government members found the Company organizing rallies and protests in their constituencies against government programs or policies which, of course, was not popular with politicians hoping to be re-elected.

The Coady Institute named after a catholic priest from the east coast of Canada Rev. Dr Moses Coady was devoted to the development of individuals and communities in an effort to institute cooperatives, resisting the dominance of the company store, which would sell overpriced goods to the poor workers of the region. This movement became known as the Antigonish movement, and was based in Nova Scotia after its inception in the 1920s. The six principles on which the movement was based were: the primacy of the individual; social reform progressing through education; the centrality of economic education; the importance of communal action within education; the importance for social reform of fundamental change in social and economic institutions; and the ultimate objective of the movement – namely, full and abundant life for everyone in the community. The movement was a grass-roots organization which stressed transformative learning. Sessions were organized and held in people's living rooms and kitchens, bringing citizens together for discussion, debate, and sometimes for formal or informal education. In its early stages, at least, the movement was truly a community development, grass-roots institution. The Institute describes its mandate today as 'a people's movement for economic and social justice' (see www.stfx.ca/institutes/coady/). An important feature of the Institute is that it understands that social change is a long-term proposition and that it can only come about through education in the social and economic issues plaguing the community and its development. It is truly committed to building civil society and civil institutions.

Tourism has been slow to adapt to this type of framework. The tourism industry does not view itself as a vehicle for the achievement of community development. Traditionally, communities have been seen as obstacles to development, not partners in the process, and have been subjected to the negative consequences of business-driven tourist development. Only recently has tourism started to become a dominant industry in some communities – so much so that the local area is often unable to digest the externalities it is creating. Communities are becoming increasingly aware that the community development approach is an option for tourism development (see Reid, Mair and Taylor, 2000). Moreover, various NGOs interested in such issues as the environment, and active in both LDCs and developed countries, are making the connection between their interests and the welfare of the people living in the areas concerned. They understand that if environmentally sensitive areas are to be preserved and protected, then people living in such areas need to make a living from efforts to achieve this outcome. Ecotourism is an example of this type of development. Community development, in this case, is a method for focusing on people and their development, with the secondary outcome of preserving an ecological or cultural system.

The 1980s witnessed a shift in ideology from the collective to the individual. Some argue that this shift was a result of the inability of governments to provide services constructed on the new technologies that were proliferating at the time, and the overwhelming budgetary deficits the welfare state tended to create. This is particularly true in the case of healthcare, for example. New technology helps to add years to people's lives which in turn makes it likely that people extend their use of the healthcare system putting more pressure on the system and mounting up costs to society. Whether this crisis was real, or rather invented by forces in society that favored a more individualistic and market-driven approach to social organization, will be debated for years to come. Much of the debate centers on whether or not the individual choice through the private sector and the market approach is more efficient and effective than government rationing. What is important for the purposes of this discussion is that a shift in approach occurred in this period, and most institutions in society have adjusted their behavior to accommodate it. As the forces for corporate globalization and liberalization became predominant, those involved in community development turned their attention increasingly towards economic issues. One of the central features of the community development approach – problem identification – was modified to focus strictly on economic matters, and became known as community economic development (CED). This approach defined all problems as economic, thereby bounding the focus of the discourse, and the central tenet of community problem identification was narrowed to economic issues. Using Sanders' rubric from the earlier quotation as a template, the designation of method and program rather than as a process or a movement would characterize the present CED approach.

Despite the claims of practitioners of community economic development that their practice is true to the principles of the community development process, their perspective severely limits the definition of the community problem to be addressed. This move from community development, which encourages the community to define problems in whatever form it thinks best, to CED and a narrow focus on the economic perspective alone can be attributed to a number of factors. Certainly, practitioners are encouraged by agencies of government to focus on the economy, and particularly on job creation, because unemployment is such a problem for many countries. When economies decline National governments reoriented the objectives of their grant and loan programs to fit in with economic priorities, and reduced their assistance to the more nebulous social domain. Practitioners and researchers also found it more prestigious to focus on economic rather than social issues. Moreover, national governments encouraged by trans-national companies begin to think that all human problems have economic solutions. It is generally considered by these institutions that if poverty and low income can be addressed, all of humanity's problems would be reduced significantly, although perhaps not eliminated completely overnight. Concomitantly, as the global economic system changed, with increasing reliance on intellectual work and a move away from the manual and extractive industries, many resource-based countries, such as those in Canada, became concerned about their long-term welfare. As Douglas suggests when he analyses the position of Canada:

It is one of the wealthiest, most stable and healthiest societies in the world. It is a country of many and very significant achievements in the arts, industry, the sciences, political development and social policy, and in many other fields. However, it is a country harbouring a crisis. *Canadian communities are in trouble.* Some have seen trouble coming for some time. For others, the economic crisis is new and at times confounding. For a very significant portion it is literally a life-or-death situation. For another group, their basic quality of life is being threatened. [Author's italics]

(Douglas, 1994: xiv)

The repeated use of the word 'crisis' here underscores the dramatic nature of the change – either potential or actual that confronted

Canada, along with many other countries throughout the world. Whether these changes constitute a crisis is a matter of contention, but the mere fact that the word crisis is used indicates the psychological perception of the issue. The response by governments in concert with trans-national corporations to all modern problems assumes that the economy is the underlying problem requiring attention, so the practice of community economic development confines its attention to economic issues.

From the late 1970s, productivity gains in the manufacturing industry and in the mining and agricultural sectors came to be associated with the increased use of technology. This approach was so successful that it has considerably impaired employment levels, and – perhaps more significantly – resulted in the overexploitation of what are considered to be non-renewable resources such as trees and fish. As Douglas makes clear:

Now with the apparent exhaustion of the resource base, more than 25,000 fishing people in Newfoundland, and even more throughout other parts of Atlantic Canada, have been rendered economically irrelevant and wards of the state. The first signs of overexploitation of resources are appearing in the west-coast fishery. Grossly inadequate forestry management and a persistent lack of value-added production will spell the same fate for this sector if there is not a radical turnaround in public policy.

(Douglas, 1994: xvi)

Certainly, these developments have caused a great deal of concern both within senior levels of government and to those living in the affected communities. In Atlantic Canada, fishers could no longer fish and found themselves in need of not only a new source of income but also a new way of life. Unemployed fishers had two questions which needed to be answered: How will I earn a living?, and What will I do with myself tomorrow morning when I get out of bed? The former question is a economic issue but the latter one is a psychological concern. For many, tourism became the answer to both questions. Fishers converted their trawlers into boats to transport visitors to view whales, and to service other water-based tourist activities. Picturesque towns are turned into tourist attractions with regionally unique cuisine, and private houses adapted to provide bed and breakfast accommodation. Community economic development practitioners therefore focused on these types of solutions. What they did not consider was the social upheaval and psychological turmoil that this would produce. It is no small task to turn people steeped in such long-standing resource based working traditions into providers within a service industry, and it is fraught with the same difficulties and consequences involved in turning the Maasai cattle herding culture in the Amboseli region in Kenya into a tourist attraction. This transition does not happen simply by a change in employment patterns. Whatever underlying anxiety these changes may have produced, those in political authority drove this economic change forward at the community level. This path was thought to be preferable to the alternative, which called for government intervention and financial assistance for those most affected by these drastic changes in their lifestyle.

In the strictest sense, it is probably more accurate to refer to this process as community-*based* economic development, since this recognizes that community development is strictly process oriented, while CED is driven by a predetermined problem and outcome. What community-based economic development (CBED) recognizes is that development should be driven by the community and not outside forces. This in itself is an important concession, given that many of the problems of the extractive industries were created by non-community global forces. In the fishing industry, for example, trans-national corporations were demanding expanded fishing rights. Any effort to hand control of the resource, and responsibility for it, to those living near or on it is an important strategy but not the sole focus of community development in general. What has often been missing in CBED are the social and psychological supports needed to support the economic changes.

Community economic development strategies, in which tourism has played such a major part in both developed countries and LDCs, is defined by Douglas as follows:

> Community economic development involves purposeful interven-
> tion by the community (or its representatives) in selected aspects
> of the community's economy, for the community's welfare. It is
> about communities addressing problems and opportunities, on
> their own behalf, which they perceive to be of importance to their
> quality of life or their community's viability ... [Q]uestions of what
> is being developed, by whom, how it is being developed and on
> whose behalf, are central issues in the definition and the practice

of community economic development. The community is central, as both the object of development and as the prime moving subject defining development and making it happen. Implicitly we see community economic development as a subset of community development. The former must serve and, in effect, be grounded in practice in the latter.

(Douglas, 1994: 3)

While Douglas views community economic development as a type of community development, the focus on economic matters precludes the community's problems being defined in any other way. It also conforms to the wider business community's orientation to regard all of humanity's problems as rooted in the economy. While CBED does emphasize control at the community level, it restricts it to only one domain and the range of potential problems to be identified. Once again, as Douglas makes clear:

Community economic development entails purposeful design and actions by community residents to influence the characteristics of their local economy. Whether increasing the rate of growth, restructuring the economy, maintaining the current direction or taking other initiatives, community economic development involves setting goals and objectives, organizing resources, getting commitment and implementing concrete action. The focus of the intervention is the community's economy.

(Douglas, 1994: 7)

Douglas is explicit in the last sentence about the fundamental orientation of CED; all non-economic community problems are excluded from the analysis. However, in many cases these other problems are caused by the focus on and change to the economy producing social alienation.

This exclusive focus on economic development – whether at a community, national or international level – is a result of corporate globalization. The generation and consequences of corporate globalization provide the subject of an earlier chapter in this book, but it is important to point out yet again that in order for globalization to occur successfully, from the point of view of capital, the groundwork needs to be put in place by means of treaties among nation states which focus on a variety of matters including the environment and labor regulations. Instead of broad treaties and arrangements, what we recently got in the developing world are 'structural adjustment programs' (SAPs), while in the developed world it was referred to as 'restructuring' or the 'new economy'. Bello outlines the major conditions of structural adjustment that LDCs had to accept if they were to continue to receive loans from the international community:

- Removing restrictions on foreign investment;
- Reorienting the economy towards exports in order to earn foreign exchange;
- Reducing wages or wage increases to make exports more competitive;
- Cutting tariffs, quotas, and other restrictions on imports, to grease the way for global integration;
- Devaluing the local currency against hard currencies such as the US dollar in order to make exports still more competitive;
- Privatizing state enterprises, thereby providing further access for foreign capital;
- Undertaking a deregulation program to free export-oriented corporations from government controls that protect labor, the environment, and natural resources, thereby cutting costs and further increasing export competitiveness.

(Bello, 1996: 286)

While many, if not all, of these measures were beneficial to offshore corporations and national governments of the countries engaged in SAPs, they were of little benefit to local communities existing in a state of poverty. In fact, SAPs generally made life more difficult for those at the bottom of the income pyramid. In many of the countries subjected to SAPs, the stated ambitions were not achieved. As Bello reports:

(F)ocusing on the African experience in the 1980s, UNICEF economist Eva Jespersen assessed a sample of twenty-four countries that were subjected to structural adjustment programs, on three counts: the rate of capital accumulation, the share of manufacturing in Gross Domestic Product (GDP), and the growth of exports. The data [sic] showed that capital accumulation slowed in twenty countries; the share of manufacturing in GDP stagnated in eighteen countries; exports fell in thirteen countries; and the increases experienced in eleven countries did not compensate for the increase in imports.

(Bello, 2000: 287–8)

In relation to tourism, SAPs had the effect that national governments could not subsidize or protect national firms in order to assist their growth or secure their initial stability. As a result, locally generated cash-strapped firms were at a disadvantage in competing head-on with foreign-owned corporations enjoying healthy capital resources. Regulations such as 'performance requirements', which could reduce the amount of leakage characteristic of tourism, were not possible because of the commitment to SAPs by national governments, imposed on them by the IMF and World Bank.

It is clear in hindsight that the mentality which created structural adjustment, and enforced it in the developing world, also created the notions of 'restructuring' and the 'new economy' prevalent in developed countries, with perhaps less dramatic results, but nonetheless it inaugurated major changes in social structure. Certainly, social programs – such as universal healthcare, labor protection and compensation during periods of unemployment, and environmental protection – were negatively affected. Moreover, this change in economic, social and political orientation prompted the modification of community development, which focused on community capacity-building and on associated processes, to the community economic development orientation, with its exclusive emphasis on economic issues. Interestingly enough, tourism has often been the vehicle for responding to this large-scale process of change in both LDCs and developed countries, at the community and regional level. While it produces jobs – albeit at the bottom end of the wage scale – it encourages trans-national companies to invest in infrastructure in the host country, and increases foreign currency earnings for national governments. What is less clear are the benefits to people at a local level. It is in this area that analysis, and probably change, must occur for any benefits derived from tourism to be equally shared, rather than consumed at the national and international level.

More recently, the academic literature has noted a new initiative. The discussion of human and social capital in the literature further strengthens the connection between economic development and social development. 'Human capital' relates to individuals, while 'social capital' refers to the analysis of relations between and among people. In the former, individuals are seen purely as an input to the production process. The idea of social capital envisages the social element as an input to economic development, and not only as the focus of such development. As Schuller suggests, social capital is:

> defined in terms of networks, norms and trust, and the way these allow agents and institutions to be more effective in achieving a common objective. The most common measures of social capital look at participation in various forms of civic engagement, such as membership of voluntary associations, churches or political parties, or at levels of expressed trust in other people. ...Despite some ambiguity, social capital is generally understood as a matter of relationships, as a property of groups rather than the property of individuals.
>
> (Schuller, 2001: 19)

The creation of the term 'social capital' is yet another indication of how planners and society as a whole are moving towards identifying all human conditions in purely economic terms. Community development began as a comprehensive approach to community problem-solving by communities, stressing process over product. It moved into the economic realm exclusively by placing the E between C and D, which narrowed the scope of problem identification to the economic realm. The introduction of the concept of social capital moves the focus of community development emphatically into the economic sphere, where all terms are defined using economic language. Schuller warns us that:

> exploring the notion of social capital runs a number of risks. It is a relatively new concept, which has not yet had time to bed down. It is proving to be extremely versatile, applicable to many levels and in all kinds of policy fields – so versatile, indeed, that it may appear at times to lose coherence. It is also vulnerable to simplistic application.
>
> (Schuller, 2001: 19)

Schuller's assertion that social capital is subject to 'simplistic application' could also be made about community economic development. Issues of mental health and of the intellectual and social capacities of the marginalized go unattended by adherents to this approach. There is a great risk in defining all human relations in economic terms, which has often been to the detriment of the tourism industry, which became frustrated when its economic contribution to communities appeared to go unappreciated by their residents, especially when the social and environmental costs of economic development have become unacceptably high. In many cases, the antagonism between the tourism industry and the residents of an area could have been avoided, or been addressed at an earlier stage, if problems had been defined in multiple ways, and not simply from an economic perspective. Changing fishers into tour guides demands a change in education and, perhaps more fundamentally, in life-style. However, these fundamental issues go unaddressed.

While I have separated out the fundamentally different ways development has been approached in LDCs and the developed world, it would be a mistake to think that they are mutually exclusive; in fact, there is a considerable overlap between them. Jane Jacobs (1984), for example, has suggested very clearly that the countryside is nothing more than a resource to the metropolis in developed countries – a concept not dissimilar from the center–periphery model often used to describe the situation of LDCs in relation to the developed world. By contrast, and probably because of the influence of donor governments and NGOs, the community development model is often understood as an implementation theory in LDCs. Perhaps the unifying force that will bring together the approaches in LDCs and the developed world will be continued resistance to the hegemonic culture of corporate globalization which will surely be the ultimate result of the direction in which we are headed at present.

4   Concepts of Tourism

INTRODUCTION

This chapter reviews the various ways tourism is defined. Many of the scholarly disciplines attempt to define tourism as a self-contained subject, and from one disciplinary view. This chapter examines these disciplinary definitions with the intention of integrating them into a program of analysis, discussed later in the book. The concept of community tourism will be explored, and the commodification of culture through tourism will also provide a theme of discussion. The chapter concludes with an examination of the theme of coexistence between human and non-human species, as outlined by David Western in his recent work on the Amboseli National Park and World Biosphere Reserve.

DEFINING TOURISM

A rigorous definition of tourism is, at best, an elusive goal. As Weaver suggests, '[u]nfortunately, there is no one single definition of tourism that can be cited here as the definition that everyone adheres to'. (Weaver, 2000: 1) Weaver therefore provides a general definition based on some fundamental principles which represent the most concensus in the field. He states:

> Tourism is the sum of the phenomena and relationships arising from the interaction among tourists, business suppliers, host governments, host communities, origin governments, universities, community colleges and non-governmental organizations, in the process of attracting, transporting, hosting and managing these tourists and other visitors.
>
> (Weaver, 2000: 2)

This definition is not adequate either for the research requirements of academics, or for the many tourism agencies that require a definition on which to construct their mandates. Specific definitions are often invoked to suit individual circumstances and for estimating levels of consumption. When forced to make these types of calculation, many government agencies utilize distance traveled and time spent in tourism activity as the variables to estimate consumption patterns. The Ontario Government in Canada, for example, suggests that a tourist is someone who travels at least 25 miles from their home, or alternatively stays at a destination overnight, regardless of the distance traveled. This type of definition suits the government's need for record-keeping and statistical calculations, but it is not so suitable for academic purposes. In fact, as mentioned previously, there is no single definition which includes all perspectives, and through which all interests could be satisfied. What we are left with is a number of approaches to defining tourism. Each provides a piece of the puzzle, contributing to an overall understanding. The remainder of this chapter provides a typology of tourism definitions and each of their roles in collectively defining the concept of tourism.

SOCIAL–PSYCHOLOGICAL DEFINITIONS

Tourism researchers and planners take an understandable interest in the perspective of the tourist in formulating a definition of tourism. One argument suggests that tourism is rooted in the psyche of all individuals, especially those who live in modern societies. It can be argued, for example, that a great many tourists are seeking to explore their own 'humanness' and self-understanding by experiencing alien cultures and peoples. Certainly, much of what is often called 'ethnic' tourism consists of travel to ancestral homelands, even by those who are generations removed from the part of the world concerned, but who have grown up with an idyllic version of that culture in their adopted homeland. Perhaps this quest to rediscover one's ancestral roots and culture goes even deeper, driven by what Jung called the 'collective unconscious' (Jung, 1990), the seeking of one's collective identity. This analysis finds some support, from the case of those who traveled to parts of Africa considered to be the cradle of humankind, many of whom volunteer to work on archaeological sites in that and other parts of the world for just such a reason. Such motivations do not account for the behavior of most tourists, however, and more mainstream explanations must therefore be sought.

John Urry (1990: 2–4) provides nine criteria of social behavior leading towards a definition of the tourist, outlined in Figure 4.1. What is of interest in Urry's attempt at defining tourism from the social–psychological perspective is the complexity with which the subject is approached. In Urry's view, tourism is a complex social and

Table 4.1   Social Practices Defining Tourism

1. Tourism is a leisure activity which presupposes its opposite, namely regulated and organised [sic] work. It is one manifestation of how work and leisure are organised [sic] as separate and regulated spheres of social practice in 'modern' societies. Indeed acting as a tourist is one of the defining characteristics of being 'modern' and is bound up with major transformations in paid work. This has come to be organized [sic] within particular places and to occur for regularized [sic] periods of time.

2. Tourism relationships arise from a movement of people to, and their stay in, various destinations. This necessarily involves some movement through space that is the journey, and a period of stay in a new place or places.

3. The journey and stay are to, and in, sites which are outside the normal places of residence and work. Periods of residence elsewhere are of a short-term and temporary nature. There is a clear intention to return 'home' within a relatively short period of time.

4. The places gazed upon are for purposes which are not directly connected with paid work and normally they offer some distinctive contrasts with work (both paid and unpaid).

5. A substantial portion of the population of modern societies engages in such tourist practices; new socialised [sic] forms of provision are developed in order to cope with the mass character of the gaze of tourists (as opposed to the individual character of 'travel').

6. Places are chosen to be gazed upon because there is an anticipation, especially through daydreaming and fantasy, of intense pleasure, either on a different scale or involving different senses from those customarily encountered. Such anticipation is constructed and sustained through a variety of non-tourist practices, such as film, TV, literature, magazines, records and videos, which construct and reinforce that gaze.

7. The tourist gaze is directed to features of landscape and townscape which separate them off from everyday experience. Such aspects are viewed because they are taken to be in some sense out of the ordinary. The viewing of such tourism sights often involves different forms of social patterning, with a much greater sensitivity to visual elements of landscape or townscape than is normally found in everyday life. People linger over such a gaze which is then normally visually objectified or captured through photographs, postcards, films, models and so on. These enable the gaze to be endlessly reproduced and recaptured.

8. The gaze is constructed through signs, and tourism involves the collection of signs. When tourists see two people kissing in Paris what they capture in the gaze is 'timeless' romantic Paris. When a small village in England is seen, what they gaze upon is the 'real olde England'. As Culler argues: 'the tourist is interested in everything as a sign of itself ... all over the world the unsung armies of semioticians, the tourists, are fanning out in search of the signs of Frenchness, typical Italian behaviour [sic], exemplary Oriental scenes, typical American thruways, traditional English pubs' (1981:127).

9. An array of tourist professionals develop who attempt to reproduce ever-new objects of the tourist gaze. These objects are located in a complex and changing hierarchy. This depends upon the interplay between, on the one hand, competition between interests involved in provision of such objects and, on the other hand, changing class, gender, generational distinctions of taste within the potential population of visitors.

psychological relationship between the individual and society, having a great deal to do with extricating the familiar from the novel.

Leisure behavior is used to explain social behavior more generally, rather than being seen simply as an escape from the more serious events of everyday life. Tourism provides an important component in the debate on the contributions of work and leisure to the individual and society. In modern societies, work is revered, while leisure describes that part of our lives unencumbered by more serious activities. Tourism, however, is one activity among many which can lend seriousness to leisure (see Stebbins, 2000). Tourists are ascribed status, viewed by others as more worldly than those who confine themselves to their permanent place of residence, and thought to possess an advanced understanding of the world because of their experience of travel. Whether this is true is a matter of debate, but the many conversations around workplace water-coolers inspired by tourist activity suggests a change in the conception of life, no matter how short-lived, on the part of the returned tourist.

Tourism, then, is a form of leisure which demarcates the classes from one other and separates the enriched life from the ordinary person. Certainly, if Veblen were still alive, he would argue that exotic travel functions as a conspicuous display of wealth, and constitutes a class-identifying activity (see Veblen, 1953) .People create a personal image through the places they visit; relaying the experiences of travel is like displaying a badge of honor. Certain destinations have more saliency among members of a certain class than others.

Leisure analysis, like other social sciences, attempts to explain the motivations and behavior of humans. The 'tourist gaze' (Urry, 1990) is a euphemism for the activity of reification. It is an attempt by individuals to bring order to their existence and to explain to themselves the importance of their own life in juxtaposition to others from different parts of the world, and in comparing world-views. Tourism is seen by most travelers as a search for meaning to modern life, when we are no longer preoccupied exclusively with the struggle for survival in an inhospitable world.

Tourism defines culture and is defined by culture. As Rojek and Urry suggest, 'tourism and culture now plainly overlap and there is no clear frontier between the two. They cannot be kept apart'. (Rojek and Urry, 1997: 3) This comment suggests that tourism has taken on a new significance as disposable income, at least in industrialized countries, has increased to the point where tourism is now a significant activity throughout the global economy. As a result, the definition of tourism is in a state of constant change as it becomes a dominant theme in the new world order. The question of whether contemporary tourism is a product of globalization or a force in its development will continue to provide material for discussion in the remainder of this book.

The contact between travelers and their neighbors in earlier periods of history was the predominant method for the social diffusion of cultural artifacts and tools from one society to another. While this model of innovation and diffusion may not have much relevance to societies today, travel nevertheless affects individuals from an educational point of view. Learning how others view the world, and understanding their interpretation of events, can be very enlightening experiences for visitors to alien societies. The tourism industry has often been criticized for the isolation of tourists within compounds and private facilities, and for not encouraging its guests to come into contact with the host culture (see Rojek and Urry, 1997). Too often, tourist enterprises attempt to reproduce the home environment of their guests, while at the same time providing such commodities as sun, sea and sand – or whatever other attractions the location in question can provide. In ever more cases, however, as tourists become more educated and sophisticated, they are venturing beyond the compound walls and into the local community and, it would seem, enjoying the experience. So while this critique is still valid, there are instances during many trips when most tourists do get a glimpse of the host culture, often gazing upon the local expressions of that culture, whether contrived or not.

A less useful way of defining tourism is through the activity of the tourist. As the world becomes more complex, however, and as we move into the service-based era of late capitalism, activities become a less clear way for identifying whether an individual is involved in leisure or work activity. As people move out of traditional work environments in ever greater numbers, the motivations for travel behavior are becoming less obvious. Many tourists, for example, visit farms and engage in farm-based activity that would normally be defined as work. In this instance, however, the motivations of those engaged in it clearly define it as a form of tourism. Stebbins has come to understand this seeming contradiction in behavior, and has coined the term 'serious leisure' to describe it (See Stebbins, 2000). While Stebbins' notion of serious leisure was created to explain and incorporate the recreational aspects of volunteering, of being an amateur or hobbyist, it has considerable merit in explaining many forms of tourism as well. If the process and outcome of the tourism activity is dominated by commitment and intensity, and acts as a life focusing event, then it has some of the characteristics that Stebbins describes as necessary to meet his description. Stebbins suggests that leisure can be divided into two distinct categories. First is casual leisure activity, which is described as enjoyment which is not necessarily significant in satisfying a quest for meaning or beyond simply a diversion. Not that there is anything wrong with diversions. In contrast, however, Stebbins argues, serious leisure can provide a central focus for life, out of which one can gain the psychological satisfactions usually found through work. In Stebbins' words:

> Serious leisure is the steady pursuit of an amateur, hobbyist, or volunteer activity that captivates its participants with its many challenges and inherent complexity. This kind of leisure stands in contrast to 'casual' or 'unserious' leisure, which typically poses many fewer challenges, is much simpler in structure, and rarely requires a steady commitment to perform it well.
>
> Serious leisure is further defined by its six distinguishing qualities. One is the occasional need to persevere ... Second, as indicated, participants find a (nonwork) career in the endeavor, shaped by its own special contingencies, turning points, and stages of achievement or involvement. Careers in serious leisure are also shaped by substantial personal effort based on specially acquired knowledge, training, or skill, and, indeed, all three at times. Fourth, eight durable benefits, or results, of serious leisure have so far been identified: self-actualization, self-enrichment, self-expression, regeneration or renewal of self, feelings of accomplishment, enhancement of self-image, social interaction and belongingness, and lasting physical products of the activity (e.g., a painting, scientific paper, piece of furniture). A further benefit – self-gratification or pure fun, which is considerably more evanescent than the preceding eight – is the only one shared with casual leisure.

(Stebbins, 2000: 314)

According to Stebbins, the fifth quality of serious leisure is the unique ethos and special social world that grows up around each instance of it, while the sixth flows from the preceding five: participants in serious leisure tend to identify strongly with their chosen pursuits. For many tourists, the activity is more than just a casual one, and belongs clearly in the realm of serious leisure. The amount of planning that goes into arranging a trip is as much a part of the tourist experience as the actual journey. Much learning occurs during this period, which sets the parameters for the experience. After such a trip, tourists are commonly eager to share their experiences with others, both at work and among their circle of friends. Often, contacts with people met during a trip are kept up, and a new circle of friends develops.

SOCIOLOGICAL DEFINITIONS

In spite of the difficulties in defining tourism in terms of activities, there are some categories of behavior which most scholars and planners consider to fall clearly within the domain of tourism. These are broad categories, and are useful in an overall framework for analysis. One model is provided by Reid, Fuller, Haywood and Bryden (1993).

The usefulness in this understanding of the categories of tourism activities is in its integration of leisure, recreation, and tourism into

Figure 4.1   Categories of Tourism Activities

Source: Reid, Fuller, Haywood and Bryden, 1993

a holistic model. Sociologists have traditionally concentrated on two areas in their analysis of tourism: first, on travel as a means of escape, and second, on its benefits as a means of self-development (see Wearing & Neil, 2000: 394). The activity itself, and the motivations driving the performance of it, provide the material for analysis. Often, the difference in motivations of tourists and locals engaged in the same recreational activity, and what distinguishes each of them, is difficult, if not impossible, to articulate. Most commentators would simply use time or distance traveled to make such a distinction, but that appears to be too simplistic. The same activity might take on a different psychological significance for each of its participants. For those traveling from a distant location, the activity may be novel, perhaps not available on a regular basis. For those pursuing a leisure activity in their own locale the activity may seem routine and familiar. Skiing, for those who live on or near a mountain and may ski 45 or more days in a year, is a very different experience to that enjoyed by those traveling long distances by air for a one-week skiing trip each season. The complex overlap between leisure, recreation, and tourism is thus in need of further study.

The relationships between the local resident and the visitor are often an important factor defining tourism and its outcomes. While both may be engaged in the same or similar activities, the customs surrounding that activity may be very different for each. There are ethnic differences, for example, in the ways that people engage in any given activity. Asian skiers, for example, are more likely to ski in larger groups than their North American counterparts. The latter still prefer the solitude of the mountain, while Asians are much more social in their approach to this activity. Again, more research is required on this subject in order to define more clearly such differences and their origins.

Primarily, sociologists have traditionally concerned themselves with issues of class, race, ethnicity and gender. This is no less true in the study of tourism than in the examination of any other area of social enquiry. More specifically, sociologists tend to be interested in the impact tourism has on the host community or society. For the most part, they see the tourist as a disfiguring influence on traditional societies. However, there appears to be some movement away from that position and a new sense that tourism needs to be explained as much as criticized (see Harrison, 2001). Tourism is coming increasingly to be viewed as one economic activity among many, to be analyzed for its impacts on both the host and guest, with policies then designed to mitigate the negative and accentuate the positive aspects of that social encounter.

Sociologists continue to strive to find a grand theory to explain tourism and the tourist. The elusiveness of the subject matter provides great problems for the development of such a theory. However, as Lengkeek suggests, '(t)ourists, even if they look the same, experience their vacations and the places where they are on holiday in different ways'. (Lengkeek, 2001: 174)

Adapting Cohen's (1979) scheme incorporating recreational, diversional, experiential, experimental and existential categories, Lengkeek creates a more precise typology to distinguish the various types of tourists. His typology includes the following categories:

> *mode of amusement* – the stories and metaphors that suspend reality are so well known and trusted that they do not create any tension with everyday reality; *mode of change* – the difference with normal, everyday life is more strongly felt. ...sometimes breaking lose (dis-association) from paramount reality...; *mode of interest* - out-there-ness is created in the sense of attractions. Fantasy is brought into being by signs, clichés and travel guides; *mode of rapture* - here the tension between the suspension of the ordinary and the inaccessibility of the Other reaches its climax. Amazement and rapture flow from this confrontation; *mode of mastering* - the unknown and inaccessible are opened up, thanks to a new masking of doubt.
>
> (Lengkeek, 2001: 182–3)

In some ways his typology follows the template provided by Cohen, but provides more depth to the explanation. It can also be argued that parts of Lengkeek's scheme – particularly the latter elements – complement or even incorporate Stebbins' notions of serious leisure. The gradations within the system are contingent on the ability of the tourist to move from the recreational to the existential in their association with the attraction. Stebbins' concept of serious leisure (Stebbins, 1983; 2000) helps to explain this transition.

When speaking of tourism as both casual and serious Wearing and Neil make the suggestion that, '(o)n the one hand there has been an emphasis on tourism as a means of escape from the everyday, even if such escape is temporary. On the other, travel has been constructed as a means of self-development, a way to broaden the mind, experience the new and different and to come away in some way enriched.' (Wearing and Neil, 2000: 394) This gives support to Stebbins' concept of serious leisure, applied specifically to tourism. Volunteer tourism is a fast-growing segment of the tourism market which demands explanation, and Stebbins' concept is certainly one place to start.

In a study by Mannell and Reid (1992) approximately one third of their sample of over 1,500 workers in Canada were identified as individuals who would fit into Stebbins' serious leisure category. For these people, leisure, rather than their paid work, provided psychological meaning to life. For them, work was significant only in that it provided them with the resources to pursue their chosen leisure activity. For many tourists, travel itself – or the activities it facilitates – would presumably constitute 'serious leisure'. Many so-called tourists devote their travel activities to projects in the developing world; many archaeological digs around the world are dependent on volunteers for a supply of labor. This type of volunteerism would constitute one of Stebbins' categories of serious leisure if the other criteria were also met.

ECONOMIC DEFINITIONS

Host countries and entrepreneurs define tourism from their own perspective. For the nation-state, especially in the developing world, tourism is defined by the issues of economic growth and employment, which are of paramount concern. This, of course, is coupled with the need of many developing country governments to raise substantial amounts of foreign currency to pay down debilitating debts.

Tourism is also defined economically among entrepreneurs, according to consumption patterns, and by profit and loss. In many developing countries, the prices charged for many exhibits maintained by government agencies changes based on whether the visitor is a non-national tourist or a citizen of the country. In a sense, then, there are two distinct types of visitors to such exhibits, even though the attraction may be the same. For these purposes, domestic tourism is seen as much as a recreation as it is a form of tourism.

Entrepreneurs represent the host in the host/guest relationship inherent in tourism. It is with the entrepreneur that products and services are created, developed, and marketed in the hope of attracting the tourist. The entrepreneur tries to interpret what the tourist is seeking, and this interpretation leads to the commodification of all types of local environmental resources, industries, and cultural products. The tourism entrepreneur also attempts to discern the social and psychological needs of the tourist. Sophisticated research is often undertaken to determine which tourists would be interested in what types of product. The attraction is constructed by business to blend the familiar with the unusual, creating an avenue into the unknown and inaccessible, as described by Lengkeek (2001).

Depending on the attraction to be marketed, market segmentation – the division of the tourism market into sub-groups composed of tourists who have similar characteristics and interests – is a major factor in defining tourism from the business point of view. In many ways, this method incorporates the typology of Lengkeek, outlined above, while many of these sub-groups would constitute homogeneous groups with unifying characteristics, as described in relation to the social–psychological dynamics discussed earlier.

Issues of supply and demand play a critical role in defining tourism from the economic and entrepreneurial point of view. When demand fluctuates, many types of business, such as bed and breakfasts, come into, and pass out of, existence. It is not difficult to use one's house for such a purpose when demand is high, and then use it for some other small business when it is low – particularly in rural areas and LDCs. In more sophisticated jurisdictions this flexibility can be reduced by government health and safety regulations (particularly as they relate to fire safety). However, in less restrictive settings this dramatic change in occupation defines the pattern of life for small entrepreneurs, who will often be transformed from primary economy workers to service workers.

COMMUNITY DEFINITIONS

Communities define tourism from their own point of view. Priorities move here from issues of demand to those of supply, since the community is the supplier of any attraction, whether it is natural or human-made. Tourism is not separate from other aspects of life for those living in a community dominated by tourism. Many of the irritants of life stem from tourism development, particularly if it is excessive, overwhelming the carrying capacity of the community. Often, what draws people to take up permanent residence in a tourism community are the same amenities that also attract tourists; but residents often feel a desire to retain the 'quaintness' conferred by the features which were so appealing to them in the first place, while the business community wants to grow and expand its operations, thereby fundamentally altering community dynamics; and herein lies the basis for potential conflict.

For many residents of a tourism community – and particularly those in rural areas – it is the pristine back country off the beaten track and nature-based recreation that are most appealing. Often, these attractions are not in the residential part of the community but in nearby areas. If such facilities are upgraded or altered to accommodate increased volumes of traffic, and eventually overrun by tourists, the aspects of the area which lured the residents to it in the first place may be changed beyond recognition, and hence lose their appeal.

Golden, British Columbia provides such an example. Golden is situated in the Purcell Mountains, next to the Rockies, in British Columbia, Canada. At the time of writing, a local skiing area is being developed to international standards in order to capitalize on this excellent resource. While many Golden residents ski, they are also interested in back country recreation, including hunting, snow-mobiling and hiking. While the residents are keen to expand the skiing facilities to capitalize on tourism, they also expressed the desire, at a recently held planning meeting, to make sure that their recreational pursuits were not overwhelmed by the expansion. Local residents are thus usually accommodating, and often enthusiastic, about sharing what they enjoy with the outside world; but they are also vigilant about the protection of their primary recreational interests. This protective spirit becomes even more pronounced when what they are protecting is a result of a serious leisure project, and not just casual leisure.

Community tourism is also often a product of a particular, unique lifestyle that may be the result of a long history in a particular part of the world, or the story of a migration by an ethnic group. Tourism product development in this context is an attempt by the descendents of a group of people who migrated to a far-off land to preserve their cultural heritage, which may be in danger of being lost. Community members are often quite proud of their heritage, and take great pride in displaying their culture to visitors. In Canada, for example, this sense of place and pride can be readily seen in many First Nations communities during pow-wows and other festival events. The same is true for the Maasai in Kenya and Tanzania. In the case of the Canadian First Nations, tourism is often the vehicle and motivation for many younger native people in learning their ancestral language and traditions, which would otherwise be lost as older members of the community passed away. Cultural display, either in terms of mores and traditional practices or in the form of a built heritage, often defines tourism from the point of view of a community. Many of the tourism activities of a community also provide social recreation or serious leisure for the residents.

In the case of rural, farm-based communities, tourism provides another outlet for farm produce. Local farmers' markets, which are a tourist event for many of their patrons, provide cash income for locally grown produce. Much of this produce is a result of the over-production of farms supplying the major traditional outlets such as supermarkets, and would go to waste if not for tourists' purchases from farmers' markets. Cummings, Kora and Murray present the results of their research into the economic impact of farmers' markets in Ontario. They report that 'combined annual sales for the 19 Farmers' Markets [sic] amounts to approximately $73 million'. (Cummings, Kora and Murray, 1999: 54) Their research randomly surveyed 19 of the 127 farmers' markets in Ontario. When calculations were completed for all markets in the province, the researchers' estimated that the value of sales in farmers' markets across Ontario stood at $500 million annually. The researchers also stated that

(m)any businesses we spoke with acknowledged that the presence of the market stimulates additional sales for neighbouring businesses and although we are unable to quantify this, it is important to emphasize that close to 50% of customers stop to shop at various businesses on their way to or from the Farmers' Market.

(Cummings et al., 1999: 56)

The researchers also reported that annually, 'multipliers associated with agriculture and other special events like agricultural fairs, suggest that for every dollar spent in the market, another two dollars ripple through the provincial economy'. (Ibid.: 56) Given that 2:1 multiplier, the researchers estimate the economic impact of Ontario farmers' markets in the annual provincial economy is $1.5 billion. Equivalent estimates can also be made for employment in this industry. Again, the researchers stated that

(p)rovincially, we estimate that on an average summer market week, approximately 8,000 people are involved in sales and related tasks at farmers' markets across the province. This would suggest that a total of 24,000 people are directly and indirectly involved in preparing and selling the goods we find in farmers' markets.

(Ibid.: 59)

At the individual level, tourism also provides some farms with a second – or for many a primary – source of revenue to support the farm. In some parts of Canada, farming no longer provides a sufficient living to maintain a family farm, and so most farms engage in some form of economic diversification involving non-traditional enterprise. Tourism is often the economic activity of choice in this circumstance. There are now farms which do very little farming other than what is needed to support tourism, so that tourism is now the primary activity on those farms. Likewise, many east coast communities in Canada have been economically devastated by the loss of cod stocks due to over-fishing. They have developed a tourism industry based on their industrial heritage, centered on the unique lifestyle their lost way of life produced. The commodification of their history and traditions may help such communities not only eco- nomically, but also in the preservation of a portion of a way of life revered in memory. It is in cases where a tourism activity closely resembles or displays a historical lifestyle that tourism seems to work for both the tourist and the community.

ECOLOGICAL DEFINITIONS

Tourism has many implications for the environment. On the one hand, hard-core environmentalists decry tourism as a major cause of the depletion of natural resources, and of pollution. They argue that international travel uses exorbitant amounts of fuel in conveying modern jets to their destinations, while the destination sites for such trips are often inadequately equipped to handle the human waste produced by tourists. When managed well, however, tourism can be one of the most benign and sustainable uses of the natural environment, compared to competing uses such as forestry or mining. In his book *The Future of Life*, Edward O. Wilson, one of the world's most respected biologists, argues that tourism is worth more to the economy in the long term than many of the extractive uses of the natural environment to which it is otherwise put. As is often the case, the proper use of any resource or facility will extend its life, while improper use is likely to destroy it.

Many environmental organizations now advocate certain forms of tourism as a means of conserving the natural environment. The World Wildlife Fund in Central America, for example, has often supported the use of tropical forests for ecotourism, rather than seeing it cleared and used for coffee or banana production. Ecotourism operations developed in a manner that protects the natural resources it takes advantage of, and educates visitors about their fragility, are seen by many environmental organizations as often the most appropriate use of the resources in question.

One example of the role of tourism in supporting environmental sustainability is the Sustainable Development Agreement (SDA) between the Netherlands and Costa Rica. This bilateral treaty was completed under the auspices of the United Nations Conference in Environment and Development (UNCED) in Rio de Janeiro. The SDA attempts to establish a cooperative agreement between countries of north and south which focuses on sustainable development through engaging the principles of participation (see Reid, Mair and Taylor, 2000), equality, and reciprocity between the signatory countries. One of the initiatives between the Netherlands and Costa Rica is a tourism program. This project, unlike others, makes sustainable development, rather than tourism per se, a central concern. As the authors of the report *Developing Sustainable Tourism: The Case of Manuel Antonio and Texel* suggest:

> The program takes a different approach from the 'mainstream' approach to sustainable tourism. It stresses the potential contribution of tourism to sustainable development, not the negative impacts.
>
> (van der Duim et al., 2001: 34)

From the environmental perspective, tourism is viewed in this model as the vehicle through which issues of the environment and sustainable development are addressed, rather than as the subject of development; the subject is the environment, and tourism is the mechanism for conservation. This method of defining tourism sees its role as that of a support to the larger goal of sustainable development and environmental protection, and not as an end in itself. Likewise, tourism is viewed in this book as a vehicle for community development, and not as the main focus of development, or as an end in itself.

The relationship between tourism and the environmental movement has often been strained. Mass tourism has been viewed by many environmentalists, for example, as just as damaging to the environment as the extractive industries of forestry, fishing and mining. Environmentalists have searched for alternative forms of tourism which are more compatible with protecting the environment. Often, however, tourism has been developed in the same destructive manner as have other more traditional industries.

As it becomes a major force across the world, new and alternative forms of tourism are appearing in the literature. Ecotourism is one of the most successful new forms of tourism, especially from a marketing point of view. The expression itself is certainly designed to reassure, but whether or not it is more ecologically sound than other types of tourism is a matter for debate. An increasing number of scholars are attempting to define ecotourism, but the definition most often quoted is that offered by Ceballos-Lascurain, conceiving of ecotourism as

> a scientific, aesthetic or philosophical approach, although the ecological tourist is not required to be a professional scientist, artist or philosopher. The main point is that the person who practices ecotourism has the opportunity of immersing him or herself in nature in a way most people cannot enjoy in their routine, urban existence. This person will eventually acquire a consciousness that will convert him/her into somebody keenly involved in conservation issues.
>
> (Ziffer, 1989: 5)

Much of what passes for ecotourism today is far removed from the strict parameters of this definition. The tourism industry has been criticized for using the ecotourism label when its real activities clearly violate the principles enunciated above. As Jaakson suggests, '(e)go-tourism has become a word-play on ecotourism' (Jaakson, 1997: 33), to capture the misuse of ecotourism as an environmentally friendly activity. He goes on to note that:

> [a]n insistent equating of ecotourism with nature overshadows a human dimension of deep spirituality which I speculate is the motivation, conscious or subconscious, for all ecotourism travel. This spirituality is akin to the travel of devout pilgrims to worship at sacred and holy sites. Ecotourism in pristine natural sites is a

form of secular pilgrimage where nature is the sacred holy site. The premise here is that the essence of ecotourism is an ethic that makes ecotourism different from other types of tourism.

(Ibid.: 34)

Unlike Ceballos-Lascurain, Jaakson combines the definition of the secular with the sacred. This clearly distinguishes ecotourism from other forms of tourism. The ecotourist has a special orientation towards nature. It is conceivable that those engaged in this type of tourism are clearly engaging in what Stebbins (2000) calls serious leisure, and Lengkeek (2001) associates with 'rapture' and 'mastering'.

Defining tourism from an ecological point of view requires the establishment of a set of criteria according to which the participant acts, and which can be understood to define him or her as an ecological tourist. One set of such criteria governing the priorities for a given development are set out by Wight:

1. It should not degrade the resource and should be developed in an environmentally sound manner;
2. It should provide long-term benefits to the resource, to local community and industry (benefits may be conservation, scientific, social, cultural, or economic);
3. It should provide first-hand, participatory and enlightening experiences;
4. It should involve education among all parties – local communities, government, non-governmental organizations, industry and tourists (before, during and after the trip);
5. It should encourage all-party recognition of the intrinsic values of the resource;
6. It should involve acceptance of the resource on its own terms, and in recognition of its limits, which involves supply-oriented management;
7. It should involve understanding and involve partnerships between many players, which could include government, non-governmental organizations, industry, scientists and locals (both before and during operations);
8. It should promote moral and ethical responsibilities and behaviors towards the natural and cultural environment by all players.

(Wight, 1994: 339–40)

These principles, if followed strictly, clearly locate ecotourism in the camp of serious leisure. As already suggested, however, many so-called ecotourism operations follow these principles only loosely, at best, and in some cases simply use the term 'ecotourism' as a marketing label while continuing in the old, exploitive tradition.

The ecological definition of tourism incorporates the notion that humans are a part of the natural world. Accordingly, it does not give primacy to humans, or separate them off as dominant. Ecotourism, by its very nature, seeks coexistence with the natural world, rather than domination of it. David Western, former head of the Kenya Wildlife Service, is an advocate of treating the environment holistically rather than as a series of individual, unconnected parts and for the need to incorporate social and conservation issues when planning the use of the natural environment. He also stresses the role of tourism in conservation efforts. This is demonstrated in a conversation he had with an attendee of a meeting where he was giving a lecture about the problems with Kenya's Amboseli Park, where his work takes place:

> What I'm trying to say ... is that we have to think about the entire ecosystem, not just the dry season range. To conserve the ecosystem we must win Maasai support by accommodating their interests. We don't really have any alternative. Besides, we know that coexistence worked in the past, so why not now? My ideas are admittedly tentative, but there's reason to think the Maasai could be persuaded to preserve Amboseli if they got a share of the tourist revenues, social services, and jobs.
>
> (Western, 1997: 101)

Western is quite right. The ecology of an area must be understood as a whole, not just from one particular point of view. His notion of coexistence – that is, humans and animals interacting together without disruption – is the only way forward, and tourism is in many cases the best mechanism for coexistence. Naturally, cattle-herding will always be a part of the lifestyle of the Maasai but they will also benefit from tourism if given a chance, and included in the planning and development process. The underlying insight here is that diversity is the key to sustainability. Success will not flow from the exploitation of any single industry beyond the limits of the environment – either natural or cultural – to absorb its effects and rejuvenate itself.

5 Planning and Development Theories and their Relation to Tourism Development

INTRODUCTION

While the first four chapters took an analytical approach towards tourism, this chapter takes a prescriptive turn. The shortcomings of the entrepreneurial approach to tourism development, which has dominated the scene to the present, will be outlined. I will argue for a bottom-up, community-driven and community planned approach to development which, in my view, will produce an integrated and sustainable industry over the long-term. This approach must balance the economic, environmental and socio-cultural aspects of tourism development if sustainability is to be achieved.

While this text has so far provided a critique of tourism development, it is also important to provide a normative planning model that will deal with those aspects of development which have been injurious to host communities. It is easy to criticize an industry such as tourism, but more difficult to provide a basis on which development might proceed in such a way as to benefit those most affected by its consequences. Many communities around the world are in need of economic development. Modern technology is changing the organizational nature of social systems and the way in which economic development is pursued. Tourism represents a possible path of development which could provide important benefits in the many communities which, relatively suddenly, have found that their traditional industries are no longer viable due to changes in the world economy or the exhaustion of a basic resource. Rural areas are suffering, with towns and cities becoming ever more dominant around the world. While this is not a new pattern, but has in fact been playing itself out for several decades, it is now at a critical stage, and new ways of surviving in the countryside in both developed countries and LDCs are sorely needed. In many cases, tourism seems to be fulfilling that role. However, it is not always pursued in the interests of the population, but is often a hostage to other interests, as I outlined in the first three chapters of this book. But tourism does have the potential to provide benefits to both rural and urban communities alike if it is developed and managed with the interests of citizens and communities at heart. This chapter, and those that follow, will attempt to provide a model for tourism development that is community-friendly and 'people-centered'.

It will also introduce learning theory as a mechanism for planning from below. The position of this book is that communities are potential learning systems, and if tourism is to be sustainable then a community must reach a collective decision – through the identification of commonly held values and aspirations for development – as to what is the appropriate level of development in their community and which suits their particular circumstances. This process also embraces the idea that there are some communally held values which need to be protected from tourism development, while others can be commoditized and shared with outsiders. If the whole issue is approached in a sensitive manner, there may not be too many areas which demand complete protection, and most may fall into the latter category.

THE NEED FOR THEORY IN TOURISM DEVELOPMENT

Tourism development, both in LDCs and in the developed world, has been initiated mainly by business people, in cooperation with national governments or their emissaries. Tourism is not a field of development that has been widely adopted by non-governmental organizations (NGOs) as a focus for their efforts. While they have often been critics of tourism, they have for the most part left development in this area to the private sector. Recently, however, NGOs such as the World Wildlife Fund have shown an interest in tourism development as a vehicle for achieving their goal of environmental preservation. It can be argued that tourism provides a less destructive developmental alternative to the unsustainable practices associated with forestry, mining and intensive agriculture.

We often hear politicians and other leaders in society today speak about the future in purely teleological terms, as if it were not subject to human choices. They urge us simply to accept the inevitable and to make the best of it. Since the domination of society by the forces for neo-liberalism, that future has been portrayed espousing a business or capitalistic framework: we are led to believe that progress can only occur when markets are free and barriers to trade reduced.

Programs such as structural adjustment in the developing world, and economic restructuring in the developed world, are a product of just such teleological convictions. Progressive planners, however, see the world a little differently. The philosopher John Shaar sums it up best:

> The future is not a result of choices among alternative paths offered by the present, but a place that is created – created first in the mind and will, created next in activity. The future is not some place we are going to, but one we are creating. The paths to it are not found but made, and the activity of making them changes both the maker and the designation.
>
> (Shaar, source unknown)

The message of Shaar's comment gives rise to the principles laid out in this chapter. Planning is about creating visions of the future from a normative perspective, and then determining how best to achieve that goal; it is a negotiated process and about social interaction, capacity-building and community decision-making which may change the end state from one which focuses on a physical product to one which is more educational and life enhancing. Planning is a transactive activity which features an open dialogue between the planner and those for whom the plan is being constructed, changing both the desired destination and those involved in the dialogue; it is less a technical activity than a social one; it is creative and partially, at least, artistic. It is comprehensive in its approach, seeking to understand and give expression to a wide range of desired outcomes and the possible paths to their realization. Transactive and open planning is the crystallization of the desires of human beings, rather than the usual routine which results in the domination of one sector of the community over the others. Transactive and open planning is political in the good sense of that word in that it features open negotiations, unlike much of what passes for politics today.

All over the world people aspire to the principles of open and negotiated planning, but the strategies and techniques for implementing them are conspicuously lacking. Viewing all life in economic and competitive terms is in direct opposition to these principles. Cooperative practices have seemingly lost out to the philosophy which embraces the notion of absolute unfettered competition, and to the supposed superiority of the free market as a substitute for political decision-making. When left to the market, decisions are made by those who can manipulate the system most effectively.

Those at the bottom of the social hierarchy and perhaps less skilled at market manipulation may be forced to the margins. Planning, on the other hand, offers society a process in which all can participate in decision-making, and perhaps achieve at least some of their aspirations. It is the art of compromise and the integration of multiple goals through an intentionally designed inclusive process. Planning a future requires specific methods and skills in order for it to run smoothly. It is also based on the fundamental belief that humans, if given a chance, can act rationally and in the interests of the majority of community members, and that their fate is not totally subject to the self-interest of the few who stand to gain financially.

THE CONTRIBUTION OF PLANNING THEORY TO TOURISM DEVELOPMENT

Tourism planning relies on many theories constructed for purposes other than tourism development. These theories are often treated in isolation from each other and, consequently, fail to be implemented in an integrated or systematic way. Figure 5.1 shows a set of theories which suggest a framework for the planning of community tourism. Each of the columns denotes a body of theories conceived by their authors in isolation from the others. It connects components of each set of theories with compatible aspects of other models by the use of connecting arrows, and thus suggests an integrated, consistent, process in which planning can unfold at all levels simultaneously. These concepts are important in explaining different aspects of the community processes inherent in community tourism planning, and have been combined in a systematic way to indicate the choices that need to be made at different stages of the planning process.

Friedmann (1987) offers six theories which can explain the major approaches to planning. Planners select one or a combination of these approaches – either consciously, according to what they perceive to be the best approach to the problem they are attempting to solve, or simply out of habit. The selection of the most appropriate general approach depends on the nature and context of the problem to be solved. This method of implementing theory is often referred to as the 'contingent' approach to leadership. More will be said about the basis on which each general approach is selected after explaining each of the stages in Friedmann's model.

According to Friedmann (1987), social reform is a top-down activity constructed on the principles of scientific rationality,

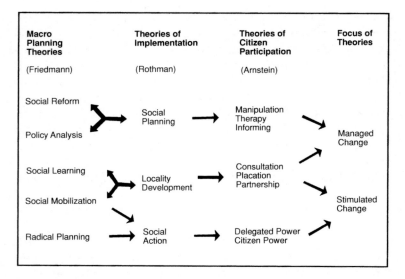

Figure 5.1 Integration of Planning Theories

Source: Friedmann, 1987, Rothman, 1979, and Arnstein, 1969

scientific management and public regulation. It is based on the belief that without state intervention and control the market economy would produce inefficiency, waste and injustice. This type of planning is directed from the top by experts in the field. According to this model, the expert undertakes scientific analysis of the situation under investigation, develops comprehensive plans of action and implements those plans. This is often achieved in isolation to the real world as experienced by the majority of citizens and their day-to-day aspirations. It is based on the premise that those in charge of policy are best placed to understand the particulars of the situation, and possess appropriate training to design adequate solutions for their resolution.

The category of policy analysis, another of Friedmann's general planning distinctions, is a variety of social reform also which relies on the top-down model of development. This model brings together three academic fields: systems engineering and quantitative modeling; management science and general systems theory; and political and administrative science. It is based firmly on the belief that rational decisions would improve the problem-solving abilities of any organization or system, and views society in the image of the machine. The emphasis of this approach is placed on the analysis of data and not necessarily on the particulars of the issue under review and the intricacies of the people it will affect. Policy analysis uses the language of systems theory, deploying such terms as 'steady-state', 'feedback', and 'boundaries'. The approach is very much driven by technical expertise, and there is little room for public consulta-tion or input, let alone control. It lacks any recognition of the value of lay people's perceptions of the problem and their involvement in its resolution.

The social learning model represents a drastic departure from the two previously outlined theories. Its approach is learner-centered rather than top-down. It follows the Freirian model of problem-centered learning (see Freire, 1990). It links collectively constructed knowledge to action and recognizes the political realities when solving social problems, including those of tourism. Perceptions of reality are not limited to those constructed by the experts and are as numerous as the participants in the planning process: no single agent has the exclusive right to represent reality. This approach, unlike the first two, is based in commonly held values and not solely on science or technique. Its most determining characteristic is its dependence on transformative practices originating within civil society. Stankey, McCool, Clark and Brown set out what they believe to be the fundamental characteristics of the social learning model:

(1) Providing opportunities for interaction and deliberation.
(2) Being inherently political, in that they involve questions of the nature and distribution of values.
(3) Representing all interests who ultimately hold veto power in the discussion and decisions....
(4) Integrating perspectives, knowledge, and interests.
(5) Honoring a wide conception of relevant knowledge, admitting both the formal knowledge of science as well as the experien-tial or personal knowledge held by citizens.
(6) Centering on a task-oriented action group – a dynamic, interactive group focused on an issue.
(7) Involving a decision that feeds back into the learning process. Indeed, the fundamental purpose is to build learning among group participants in a way that facilitates action.

(Stankey et al., 1999: 443)

The social learning model recognizes the legitimacy of personal knowledge in the decision-making system. People live in unique circumstances and each society may possess special knowledge about their particular environment which is not in the purview of science. This knowledge needs not only to be legitimized in the planning process, but may, in fact, be made principal in it.

Social mobilization, according to Friedmann, extends the basic philosophy of social learning into the realm of action. It is constructed from the three great oppositional movements of history: utopianism, anarchism, and historical materialism – or Marxism. It developed as a counter-movement to reform, so it is revolutionary in spirit. Its perspective is that of the victims and the underclass in society. Its purpose is the political practice of human liberation. This model views the role of the individual and the community in the problem-solving process as paramount.

Lastly, Friedmann identifies radical planning as a separate general planning theory. In this model, planning focuses on the structural problems of society, providing a critical interpretation of existing reality. Radical planning attempts to chart the future course of a problem and then act to alter it. It elaborates conceptions of a preferred outcome based on emancipatory practice. Perhaps its most outstanding feature is that it suggests the best strategy for overcoming the resistance of established power structures. Radical planning is an amalgam of analysis, social vision and strategic thinking.

Social reform, and to a lesser extent policy analysis, are often the planning models of choice for national governments who wish to be prescriptive in dealing with what they understand as local or regional issues. National governments will develop tourism responses to a local problem which are often generated from outside the community, and without meaningful input from those most affected by the situation, the citizens themselves. They are often surprised when local people reject their proposed solutions, and even the description of the problem itself. This approach is top-down, even though it may attempt to garner input from those affected. Usually this type of input activity simply seeks the uncritical acceptance of the plan by the local people.

Tourism planning, as traditionally practiced by the business community, relies mainly on the second of Friedmann's theoretical models. Tourism businesses are interested in the analysis of markets through modeling the variables which are thought to play a role in producing financial success. Less important to the tourism corporation are the social learning and community capacity building goals which might also be part of a tourism development activity.

Tourism planning has generally been a top-down exercise, characteristic of social reform but more in the tradition of policy analysis. While this approach has theoretically worked well initially for the corporation, it has often encountered opposition in communities where citizens have come to feel that their culture and environment are under threat.

Social learning and social mobilization, on the other hand, are bottom-up planning approaches which place as much, or more, value on the psychological and social growth of the citizens involved as on the establishment of a particular tourism project. Tourism planning, therefore, does not make the same mistake as community economic development and take a tourism response to all social problems. The planner in a tourism context is prepared to alter course or terminate the tourism project if the community determines that a different destination is right for them. Those engaged in this approach have faith that if the process is correct the outcome will also be right. These approaches consider problem-identification to be the prerogative of the community involved, and the solution of problems as a vehicle for capacity-building within the community. The whole process is a collective learning experience which will carry over to other projects in the community.

Finally, radical planning involves designing social actions with the explicit aim of emancipating a group of people from a clearly identified oppressive social force. This method is used when tourism issues such as overcrowding or pollution have not been resolved through more traditional channels. Citizens within tourism communities have been known to block buses from entering tourism districts or poison animals to destroy the tourism product, when conditions have become intolerable to them. This has usually occurred when all else seems to have failed, and when citizens have become frustrated by their inability to resolve the dispute by other, more conventional means.

Any one of these approaches may have more appeal than the others to a particular planner. However, adopting a single approach and applying it to all tourism problems is not an appropriate strategy. The nature and context of a given problem are the criteria according to which one of Friedmann's overall approaches is selected. The legitimacy of each of Friedmann's designations is evaluated on their selection appropriate to the unique set of circumstances being addressed. The selection by the planner of a social reform approach when the diagnosis of the situation to be addressed clearly warrants a social mobilization approach would likely produce a less than adequate outcome. That said, when a community is the subject of concern it is likely that the social learning and social mobilization strategies will have some role to play in the planning process.

Friedmann's formulation can be very useful to the scholar interested in tourism planning, as well as to the practicing tourism planner. Destination areas can be analyzed and explained using Friedmann's concepts. More importantly, perhaps, the problems found in many destinations can be directly tied to the particular planning approach used in the initial development process. Equally, strategies for solving these problems must also be selected based on a sound diagnosis of the problem. All too often, planners have favorite approaches and will implement them no matter what the situation may call for. The repertoire of theories presented by Friedmann is not merely interesting and esoteric, but provides a guiding framework which may play a vital role in the ultimate success of any intervention. More will be said about these general planning theories later, but first the other theories in the planning system and found in Figure 5.1 need to be reviewed.

Jack Rothman (1979) presents a set of theories which can guide the implementation of the planning process. Like the theories provided by Friedman, each of Rothman's constructs provides the tourism planner with a different set of strategies for intervening in the tourism system, designed according to the nature of the problem being addressed.

Rothman refers to the stereotypical version of planning, in which the 'expert' planner enjoys a high degree of control over the process, as 'social planning'. The function of the planner in this regime is to collect and analyze data, formulate a plan based on these data, and then present it to decision-makers. While there is often citizen participation in this process, it is generally at the level of what Arnstein calls 'manipulation' and 'therapy' (Arnstein, 1969). Concepts of manipulation and therapy embrace the notion that those in power are in a position to know what is best for the community or nation as a result of their expertise and access to special information and, therefore, will only inform citizens of what needs to be done. The planner is simply providing information about the plan to those who are likely to be affected without meaningfully seeking their input. This type of token participation is implemented to pacify and inform the public for what is about to transpire, and not necessarily to involve them in any meaningful way in the process of decision-making. In some cases, it may take on some of the characteristics of consultation but, for the most part, the social planner rarely if ever carries the consultation process to its proper conclusion, in which citizens provide meaningful input and potentially change the nature of the relationship between those with power and those without, or where they can affect the outcome of the proposal.

What Rothman calls locality development is often thought of in wider circles as community development. It places the community in question at center-stage in the planning exercise, rather than giving that status to the outcome of the discussion, or the plan itself. This represents a major shift in focus from the approach entailed in social planning. This shift moves away from a focus on product creation to empowering local communities through the building of individual and collective capacities. Arnstein's notions of consultation and partnership between the planning agent and those involved in the process are central to this approach.

Finally, the social action model in Rothman's scheme emphasizes the importance of the marginalized and disadvantaged members of society taking control of the planning process. Whether power is delegated to this group by someone in authority, or actively taken by them, the location of social power is critical to this approach.

Figure 5.1 links these separate theoretical constructs into a system connecting all of the approaches together into a coherent system. The relationship between the various theories, rather than any single theory on its own, confers particular power to this perspective. It is often when planners acting according to a particular planning approach offer citizens an incompatible participation process that the planning exercise runs into difficulty, and has the potential to break down completely. If, for example, a representative of a government agency which embraces the social reform model of development – within tourism or elsewhere – suggests to participants in the process that they will have control of the decisions leading to the final outcome of the plan, they are offering an incompatible participation strategy given the fundamental orientation of the foundational theoretical approach established initially. As a consequence, when the government agency makes decisions which are contrary to the ideas expressed by the involved groups of citizens, feelings of frustration and a sense of betrayal may ensue, severely damaging the prospects for the success of the plan, as well as the relationships between the parties involved in it.

In essence, Figure 5.1 provides three streams leading to two distinct processes of change. The first is managed change, which derives from social reform and policy analysis, and utilizes the citizen participation approaches of manipulation, therapy, informing, and a truncated form of consultation. To offer any other form of citizen participation strategy would be disingenuous given the top-down and tightly controlled features of the social reform and policy analysis models. The goal of these approaches is to produce a tightly controlled, top-down planning process, based on such practices as market analysis which leads to the implementation of decisions which are made by those in charge. The legitimacy of these approaches which is often argued by those in power is that community officials are put there through a democratic voting process for the purpose of making such decisions and, therefore, only a limited amount of citizen participation is needed to inform the public on what is to unfold. Those in power would argue that this is the essence of the democratic process. The planning exercise focuses solely on the end-product and does not concern itself with issues of process other than getting the agenda of those in power implemented and the job done. It is not concerned with instituting a highly participatory process or in designing an approach which transfers power from the elite to the majority of the community. This approach is commonly found in tourism development throughout the world. Those in charge of the process are often government officials, but are most likely to be entrepreneurs and large trans-national corporations as well.

In addition to the first set of processes found on the extreme right of Figure 5.1, which are essentially designed to manage change, the second set of processes is to stimulate change. The planner is not in control of these processes but acts as a facilitator, stimulating change but not responsible for its fundamental orientation or outcome. The various strategies of participation in this section of the model include full consultation, placation and partnership. Also in the approach of stimulating change, the possibilities of elites delegating power to citizens or citizens taking control of the process are now possibilities. Cases where control resides exclusively in the hands the community are rare in number, particularly where tourism is concerned. *Visiting Your Future: A Community's Guide to Planning Tourism* (Reid, Mair, George & Taylor, 2001) is an example of a self-help manual offered to communities who have some idea about taking control of a tourism development project. The application of such processes allows for a wide range of possible outcomes, and whether or not they lead to true delegated power or control varies between communities who have implemented them. Whether or not the objective of absolute citizen control in tourism enterprises is desirable is much contested, and will form part of the debate in this book.

Figure 5.1 connects the various theories horizontally by means of connecting arrows, which are meant to suggest that certain aspects of each theory connect best with specific parts of other theories. When planning fails, it is often because certain aspects of theories don't work well with features of other theories. It is important to match theoretical frameworks which work well together, and not to cross impossible philosophical and ideological barriers. For example, it is dangerous to suggest to community members that they can expect to control a tourism planning process that is designed according to the approaches embodied in the social reform or policy analysis models whose outcomes are determined through other methods like input-output analysis or marketing. This would be promising a citizen participation strategy which does not agree with the decision-making methods of those who control the process. However, given the emotional appeal of the ideas contained in the notion of full citizen participation, citizen control is often promised but not implemented in the final decision-making process.

A final word needs to be said about combining the approaches which are outlined in Figure 5.1. As the phases of any given project change, the approach to planning and decision-making may also need to change. It is not unlikely that the shifting situation may demand movement throughout Friedmann's typology thereby dictating different implementation and participation strategies which correspond to the change in overarching theory. What is important is that continual diagnosis of the situation be constant throughout the project and that the planner is sufficiently skilled to make the appropriate changes in approach as dictated by the shifting dynamics and situational requirements. Any shift in dynamics and hence approach, needs to be communicated to all those involved in the process. Making changes in approach is consistent with the notion of 'contingent' leadership referred to earlier in this chapter.

GENERAL ORGANIZATIONAL STRATEGIES

While all of the approaches to planning are legitimate in the appropriate circumstances, I would argue that too many planning projects are completed using the social reform or policy analysis approaches, without due consideration being given to bottom-up strategies which may often be more suited to the circumstances at hand. It is the contention of this book that most tourism projects of a local nature call for the application of the social learning or social mobilization approaches outlined in Figure 5.1 at some point in the process. The fact that many such projects do not adopt these approaches may partially explain why so many of them end in failure, or at least encounter considerable resistance from community members and other stakeholders in the process. Such circumstances may even produce rare cases in which a radical planning approach is appropriate. However, this would only be suitable where a tourism development was creating intolerable living conditions for the local citizens, or negatively affecting the environment in an extreme way. As mentioned at the end of the last section, what must also be constantly kept in mind is that situations change, and the tourism planner will therefore need to move from one theoretical model to another within a given project. A fatal mistake is to adopt a particular approach and maintain it throughout the course of the planning project while the situation, or the people involved in the process, change. The tourism planner must continue to monitor and diagnose the dynamics of the process and be ready to move between theories when the situation warrants that type of movement.

In addition to the theoretical approaches to planning outlined above, an overarching strategy must be created in keeping with the spirit of the planning theory stream selected. Tourism planning has relied mainly on the social reform and policy analysis models of planning and, therefore, many planning process models have been created (Innskeep, 1991; Mill & Morrison, 1985) which give expression to these constructs. Models which can be used to implement the social learning and social mobilization approaches to planning, which provide the focus of this book, have remained less well-defined. Reid, Fuller, Haywood and Bryden (1993) have created such a model which, in turn, has been employed as the organizing framework for the case studies outlined in Chapter 7. Figure 5.2 provides a conceptual model of that strategy.

The main objective of this approach is to interrupt the normal course of events characteristic of the entrepreneurial approach to tourism development, which moves through the first two stages represented in Figure 5.2 and then immediately to the fourth, which is shown as the organizational structure and product development

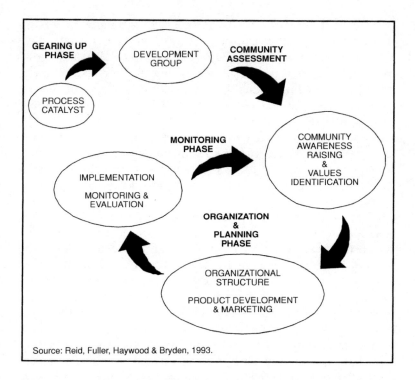

Source: Reid, Fuller, Haywood & Bryden, 1993.

Figure 5.2 Community Development Tourism Planning Strategy

and marketing stage in the diagram. The third stage focuses attention on involving stakeholders in the process, not just as a tokenistic exercise but in a real and constructive manner. It is when this stage is missed completely, or glossed over, that the seeds of discontent, and eventually resistance to future development, are sown.

The third stage represented in Figure 5.2 relies heavily on Arnstein's concept of citizen delegated power and control and Aria's and Rocha's ideas about empowerment (see Chapter 3). Certainly, the third stage is more important to the social learning and social mobilization approaches outlined by Friedmann, than to the social reform or policy analysis approaches. The implementation of this part of the overall structure of the planning process requires great skill in the subject areas of community development and group facilitation. The implementation of this stage of the process demands time and energy in organizing the community to take charge of the process.

In many tourism destinations there are generally two major interest groups in the planning process. The first is what I have termed the supplier of the product or destination – often an international hotelier or a company specializing in the construction of hotels, or related infrastructure such as airlines. Also representing the supplier are national governments, who can facilitate or inhibit the proposed development.

The second actor in the system is the consumer, who is represented by travel agents advertising and selling destination packages. They have great influence in the system and are often guided by what they believe consumers want and need, in turn producing profits for the investor.

What is often missing in this system is any thought given to what I call the producer of the product – namely the environment or the culture that is visited. Rarely, if ever, is the producer included in the planning process, unless the product is artificial – as in the case of Disneyland, for example – and created by means of large-scale capitalization. But the many people living in traditional societies adjacent to national parks and game reserves throughout the world are not considered by the two major – and often foreign – actors in the system as having a substantive interest and, therefore, a legitimate voice in the decision-making process. Often, local communities are assumed to be represented by their national governments, but, as we have seen, national governments have their own agenda, usually having to do with earning foreign exchange in order to pay down debt held by foreign banks, but not necessarily related to issues like regional development and income generation at the local level. All too often, national governments are too eager to sell off local culture and the environment cheaply, because they do not themselves see the value in it, or feel they have any alternative because of their drastic need for foreign currency in order to keep their commitments towards the payment of foreign loans. The community therefore needs to speak for itself, and environmentalists need to be recognized as a surrogate voice for the environment, which obviously cannot speak on its own behalf. This process depends on highly-developed group facilitation skills, and focuses on raising awareness of local conditions and issues, as well as on developing greater social interaction, aside from the physical outcome of the planning process. First, building functional capacity in the community through participation is a key goal of the process. Skills should be developed which will be useful in future projects, whether related to tourism or not. Building social, political and entrepreneurial capacity in the community encourages them to take charge of their own development, and not to rely on government agencies or transnational corporations for direction and control. While governments and outside corporations are likely to be involved with development issues at the local and regional level, they must support rather than control local development itself. According to Freire (1990) learning occurs best when it is directed at concrete problem-solving. People will learn social and entrepreneurial skills most effectively if they can see some short-term advantages, as well as the long-term benefits. Communities will contribute and take charge of their development if it is clear that the ownership of the eventual tourism project will remain in their hands, and that they will benefit from it. The project must be based on a comprehensive vision of the future, and on both the long- and short-term objectives of the community, but implementation of the vision must be accomplished in incremental steps. Frustration will soon set in if these steps are too large, and failure to accomplish part of a plan may sabotage the entire process. Equally, the steps must be sufficiently small to assure success but not so small that they do not seem to make significant progress towards the overall goal. Finally, the community must have access to a variety of resources in order to implement their goal; these may include development funds to assist them with their tourism project. It is important for governments not to dictate the conditions of the tourism project or to micro-manage the plan, but simply to support the ingenuity and resourcefulness of the community. See Figure 5.3 for a graphic illustration of this relationship.

It is a simple matter, however, to say that the process should be as inclusive as possible; it must also be remembered that the community is not a single entity, but is composed of a number of distinct groups with divergent interests. The antagonisms often found in tourism communities are not simply dichotomous, but multi-faceted, and the product of many competing interests.

Individuals have varying levels of skill in tackling such a community development process. Often, communities do not already have an inclusive decision-making process in place. As a consequence, they are forced to rely exclusively on the official local political system for all decisions that affect their day-to-day lives. When this total reliance on the formal decision-making system has not worked well for them in the past community members and other stakeholders may become cynical, and lack trust in the official

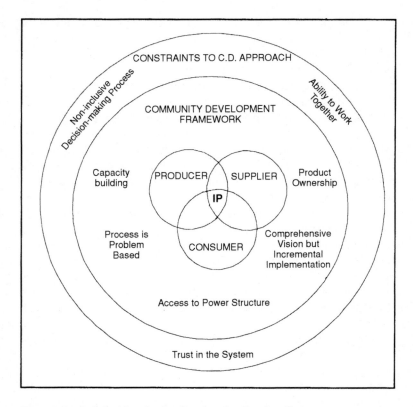

Figure 5.3   Stakeholders in the Community Tourism System

system. Embarking on a path of developing an inclusive process is a viable alternative to this type of system. However it is also time consuming and requires great quantities of leadership. Tourism planners must therefore be versed in adult education and group facilitation theory and practice, and understand how to develop cultural specific strategies so that communities can engage effectively in community development processes. There is nothing more frustrating to community members and planners alike than a community development process that fails because of the lack of process skill or disregard for the needs of the population the plan is supposed to serve.

As a result of structural adjustment programs in the developing world, and economic restructuring in the developed world, we are witness to the 'downsizing' of national government, and its withdrawal from the development process. While this may in some circles be seen to have certain advantages in the long term, it can leave communities adrift and open to exploitation by corporations. Prevailing ideologies suggest that less government regulation and greater dependence on the private sector produce better results in both the long and short term. While the evidence to support this position is lacking, its premature implementation seems to have created a vacuum in many areas of development. This is particularly evident in areas such as worker training – a critical factor for development, particularly in LDCs. There is a natural role for government here, whether it is through funding NGOs to do this work on their behalf or for government ministries and agencies to do it themselves.

In traditional societies, training is not a simple or quick process. The development of tourism often implies a transition from subsistence agriculture to an economy that is dependent solely on monetary transactions. This transition is not just technical, but often involves a complete change of culture. Some argue that this huge change is tantamount to producing cultural genocide, but it must be remembered that cultures are continually transforming, often as a result of Western influences infiltrating the most remote corners of the world through new technology and relentless media activity. But this transition must be planned so as not to have an overbearing effect on traditional societies. In fact, many traditional cultural traits are often important for a tourism project. A community project will perhaps need to encourage subsistence agriculture alongside the tourism project, and the two activities, which might initially appear to be incompatible, may be combined in a holistic and systematic way to the mutual benefit of those involved. But the transition from one way of approaching the world to another involves education – not only in the development of specific tourism related skills, but also in general skills such as reading, writing and numeracy.

Guests are generally asked to respect and learn from the culture they are visiting, but the same must apply to the host society if it expects to be successful in the tourism industry. Some of the practices of traditional societies can be quite foreign and frightening to Westerners, and may be avoided by guests. There is nothing more daunting for a lone Western traveler than being surrounded by hundreds of Maasai women trying to sell their trinkets. Such incidents also highlight the need for the community to organize itself efficiently in order to maximize profits and reduce the effort

and time expended. If left to national governments or foreign entrepreneurs, the tourism planning process not only tends to exclude
other community interests, but little is done to gear up the
community to be active participants in the process. I would argue
that community members should not only be participants in the
planning stage, but should also control the process and outcome of
tourism development; it is, after all, their lives that will be most
affected by it. In order to fulfill that role, the community must be
highly organized. National governments also have a role to play, as
well as NGOs – particularly foreign NGOs. Community organization
has traditionally been overlooked by all actors in the system – even
in cases where the community is asked to participate.

COMMUNITY ORGANIZATION AND LEADERSHIP

Much of this discussion relates to the implementation of Figure 5.2.
The first three stages represented in Figure 5.2 depend on community
organization. The model begins with the identification and development of a person or group of people who will provide leadership to
the project. As suggested in Reid, Mair, George and Taylor,

> people who are considered catalysts possess essentially three char-
> acteristics. They are usually people who are charismatic, motivated,
> and are dedicated to a particular idea or project. As important as
> these characteristics are, they are not sufficient in themselves to get
> the job done. In fact, if they are found in over abundance, they
> may even inhibit the project.
>
> (Reid et al., 2001: 15)

All too often, people tend to become involved in tourism projects in
pursuit of a specific business agenda. Any such point of view must
be contained within the larger community interest, and not become
the sole driving force of a tourism project. There are other skills and
overarching perspectives which are particularly important – chiefly,
perhaps, a broad perspective, which takes on board the development
of the community as a whole, rather than in relation solely to
tourism. An individual who has historically displayed consistent
interest in the overall welfare of the community may be a better
choice to lead this process than someone who may not posses this
wider viewpoint but is engaged in the tourism industry. The selection
of this former type of person will ensure a wide-ranging discussion

takes place, rather than a narrow focus being taken on a specific and perhaps self-serving objective. This selection of a person to lead the planning process is critical to its overall success. Individual skills in group facilitation and conflict resolution are more valuable at this stage than a complete understanding of the intricacies of tourism development as such. Expert knowledge of the various technical subjects relevant to tourism planning can be exploited at appropriate points along the way, but it is not necessary for people possessing that knowledge to lead the entire process. Reid et al. describe more fully the leadership role:

> The catalyst must also be a good leader. Often a good leader displays the ability to listen to others and is able to orchestrate the views of many into a single concept. This type of facilitation takes skills in mediation and compromise. A good leader in a project such as this is a person who is genuinely interested in the quality of life in the community and is dedicated to identifying and implementing processes which will help members to determine what that looks like.
>
> (Reid et al., 2001: 15)

This person will also need to be able to command the trust and respect of the majority of community members. It is highly unlikely that such a person possessing all of these attributes could be readily found in most circumstances, but there are usually individuals with impeccable reputations who are recognized as natural leaders in their community. These people can inspire and motivate others, and when their name is attached to a project people in the community take their call to participation seriously. Particularly in modern societies, people are often inundated with calls for input into many planning exercises. Consequently, many citizens have become skeptical about the sincerity of these processes, and so it is doubly important for a leader of a tourism planning process to be seen as a person of integrity within the community concerned. In these circumstances, it can perhaps be hoped that when a call for participation is made, the community will respond *en masse*.

As Reid et al. point out, not every community will contain individuals who possess the necessary attributes for this role. If that is the case, then outside assistance may be required. If an outsider is needed because of the lack of a specific skill in the community it is important to have that person partnered with a community member so as to pass on that skill. This process is an example of the capacity building which is so vital to the community development process. Given that planning is not a linear process but is cyclical in nature, these skills will be important in the long term, and must become part of the inventory of skills within the community. An adapted version of this method for determining the appropriate leadership for a project is (see Reid et al., 2001: 16) presented below:

Rate the candidate on each of the items below on a 1 to 5 scale (1 is low and 5 is high). Have we forgotten any characteristics that you think are important? Feel free to write them in and use them in your ranking. This exercise can be completed individually or with a group of people.

Characteristics	Rating 1 to 5
1. Is a highly motivated person	
2. Has a wide ranging perspective on community issues	
3. Is widely trusted and respected in the community	
4. Has a wide range of experience on programs of a social, environmental and economic nature	
5. Has demonstrated ability to listen to others and act on their suggestions	
6. Has ability to facilitate large groups	
7. Possesses a good balance between task and process skills	
8. Does not appear to have his or her own agenda or axe to grind	
9. Is willing to share leadership when clearly warranted	
10. Has demonstrated that he or she can get the job done	
Total	

Additional rows may be added to this table in order to include other skills which particular communities might deem important. It is worth pointing out that communities are unique entities, and as such require skills and abilities peculiar to their circumstances. A cookie-cutter approach to planning and development will not suffice, and the recognition of each community's uniqueness is necessary on the part of all parties involved. Because one solution works in one situation does not necessarily mean it will work in another. Too often in the past, planners have employed whatever methods worked well in one community for the process in another, and wondered why it did not achieve the same success. While we may have a natural tendency to think in generic terms, the fundamental uniqueness of a community must be a principle guiding the tourism planning process.

Once the appropriate catalyst is in place, it is necessary to start to build the planning and development group as suggested in the second bubble in Figure 5.2 who will begin to provide some leadership to the eventual planning process. This body is usually comprised of individuals who have technical expertise and, perhaps a vested interest in the eventual products of the plan. That said, it is still important to include individuals on this body who have other interests – particularly what might be defined as community interests. Generally speaking, the makeup of this group must mirror that of the community in its interests. It is important to consider such areas as gender, age, and the background of the potential candidates for this important function. Diverse and equal demographic representation of the community must be the criterion on which selections to this committee are made. Again, not only will this influence the overall work of the community, but it will also speak to the legitimacy of the process itself. The goal should be to ensure that the community buys into both the process and the tourism project, so that antagonism and resistance do not develop and place the development in jeopardy. As a consequence of this goal, this part of the planning process cannot be rushed in order to get on with product development, which forms the fourth stage of the tourism development process.

Perhaps the most crucial of the stages of the community tourism planning process represented in Figure 5.2 is the third, which is intended to see the raising of community awareness about the issues of tourism development and the building of organization to deal with those potential changes. The outcome of the third stage in this process is a public which is engaged in planning for tourism that will construct and determine the essence of the final product. This stage guarantees that the future tourism project is not a destination already conceived, but a place that is created first in the mind and then by hard work. What we too often hear today from business leaders and politicians is that the die is cast, and our only role as citizens is to get on board and help achieve that pre-determined goal. Some planners reject that single view of the world and dedicate themselves to identifying alternative futures, and then creating the means to achieve the most desirable among them. In fact, this is the sole function of the planning process as designed in Figure 5.2. As Reid et al. suggest, it is the responsibility of the development group and the catalyst to carry that philosophy to the general public and get them to buy into the general idea. This can be done in at least two ways. First, it must develop a strategy to actively communicate the idea of the need for this type of inclusive planning to community members. Second, the development group needs to recruit additional people to become involved and they, in turn, will have to recruit others for the same purpose. The goal here is to maximize participation so that all voices in the community can be heard.

The pulling together of the community needs to be completed in a slow and methodical way; simply calling a public meeting will not do. Because participation processes of this type may have led to nothing in the past except frustration with the process, there is some skepticism on the part of the public to this call for involvement. So, large scale single community forums are to be avoided in the early stages of the process and until confidence in the system is gained. Neighborhood and small group meetings are an appropriate method to begin the process. They require more time and energy, but in the long run produce better results, while they are also in keeping with the focus and goals of the social learning model. This process should focus on gearing up the population to participate in what planners call the 'exercise of the community visioning', outlined in more detail elsewhere in this book, rather than on the substantive issues of tourism development. It is likely to be difficult, however, to keep participants from immediately airing their more general sentiments on tourism or other matters, particularly if they have strong feelings or have previously been involved in a negative process. But the goal of this neighborhood or small group initiative is to arrive at an organizational structure and to create a momentum so that a large participation in the community visioning exercise which comes later in the process, will be assured.

In addition to engendering participation, the second goal of small group and neighborhood meetings is to assist citizens to begin to think about the issues surrounding tourism development in their community. They need to begin to think about the values which require protection, and the customs which they are willing to share with the outside world. It is important to remember that public participation is not a single event. It is a series of events or, perhaps put more accurately, it is continual involvement in the affairs of the community over the long term. The stage of the raising of community awareness represented in Figure 5.2 is expressed as one stage in a linear process, but it would be more accurate to represent it as one aspect of an effort to build ongoing citizen participation in every stage of the process. This aspect of citizen participation is the essence of democracy itself.

6 The Normative View of Tourism Planning

INTRODUCTION

The community development approach to tourism planning advocated in this text relies on theories, methods, and techniques which result from interpretivistic as well as positivistic science; that is, on data which are phenomenological and normative in nature, as well as purely empirical. This chapter stresses the need for the comprehensive collection of baseline data against which the impacts of tourism over time can be measured. It also reviews the literature on the economic, socio-cultural and environmental impacts of tourism development. Theories are identified from the various disciplines relevant to tourism development. The research methods required to support tourism planning are also examined, while a planning framework is presented around which impact assessments and other research activities may be pursued.

THE PLANNING FRAMEWORK

Tourism planning has suffered from two fundamental inadequacies. The first is a lack of theoretical literature specific to tourism development. There is little literature which explains and predicts how tourism behavior is altered under various conditions. Moreover, there are even fewer normative theories which specify on what basis tourism planning should proceed in order to accomplish its stated goals of profit maximization while maintaining sustainable communities and environments. In fact, there is little attention given to developing foundational and unifying theory designed to encompass the various disciplines engaged in tourism development, or even ongoing dialogue among the various actors in the system which would lead to such theory. This is particularly the case between leisure theorists and the business schools. Secondly, there is a general lack of implementation theory that can be deployed within tourism planning. What has stood in for foundational and unifying theory is a sole reliance on economic and business concepts. It is important to develop theory which provides perspectives other than the economic, given that tourism development affects the social and environmental conditions of so many people's lives. The general planning theory discussed in Chapter 5 sets out an underlying framework for community tourism planning. This chapter provides the beginnings of the lower-level theory needed to construct and implement community tourism plans inclusive of all points of view within a community, as well as cognizant of the environmental issues inherent in the task of tourism planning.

While basic planning theory outlined earlier provides the overall structure for the main planning approach, lower-level theoretical tools are needed as a framework for implementing tourism planning activity on the ground. Method and technique are critical to tourism development, as they are to other areas of planning. These types of theory provide a technical framework for what is largely a process of community negotiation – dependent on a community's organization and political will. However, even when all of the necessary organizational and human ingredients are in place, a planning structure is required in order to implement the spirit of the overall approach represented in Figure 5.2, taking into account all of the actors in the system as designated in the inner circles of Figure 5.3. This process is presented in Figure 6.1.

The process outlined here utilizes the classical approach to planning, which emphasizes a number of features: the creation of a vision to establish an overall framework for tourism development; the setting of goals and objectives to bring that vision about; the development of programs designed to accomplish the relevant objectives; an evaluation of the feasibility – usually financial – of the proposed project, and if necessary its adaptation or refinement; and the implementation and ongoing monitoring of the project established as a result of the planning and decision-making process. This process is not much different from those found in the social reform and policy analysis planning strategies outlined in the Chapter 5. What are different however, are the data gathering and analysis procedures which provide information on which this process depends for making critical decisions about the tourism system and its relation to the community and environment. In addition, a major departure from the social reform and policy analysis approach is found in relation to who controls the process, and to the basis on which decisions are made.

Figure 6.1 suggests that two types of research are required in order to support the planning process. First are the positivistic research

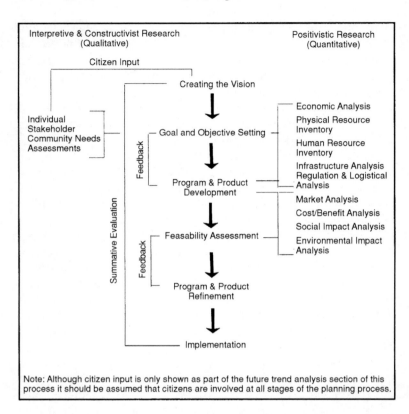

Figure 6.1   Community Tourism Product Development Planning Process

activities, involving the collection and analysis of quantified data. These activities are normally found in the more traditional, top-down approaches to planning. However, the role that data collection and analysis play in decision-making here is quite different. These data are used to support the decisions made by the actors in the system during the part of the process designed to assess the needs of the community and the state of the environment. Too often the analysis of these data and the information that analysis produces are assigned too much power. It is as if the actors in the system are looking for some force outside of their decision-making responsibilities to make the difficult decisions on their behalf when, in fact, these decisions belong in the political realm. Unique to the social learning and mobilization strategies are the interpretive and collectivist approaches to data collection, which focus on understanding the needs and aspirations of those who will be most affected by the tourism plan and subsequent development. Not only are data collected and analyzed to support these approaches, but the results drawn from these data drive the planning solutions that are developed. The changed nature of the relationship between quantitative and qualitative data and their use in the development of a plan produces a change in the locus of power from the expert to the citizen and the local community.

While both qualitative and quantitative data are useful to the planning process, the empirical, quantitative data are often overly relied upon by decision-makers to influence the goals and objectives of the project or determine the nature of the tourism products in the social reform and policy analysis approaches. They should be used to merely inform the collective wisdom of those involved in the interpretive and constructivist activities as outlined on the left side of Figure 6.1, who, in the end, will select the appropriate path to follow, relying on some parts of that analysis more than on others. This shift in emphasis also demands different skills and methods on the part of the facilitator of the process. Instead of the tourism planner possessing a set of research skills specific to a certain discipline – hospitality or food science, for example – the role of the planner is to orchestrate the various disciplines in the construction of the development as a whole. For example, a development proposal may unearth social, economic or environmental issues which need to be analyzed as part of the planning exercise. The tourism planner will assist the community and other stakeholders in the process to identify the important issues to be addressed, then engage the appropriate disciplines to undertake data collection and analysis in relation to those issues. Finally, the planner will endeavor to enable the community and the professionals involved in the process to determine the meaning of that analysis, and to decide how it will inform the plan and subsequent development. Clearly, the planner in this instance acts as a process facilitator, rather than deploying specialist knowledge in any given tourism area. His or her role is to assist people in determining the problems to be addressed, helping them gather information which will clarify the intricacies of those issues, and facilitating their resolution in the plan. The planner is like the conductor of an orchestra, in that he or she ensures that all actors within the process work in a coordinated fashion – making music out of what otherwise would be just noise.

RESEARCH METHODS

There are a number of research instruments, available both to the tourism planner and to communities interested in tourism development that could help to inform the planning process outlined in Figure 6.1. These methods will be explored under the headings of 'Individual and Community Needs Assessment' and 'Positivistic Research', as indicated by Figure 6.1.

INDIVIDUAL AND COMMUNITY NEEDS ASSESSMENT

In the schema presented in this text, tourism development rests on the fundamental principles of individual and community satisfaction. In order to accomplish these goals, individual and community needs must be identified and expressed in both the plan and the resulting tourism project. How this is to be achieved will be outlined in this section.

In the manual, *Visiting Your Future: A Community Guide to Planning Rural Tourism* (Reid, Mair, George & Taylor, 2001) the authors outline a number of exercises which can help a community to identify its collective vision and goals, and the strategies and actions necessary to realize them. Perhaps the greatest single difficulty in implementing those actions is not the lack of tools available, but the absence of the necessary capabilities and leadership in the community to administer and implement them. Leadership, in addition to the other so-called soft skills, is required at the community level on a continuous basis if the process is to begin smoothly and continue effectively. Skills such as evaluation, group work and group dynamics, conflict resolution, leadership, in addition to those associated with the general design and implementation of research protocols are examples of community capacities which need to be cultivated and maintained. It is often thought that leaders are born and not made, but recent research (Hersey, 1984) suggests that this is not the case, and that direct action on this front can ensure that appropriate leadership is available when required. Leadership is often viewed as contingent. Different actors will provide leadership in different situations, and absolute leadership is therefore not allocated solely to one person. For the purposes of a tourism project, this requires an abundance of leadership skills within a community if that project is to be truly participatory and democratic in nature.

Moreover, many community citizens have become cynical about community planning processes which have been instituted in the past, and which, because of the many problems outlined earlier in this book, have often been characterized by frustration, leading to failure. Often, tourism planners and community leaders also make the mistake of believing that communities are sufficiently organized to undertake such activities. All too often, there is a small elite group within a community which is involved in many public discussions, and it becomes too easy to rely disproportionately on this small and usually well organized group for input into the tourism planning process. An opportunity is thus lost to cast the net wider, to a more representative fraction of the total population. Citizen participation is an ongoing process, not a single event, and participants must be continually encouraged to associate with the planning process over the long term. Effective participation may also require training and education in its processes.

Planners have often fallen into the trap of conducting citizen consultation and participation in the form of a single public meeting to discuss the issues at hand. When those public meetings are poorly attended, it is often erroneously thought that the public is not interested in the discussion and the planner should look elsewhere for other explanations. Worse still, a lack of attendance is interpreted to mean that citizens are giving their tacit approval to any proposal. More often than not, this is far from being the case, and realization of that fact is only arrived at after many years of development, when resistance begins to show itself in covert ways, if not in organized overt opposition. The amelioration of many of the consequences of development then becomes the focus for planners, when much of this might have been avoided in the first instance by paying greater attention to the third stage represented in Figure 5.2.

Put at its simplest, community members need to be asked to think about what it is that they do and do not like about living in their current surroundings, and what developments they would like to see over the next five to ten years to enhance their life conditions. There are many techniques which can be employed to create a community vision. Communities that I have worked with quite enjoy the exercise of examining the important events in the community's past by drawing a representation of those events on newsprint stuck to the walls of the meeting room. This exercise can be continued by drawing the new spaces and buildings required to satisfy their future needs. Community values which need to be preserved can be written down on the same sheets as the drawings, after these have been fleshed out by the facilitator during the drawing exercise. This technique not only includes the identification of buildings and the spatial environment, but also that of community values and psychological needs.

The community self-assessment instrument outlined by Reid, Mair George and Taylor, (2001) provides a powerful tool for gauging the public's attitude towards the influx of visitors, and the other impacts of tourism (see Table 6.1). While it is presented here in simple statement form a five-point scale (see Golden case study in Chapter 7) can be added to each statement to provide a scoring mechanism. This questionnaire was tested in several communities during its development, and the respondents reacted favorably to the quantification of the statements. Scaling also provided the researchers with the opportunity to calculate an overall 'readiness for development' score for each community under examination.

Table 6.1   Tourism Self-assessment Questionnaire

---

1. There is a person or small group of people in the community who is readily identifiable and gives leadership to a tourism and community planning process.
2. Tourism plays a predominant role in the economic life of the community.
3. There is need for the community to be better organized to meet any tourism development needs that may arise.
4. Tourism is a well developed industry with a long but rocky history in our community.
5. We do not have a clear process for solving problems as they arise.
6. Tourism development is out of control and too dominant in our community.
7. The residents do not want to see any more tourism development take place in our community.
8. The residents and business community are not in agreement about how tourism should develop in the future.
9. Everyone in the community needs to be involved in tourism development; it should not just be left to the business community.
10. Most residents would be willing to attend a community meeting to discuss an important tourism issue.
11. If tourism proposals are developed by certain people in the community, they are automatically opposed by others.
12. Everyone is willing to pitch in and help when we have a tourism event.

Source: Reid, Mair, George and Taylor (2001).

While the statements in this instrument can be scaled to provide a quantitative indication of what the respondents feel about tourism development in their community, the issues themselves form a basis for community discussion on the state of tourism, and do not need to be scored in order to be effective. Where this instrument has been used with communities, responses indicate that most participants enjoy the exercise and like to compare scores between individual group members. Adding the scores provides a total value for each respondent. This in itself provides a basis for comparison which would not exist if the questionnaire was not scored. Moreover, a representative sample of the community can be polled each year in order to determine whether movement on the scale indicates improvement or deterioration of the system due to tourism.

The most important feature of this process is that group members hear a variety of different perspectives, brought to the discussion by their fellow citizens. Ideally, they will gain a wider interest in the history of the community, and a deeper respect for the aspirations of their fellow participants. During the collective drawing of the history of the community, participants are asked to include events which they feel were important to the development of their community. This exercise requires participants to recall history, including past debates over development issues, and it thus provides a context for the rest of the tourism planning exercise.

Only after this wider discussion has taken place are participants in the forum encouraged to think about tourism development, and resulting proposals must therefore respect outcomes of previous discussions. In many of the communities where this method has been used, participants were asked to rank their priorities for development by sticking colored dots to the proposals of their choice. Red dots indicated that a particular activity or development should be stopped to protect the community; green dots indicated that the project should be developed to increase its presence in the community; blue dots indicated that the feature should be protected and maintained at all costs. This voting system was not rigid, and once the first round of voting had been completed, discussion ensued with the purpose of reaching collective agreement. Once this had been achieved, strategies were developed to implement the agreed upon proposals. Workshop participants then chose which of the issues they wished to work on over the short term.

This exercise should be concluded with the actions and strategies being mapped out by means of critical path. Figure 6.2 provides a simplified example.

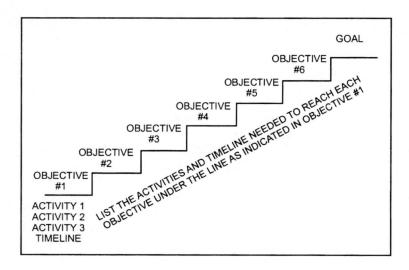

Figure 6.2   Critical Path Format

This is just one example of the many techniques that may be used to flesh out the fundamental components of the social, physical, psychological and economic perspectives of a community that is considering tourism development. The range of possible methods is limited only by the tourism planner's imagination. What is critical here is to recognize that planning for community tourism development is a process of community organization, dealing fundamentally with the aspirations and fears of the residents, who are the potential hosts for any development which may take place. The effort put into helping the community to identify those issues at an early stage in the process, rather than having to deal with the neglect of those concerns after development has begun, will provide huge dividends to all concerned. However, this process may be seen by some as time-consuming, and as an interference with the basic objectives of the entrepreneurs and their investors who will eventually take the financial risks for the project. All of this is true, but it is also true that, if sufficient attention is paid to these issues in the first place, much less time and effort will be spent dealing with problems which might never have arisen.

While much of the discussion so far has focused on process, there is also a need to get the results of this discussion on paper in a logical format. Communities are comfortable with discussing the problems encountered in the environment but less good in analyzing the nuances of those issues and in designing resolutions to those problems. It is important to move to these stages of the process, and even more important to record this discussion, including any decisions that are made which need to be implemented and then monitored over time for their effectiveness. The community can begin to incorporate these considerations into a conceptual and strategic plan immediately. This will not only facilitate the implementation of the steps outlined in the critical path framework; it will also provide a record of the history of the process as it unfolds over time. The plan can also contain any data which may be relevant to future planning activities – particularly as the actors in the process change over time. The objective here is to place on record what everyone has agreed to during the process. This will prove invaluable when future discussions emerge on issues which were initially resolved and may now need to be reconsidered because of changes in the environment. While many decisions may need to be revisited in the future it is important to understand the thinking which originally led to those decisions in the first instance.

The content of the plan includes: an introduction outlining the history of the community and the significant features of the area being planned; the articulated vision that results from the community forums described above and the subsequent goals and objectives of the plan; a statement of the strengths and weaknesses of the community as it relates to tourism development (some would also include opportunities and threats); an inventory of human and physical assets of the community; a section on the potential market, for which a separate document may be developed outlining an advertising and marketing strategy; the action steps which must be taken in order to accomplish the goals of the plan; the organizational structure for implementing these activities; and a critical path for implementing the plan. These stages of the planning process are described in more detail in Chapter 8. What is worth reiterating is that all of this information needs to be recorded, so that the rationale for the decisions made is not lost over time.

ECONOMIC, SOCIAL AND ENVIRONMENTAL RESEARCH

Research activity that can provide background and context for the foregoing discussion is an integral part of the planning process. The important categories of quantitative research are shown on the right hand side of Figure 6.1. Much of this research will be expert-driven, since very few people have sufficient expertise in each of the fields listed. What is important for the tourism planner is to have an overall concept of what is contained in each of the categories listed, and the ability to explain their significance to other participants in the process. The results of this research are not intended to drive the plan, but simply to provide information to those deliberating on the categories represented on the middle and left side of Figure 6.1 with background information and analysis that will help them to make informed decisions and select appropriate priorities. The remaining part of this section will outline the data required to satisfy the analysis categories listed on the right side of Figure 6.1.

ECONOMIC ANALYSIS

Fundamental to the economic analysis on which tourism rests is the analysis of supply and demand. Both entrepreneurs and public officials, investing either their own or the public's money, need to know the level of demand for the activity their project is directed towards. This is not a straightforward question to answer. The location quotient, which measures the locality's economic diversification against the economic structure of the region/country or province – referred to as the reference group – (see Reid, 1998), gives the researcher an idea in what economic sectors the community is over- or under-weighted in comparison to their reference group. In most cases, employment within a given sector is the variable examined in the location quotient equation. The location quotient expresses the relative specialization and concentration of labor in specific sectors of the local economy. This technique is used to estimate demand within a particular sector – tourism, for our purposes. Employment in tourism is measured against total employment at the regional or national level. The location quotient is a ratio that compares a particular economic activity's share of the local economy with the same activity's share of the national or regional economy. This is different from estimating shares by using a mean score, in that the location quotient normalizes these data so that large and small populations become comparable. The formula for completing a location quotient is set out below:

$$(\text{sect. emp/tot emp})/(\text{ref sect emp/ref tot emp})$$

where:

sect emp = local economy sectoral employment;
tot emp = total employment in the local economy;
ref sect emp = reference economy sectoral employment;
ref tot emp = total employment in the reference economy.

Location quotients greater than one indicate comparative specialization, meaning an area is more specialized than the reference economy in that particular sector. A location quotient of less than one, conversely, means that the community's tourism sector is less specialized than the reference sectors. If the location quotient of the area is equal to one, then that economy's share of the tourism sector would be equal to the reference (provincial or county economy in the example shown below) or perhaps the national economy. Location quotients were calculated by the researchers for Wellington County, Ontario, Canada, using 1991 Statistics Canada data. Statistics Canada is a federal government census taking agency providing data on a variety of social sectors including information on the structure of the Canadian economy. Most developed countries possess a comparable set of statistics on which such an analysis may be calculated, but this may not be the case for many LDCs. However, given that there was no tourism data category specifically in the Statistics Canada database, surrogate categories were required to make this measurement. In the Wellington County case, sectors used to approximate tourism data included: (1) the retail trade, (2) accommodation, food and beverage service industries; and (3) other services. After examining the contents of these divisions these categories were used for location quotient calculation in determining tourism activity (see Reid, Lee, Phillips & Duggan, 1995). Table 6.2 sets out the results of this analysis. Pushlinch Township, for example, employed 740 individuals in the tourism sector, while its tourism location quotients were slightly below (0.9) the provincial reference economy, and slightly over (1.02) the county reference.

Once location quotients have been calculated and compared, researchers can then examine how this profile would be likely to change with the introduction of a proposed tourism project. These are basic descriptive statistics of the community or region concerned, and they give the planner a basic structural understanding of the population and economy as things stand. They also provide a baseline data set which can be used to monitor changes in the economy over time for evaluative purposes.

Table 6.2   Location Quotients for Guelph/Wellington County Municipalities in Comparison with County and Provincial Location Quotients

COMMUNITY	EMP 91	PROV LQ	COUNTY LQ
PUSLINCH TWP	740	0.9	1.02
GUELPH TWP	380	0.77	0.88
GUELPH CITY	11,390	0.91	1.04
ERAMOSA TWP	765	0.89	1.01
ERIN TWP	685	0.62	0.71
ERIN VILLAGE	279	0.83	0.89
WEST GARAFRAXA	400	0.88	1.01
NICHOL TWP	520	0.93	1.06
FERGUS TOWN	1,030	0.99	1.13
ELORA VILLAGE	400	0.97	1.1
PILKINGTON TWP	285	0.75	0.86
PEEL TWP	360	0.61	0.69
MARYBOROUGH TWP	240	0.63	0.72
DRAYTON VILLAGE	155	1.08	1.23
MINTO TWP	230	0.64	0.73
CLIFFORD VILLAGE	115	1.23	1.4
HARRISTON TOWN	230	1.07	1.22
PALMERSTON TOWN	290	1.06	1.21
ARTHUR TWP	295	0.81	0.93
MOUNT FOREST TOWN	495	1.01	1.15
ARTHUR VILLAGE	235	0.94	1.07
WEST LUTHER TWP	100	0.55	0.63

Source: Guelph/Wellington Tourism Study Report, by Reid, Lee, Phillips & Duggan (1995).

Note: Communities are listed by geographic location in the county from south to north.

Ontario is divided into tourism regions by the Ontario Provincial Government. Location quotient analysis was used by Reid (1998) to compare these tourism regions using expenditure and employment data. This analysis highlighted those regions, no matter how small, that were more dependent on tourism than the other regions. This information can be used both by entrepreneurs and government agents to direct future investment towards the achievement of policy objectives. Governments may want to stimulate already strong regions further, or to help less-developed regions to catch up. Businesses may want to invest their energies in areas which have already demonstrated strength in the tourism sector or carve out a new niche for themselves where one doesn't exist at present. Location quotient analysis helps planners and entrepreneurs sort out those types of issues.

Demand is often generated in the tourism industry by some geological feature of a region. Many communities exploit local features such as a lake, forest, or mountain by constructing facilities to take advantage of those unique features. Issues such as distance decay, whereby demand is weakened by travel time, affects tourism success. Intervening opportunities – similar facilities or opportunities located between the target facility and the home of the traveler – also affects demand unless entrepreneurs can create a unique experience which differentiates their destination. Profiling demand for similar or complementary activities also gives tourism planners some understanding of the latent demand for their proposals. Research into the economic structure of the target market, so that an estimation of disposable income can be made, is also helpful in determining demand. Having this information allows tourism planners to compare their situation with those similar in the area and will fill in part of the demand picture.

In relation to issues of supply, developers are very good at estimating costs of construction and potential returns on capital. Hoteliers, for example, are able to calculate the occupancy rate required for profitability. However, as we have seen since the World Trade Center tragedy in New York, catastrophic world events can subvert the best economic analyses and projections, based on the finest research. Many of the Caribbean islands have experienced weather-related tragedies of this nature for decades, which have made the estimation of supply and demand very difficult – yet still they survive, and even thrive, today.

Perhaps most relevant to an understanding of the economic significance of a particular development are the issues of economic valuation and impact. Both of these measures are of interest both to planners and decision-makers alike, particularly when the tourism sector is in competition with other industries. Moreover, if planners and decision-makers are involved in selecting from a variety of development proposals, then a comparison between those proposals, in terms of both the value of the resource and the economic impact of each alternative, is important to the decision-making process.

There are three methods of valuation available to the planner of recreation and tourism resources. They are: (1) the contingent valuation method; (2) the travel-cost approach; and (3) the unit-day value technique. Since texts dealing with the economics of recreation are abundant (see Walsh, 1986; Graton and Taylor, 1985; Clawson and Knetch, 1966), only a brief description of these methods will be provided here.

Perhaps the best known and most used method for estimating the value of a resource or activity is the contingent valuation method (CVM). It relies on the collection of data through surveys which ask participants and users (potential or actual) what they are willing to pay for participation in, or preservation of, the relevant activity or resource. It is assumed that the most a respondent is willing to pay is equal to the benefit gained from the resource in question.

Rollins and Wistowsky (1997) used this method in a sophisticated study to determine the benefits to those participating in back-country canoeing in Ontario wilderness parks. They surveyed three sites and over 2,400 respondents, eventually demonstrating that 'canoeists receive substantial benefits (as measured by willingness to pay) at the current level of wilderness use'. (Ibid: 27) Determining precisely how much benefit they received was very helpful, since park administrators were attempting to explain to decision-makers the value of maintaining these parks for canoeing rather than turning them over to competing industries such as mining and forestry.

The other two methods are less used, but are nonetheless available to the tourism planner. First is the travel cost method, which estimates resource value by calculating the out-of-pocket expenses of the traveler and the cost in time of the excursion. It is assumed that, as each increases, the visitor will be able to take advantage of the resource less. This method of valuation is more relevant to the experience than the resource, although it can be said that the smaller number of visits – and hence the less income – a facility may receive reflects its value in terms of tourism and recreation. Certainly, such information would be very useful to entrepreneurs making decisions about where, and what type of facility, to develop.

Finally, the unit-day value approach relies on the judgment of experts to estimate expenditure. Data relating to willingness to pay are used in this process, as in the contingent valuation method. Here, a sample of expenditures is gathered for a given site for one day and then multiplied by the number of days per year on which the site is used. This provides an estimate of the benefits produced by the facility on an annual or longer-term basis.

The contingent valuation method is the most used method in calculating the economic value of a resource within the recreation and tourism sectors. This is especially true when there is competition in natural areas for recreation and tourism against uses such as mining and forestry. Foresters and miners can easily estimate the economic value of a given area. Those wishing to use that resource for tourism and recreation purposes do not have such a direct means of measurement available to them, and must thus rely on 'shadow prices', such as estimates of willingness to pay, in order to make equivalent calculations. However, these calculations will be examined alongside those of competing industries in such situations, so their reliability and accuracy must be ensured.

Walsh (1986:196) outlines

three basic evaluation problems in recreation, namely, to estimate: (1) the benefits of recreation activities at existing sites of given quality; (2) the benefits of recreation activities with changes in the quantity and quality of the resource; and (3) the public benefits from preservation of resource quality.

(Walsh, 1986: 196)

The three methods outlined above for calculating the economic value of a given tourism site are an attempt to overcome these constraints, and provide adequate measures for recreation and tourism purposes. There are certainly other variables and considerations, beyond economics, for valuing recreation amenities. However, there is a heavy onus placed on being able to assign an economic value to recreation and tourism resources, particularly when they are subject to intense competition, both within and beyond the tourism and recreation sectors.

The second economic area important to the tourism planner is the estimation of the economic impact of the given site or activity. The planner's or economist's ability to estimate the total impact of tourist expenditure on the destination site is important here. It should be noted that the beneficiaries of tourism expenditures come in many categories, usually divided into two groups, namely the direct or indirect beneficiaries. The direct or primary beneficiary of the tourist expenditure is the firm or person providing the resource or service; guides, hoteliers and outfitters all come into this category. The indirect or secondary set of beneficiaries includes suppliers or wholesalers of equipment to the primary beneficiary. Indirect benefits are also experienced by those who sell goods such as groceries and household products to tourism workers, although such goods may not necessarily be associated directly with tourism.

It is often difficult to distinguish, among these transactions, between what is directly associated with the tourism industry and what is peripheral to it. As Vaughan, Farr and Slee suggest 'the validity of any measurement process depends on the method of measurement and quality of the data used...'. (Vaughan et al., 2000: 97) Most restaurants in a rural community will cater to tourists and non-tourists alike, and will not separate out the receipts for each group, making an estimation of the specific impact of tourism very difficult. As in the earlier discussion dealing with contingent valuation, estimating impact requires the use of the available data to arrive at approximations. The precision of the data gathered will determine the reliability of any conclusions.

Multiplier analysis is the method most often used by tourism planners and economists to make these estimates, although it is not without its difficulties and detractors. What is required is an estimation of the money spent on tourism in a given site or region. Naturally as this money passes through the economy of a region some of it gets spent outside the region for supplies and other goods and services. The speed with which those receipts drain from the local area and into the outside larger economy is called leakage. Leakage characterizes the travel patterns of currency in the economy which is spent by tourists, and then distributed by those playing host to tourism both inside and outside the local economy, on supplies and other commodities which are not locally produced or available. Eventually, all of the original receipts of tourism businesses and people working in the sector leaks from the local economy to the surrounding larger one. This does not happen instantaneously, of course, but in a number of stages. As a result, tourism receipts are said to circulate in the local economy until they have completely leaked from it, producing a multiplier effect. An estimated multiplier is calculated from the number of times the currency is spent in the local area until all of it is leaked out to the larger economy. Based on that premise economists can estimate that the impact of tourism expenditures as, hypothetically, 2:1 – or whatever the calculation produces – meaning, for every $1.00 spent it has an impact in the economy of $2.00 because of being expended at least once more in the local area, for example. The generation of a specific multiplier is the function of the size of the local economy and its proximity to the regional center.

The second economic criticism of tourism is in the weak forward and backward linkages that it produces – or its failure to produce them at all. Especially in small island states and other LDCs, backward linkages are poor because many of the inputs into the tourism industry are not produced in the host country, but imported – usually from a neighboring, highly-developed industrial economy. Moreover, upper-tier management jobs are occupied by expatriate personnel rather than locals, representing a loss not only in terms of local employment, but also in terms of the development of relevant skills on the part of local people. Similarly, tourism businesses generally fail to develop forward linkages, since they do not tend to stimulate the proliferation of secondary industries – although certain large events and attractions, such as Disney World and the Olympic Games, may provide exceptions to this general pattern by acting as main attractions around which lesser tourism activities and facilities congregate.

The task of the planner using the multiplier method to estimate economic impact is the determination of total spending on tourism in the study area. A study of the economic impact of a trout fishery on the Grand River in Ontario, Canada (Smith, 1997) surveyed a sample of trout fishers on the river to determine their spending patterns while visiting the area. Smith thus estimated a daily spending amount per fisher. From this estimate, he established from community records the number of fishers present over a multi-year period and averaged that multi-year number, in order to create an estimate for an average year eliminating fluctuations due to good and bad years, and then multiplied the daily expenditure data by the average of the annual number of visitors, providing the multiplicand for the study. Next, Smith used a table from an earlier study (Reid and FitzGibbon, 1991) to estimate the multiplier effect for the community under study. Relating the size of the local economy to its geographic proximity to the regional center, this table attempts to calculate the likely speed of leakage of direct and indirect expenditures out of the local economy. Smith's study provided a good estimate of the importance of the trout fishery to the local community and its economy, and has been used by local planners to inform the public and decision-makers about the importance of this tourism destination – and thus of maintaining the trout fishery – to the local economy.

Finally, the question of which members of a community benefit from a tourism enterprise, and who bears the cost, is very important, though unfortunately seldom posed. It is often treated similarly to GDP, the calculation of which makes a number of assumptions about the economic homogeneity of the population. For example, it uses the mean to calculate GDP when a more effective measure of central tendency would be the median. Likewise, tourism planners determine and report the gross financial receipts of the industry, without considering how those receipts are distributed within the economy. A trickle-down effect is thought to apply in the tourism sector, just as in the general economy. There have been too many cases where people and their communities have borne the costs of a tourism infrastructure without reaping any benefits from it. Tourism plans need to address this issue at an analytical level, and through development of practical solutions.

PHYSICAL RESOURCE INVENTORY

One of the critical quantitative research activities in the tourism planning process is the establishment and maintenance of a physical resource inventory, whereby an attempt is made to develop a comprehensive list and description of the resources upon which a tourism destination can be developed – a more difficult task than it might at first appear. This is because people often do not recognize aspects of their landscape or culture which might appear distinctive or striking to an outsider. Often, such artifacts and behaviors will seem common place or mundane to local people, and it may take an outsider to point out their particular interest. The second difficulty in maintaining a resource inventory is the rapidity with which it is likely to become outdated. The natural and built environment is subject to constant change, either naturally or through human intervention; various features will appear and disappear with the passage of time, attracting little notice unless consciously recorded. No matter how difficult keeping such an inventory may be, it is an activity that provides an extremely important resource for the community. A simple recording sheet was prepared for this purpose by the Minnesota Extension Service, at the University of Minnesota, and appears opposite as Table 6.3.

Table 6.3 is one demonstration of an inventory recording format. There is a variety of similar formats, many of which are more sophisticated (see Ontario Ministry of Tourism, (2000). *Premier Ranked*

Tourism Destinations. Toronto: Queen's Printer). The particular format used is not important itself; what matters is the development and evaluation of the relevant physical resources that exist in the area concerned. Citizens can become more familiar with the community by undertaking and completing an inventory of the existing and potential tourism activity sites in the community, rather than employing an outside agent to do the job. Revisions may then be made continuously by them as conditions change, rather than periodically.

Table 6.3   Physical Resource Inventory Recording Sheet

Natural or Scenic Attraction or resource.	Where does it exist?	Potential for development in 1 yr , 3 yrs, 5 yrs	Description/Notes/ Problems (here describe the features of the site and ownership, etc.)
Beaches			
Bird watching sites			
Canyons and gorges			
Fall Foliage			
Farms			
Fishing Streams and Lakes			
Forests			
Headwaters			
Mountains			
Nature Trails			
Open Space			
Parks (national, prov., local)			
Rivers			
Wilderness			

Source: A Training Guide for Rural Tourism Development. 1991. Minnesota Extension Service, University of Minnesota.

The blank columns at the bottom of Table 6.3 are there for a purpose. Communities can make additions to the list, or create their own lists from scratch if that is required because of the uniqueness of the locale. In fact, the entries in the left hand column of Table 6.3 are intended only as examples, rather than as a definitive list of categories that could appear on such a list; each list will be unique to the community or region to which it relates. The example in Table 6.3 deals with outdoor features, but a particular community may be restoring, for example, a built historical site, and the list would therefore contain entirely different categories than those presented here. The items appearing on the list should represent any features of the area which might in future be useful in relation to tourism development.

The method of preparing an inventory is also important. I would encourage planners to approach this inventory in a way that involves the community; as many people as possible should be involved, because each person will have a unique point of view, and each can add flavor to the discussion. What some consider an important feature may not be considered so by others, and so it is important that there is a full discussion. In addition to developing the resource inventory, this discussion will also aid the eventual identification of the theme on which the tourism destination is to be based. Establishing a tourism theme early in the process will also help to control the size of the inventory list, and prevent it from becoming too unwieldy. Obviously, a balance must be struck between, on the one hand, creating a complete but time consuming, and comprehensive inventory and, on the other, a failure to recognize and include an important aspect of the community or area in that document. The role of the planner here may be to help prevent a group from becoming bogged down in the detail of completing such an exercise.

This process has in the past mainly considered the physical resources available for constructing the tourism product. Exactly the same process should be completed in relation to the human resources available in the community as well. Not only should individuals be identified; so also should community groups and clubs, which may be recreational in nature but still useful in developing a tourism project. For example, naturalist groups may have an interest in maintaining or expanding the natural habitat of species found in the area. What they are preserving for their own reasons may also be of great interest to tourists. Festivals and other events organized by and for the local community are often the very things that attract tourists. Artists and art groups may provide a resource to the tourism destination. Volunteerism is often an integral component of tourism development especially in rural communities. Again, it is important to determine how the various human assets of the community fit into the overall potential of the tourism destination, and to list those assets along with the physical attractions of an area.

REGULATION AND LOGISTICAL ANALYSIS

Many LDCs have developed a complex system for internal travel, in order to meet social and political requirements, such as travel permits that do not exist in the developed world – although the events of September 11, 2001, have increased the difficulties of entry into, and subsequent travel within, the US. Travel permits and visas require varying amounts of energy and money to secure, depending on the country being visited; the process is not uniform throughout the world. While the situation is improving worldwide, there are still a few countries which have very stringent entry restrictions. This represents a barrier to tourism development for these countries, and would need to be overcome if tourism was ever to be an effective tool for development.

In addition, infrastructure development is often lacking – especially in developing countries – on which a sustainable tourism industry can be built. The provision of such mundane facilities as sewage treatment plants represents a challenge for many LDC tourism areas, many of which discharge their sewage directly into the ocean, damaging beaches and coral reefs. In Africa, the burning of waste affects both air quality and the health of animals living alongside hotels and other tourist facilities. Roads, especially in some African countries, can be almost impassable, particularly following periods of heavy seasonal rains. Many roads are also infested with bandits who, while mostly not posing a significant threat to one's life, are sure to relieve visitors of their possessions. The proximity of airports to resorts is also a concern in many LDCs, since tourists do not want to travel further long distances after their arrival at an airport. In some countries, however, this is necessary due to a lack of adequate airports and transport facilities.

All of these issues combine to make tourism a difficult development option for many countries. Many high quality resorts, or potential locations for tourist facilities, are not viable simply because of the difficulties of access. A community may feel that it has an idyllic location for a tourism development, but fail to take into account these logistical issues, and consequently suffer disappointment.

In the analysis of the attractiveness of tourism destinations, the organizational aspects of a destination area are often overlooked. Except in the case of a small number of large attractions – such as Disney World, for example – most rural tourism is not dependent on a single site or installation, but is organized around a constellation of facilities or events, requiring a complex network of organizations to coordinate the overall experience for the visitor.

Community tourism organizations usually come together to perform such practical tasks as cooperative marketing, establishing business hours and other basic parameters, and acting as arbiters when organizational problems or disagreements arise among relevant stakeholders. Even accreditation and amenity rating schemes may be of concern to these bodies. Such issues can be quite divisive, however, and need to be tackled with great care. All of these issues must nonetheless be addressed by a group from within the community if the system is to maintain itself effectively. Many communities have neglected these areas, leading in many cases to paralysis in the system. Community tourism relies on a system of businesses and attractions, and close cooperation between all actors is required in order for it to work well.

A key ingredient in developing this degree of coordination is the development of leaders within the community. In rural communities, and to a lesser degree in urban areas, volunteers are required in large numbers to provide labor to the many events and festivals which form at least a part of the tourism enterprise. The recruitment, training, and deployment of volunteers are major undertakings in any community, and need special attention from well trained leaders, whether they are professionals or volunteers themselves.

The assessment of organizational concerns like the network structure, and leadership are extremely important but an often overlooked area of study by tourism planners. All actors in a system need to be identified, and their perspectives and interests clearly articulated, so that a plan can address their needs. This type of research may overlap with the individual and community needs assessment phases outlined earlier in this chapter, but it is important to remember that there may be a quantitative aspect to this research, in addition to the more qualitative task of developing goals and visions. It is possible to combine these two types of activity, particularly if the tourism system is small and consists of the same people as those involved in the vision creation exercise. A common pitfall, however, is the inclusion in the vision creation section of the planning process of only the business actors, who cannot possibly represent the wide range of values and priorities embodied by any community. While the wider community needs to have continuous access to the tourism system, when overall priorities are being established they will probably not be interested in the day-to-day operation details with which the system is confronted. While some of the activities in this section of the planning process may therefore seem similar to those outlined in the individual and community needs assessment stage, they are nonetheless significantly different in detail and function. The critical role of the leader and the network of tourism entrepreneurs is to recognize these differences, and to make sure that the stakeholders are engaged at the appropriate moments.

One of the areas of detail which it is the task of the tourism network to address is that of directional and interpretive signage. This may seem like a trivial issue, but many tourism destinations have failed to live up to their potential due to a lack of adequate signposting, whether in a built or natural environment. In most rural situations, tourism relies on a historical component, which requires sophisticated interpretation in order for the visitor to get some understanding of the significance of the events comprising the history of the area. Often, this history is not displayed on easily identified signs, in relevant locations, and so this is an area that requires the attention of the tourism planner when issues of logistics and regulation are being considered. It is in areas such as this that the human resource inventory plays a role in identifying any professional or amateur bodies that may be of help. Many naturalist clubs have taken on the problem of interpretive signage when dealing with areas of ecological interest. Likewise, local history clubs can be instrumental in developing interpretive material suitable for tourists. Signage, either directional or interpretive, is clearly an issue of special importance to the visitor. Inhabitants of an area are quite accustomed to finding their way around, but that is obviously not the case for visitors, so transportation networks and interpretive resources both need to be assessed from an outsider's point of view.

MARKET ANALYSIS

Marketing is a preoccupation of a large number of tourism practitioners and academics. Most texts on this subject focus on the issues of 'place', 'product', 'people', 'price', 'packaging', and 'promotion'. The function of this discussion is not to restate that literature, but to present the fundamental concerns of the planner and the planning process when undertaking a plan for a community destination site, whether in the developed world or in LDCs. As in the other sections of this chapter fundamental questions such as, has the market segment for this attraction been identified, will drive the basis of the research in this stage.

Weaver tells us that:

> [m]arketing involves the interaction and interrelationship among consumers and producers of goods and services, through which ideas, products, services and values are created and exchanged for the mutual benefit of both groups.
>
> (Weaver, 2000: 212)

A separate marketing plan is usually created, in addition to the development plan which has been the main focus of this chapter. With the broader plan in place, the marketing plan deals with exactly how the relevant ideas, products and services are packaged and assessed. Perhaps more important, is the assessment and creation of the marketing strategy based on honesty, truth, and transparency. In their eagerness, marketers have tended in the past to overstate the image of the market area leaving the visitor disenchanted with what is found during actual contact with the attraction. If the attraction depends on repeat visits, any false advertising, no matter how inadvertent it may be, will be counterproductive rather than useful in the long run.

Many traditional societies, particularly in the developing world, have in the past been stereotyped by advertisers and marketers who have created a distorted image rather than portraying a more accurate picture of the host community. Wels is concerned with the imagery used in marketing Africa, for example. He argues that the marketing image of Africa has been created to contrast and measure European civilization rather than accurately portraying Africa and its many cultures. Wels states:

> European imagery of Africa has often been presented in the most literal sense of the word, in photographs and art. Imagery lays at the basis of 'us' and 'them' categorizing, which has the serious danger of leading to 'us' stereotyping the African Other ... Africans should blend in [sic] an aesthetically dominated European image of the African landscape. That is why European tourists, for example, usually perceive huts with thatched roofs and African women with water buckets on their heads as 'authentic Africa' while Cape Town is considered 'not the real Africa'. Huts and women with buckets on their heads blend in [sic] our perception

of African landscapes, while bubbling, cosmopolitan city-life is alien to that image.

(Wels, 2000: 55)

Wels understands that these are the images which dominate the marketing of Africa as a tourist destination. A romantic picture is created, portraying an idealized image of the continent. Marketing and promotion have been guilty of this type of stereotyping, and have thus been counterproductive for the long-term development of the industry. Promotions which portray a more accurate picture of the culture of society are now beginning to be seen by the industry as an important ingredient for the health of the sector. They realize that an inaccurate picture creates dissatisfaction on the part of their clientele as well as damaging the host society. A set of criteria needs to be established by the industry on which to judge the accuracy of the marketing material that is presented to the public.

Tourism marketing is often more complex than marketing in other sectors, it is frequently not just one business that is marketing its products, but a number of cooperating businesses and government organizations. This follows from the fact that a destination site is nearly always comprised of a number of component parts. Moreover, a given tourism site may also be a part of a larger tourism region that is marketed by regional organizations, and is therefore even more remote from the single tourism business. This complexity calls for sophisticated coordination between actors, and a planner needs to analyze this system's structure to discover whether all of the parts of the system have been developed effectively and are functioning as they should. Gaps and miscommunications within the system can then be addressed.

It is necessary to identify not only the actual material that constitutes the marketing program including such things as advertisements and their communication system, but also the data needed to evaluate that function and organizational structure of the program itself. Important parts of the process include such elements as goals and objectives; implementation strategies – including who is responsible for which parts of the promotional program; the timeframe for completion; and an evaluation strategy from a formative and summative point of view. Formative evaluation techniques require continuous assessment at each stage of the process while summative evaluation occurs exclusively at the end of the process or cycle. Each may address different questions and survey dissimilar respondents. Most importantly, a clear and detailed identification of the target market, and the means of attracting them, should be a central feature of the strategy and form the basis on which the evaluation should progress.

A research program should support the marketing strategy, creating an extensive database identifying market segments and visitor numbers, and making use of exit evaluations of the service by its users to determine their level of satisfaction. The evaluation should also include a community monitoring program which continually assesses the mood in the community for continued development of the tourism product. This analysis should be used to assess the relevance and health of the tourism destination and its various attractions and services to both the visitors and citizens of the affected community. Data which can be applied to such theories as Butler's Product Life Cycle model (Butler, 1980) in order to judge the health of the industry need to be generated by the research team. Butler's concept proposes five stages through which a tourism destination usually passes: (1) exploration, (2) involvement, (3) development, (4) consolidation, and (5) stagnation. One of the functions of the marketing database is to monitor the destination area and its attractions so that the system never reaches the stagnation phase of Butler's model. If it does reach that stage, then steps leading to rejuvenation are indicated. Quite often rejuvenation does not happen as a natural and continuous part of the planning process but occurs some time after collapse of the initial project. This is usually a result of the lack of monitoring and evaluating the tourism system in a comprehensive manner and when there is no collective system network to make comprehensive decisions to control the trajectory of the project. It is hoped however, that attention to evaluation and monitoring the system through the development of a strong research program and detailed database will help both the community and the planner to avoid such circumstances. The research function provides the stakeholders in the system, including community officials and residents, with accurate and detailed information allowing them to establish where their community is situated, at any given time, along the continuum outlined by Butler's model. The use of Butler's model is not an exact science, but it does provide a community with a crude framework for assessing the current situation and estimating the future trajectory of the tourism project.

Of course, the marketing research should also try to identify and monitor the social composition and behavior of the tourist clientele, as it relates to the destination. These data will assist the destination site and its various attractions to improve their levels of service. Reactions by the clientele to the components of the marketing strategy can also be tested as part of this research, in order to help officials to fine-tune it.

SOCIAL AND CULTURAL IMPACT ANALYSIS

Social impact analysis requires a set of baseline data relating to (1) social conditions prior to development, (2) the changes produced after the development is introduced into the system, and (3) a detailed examination of measures that can be implemented to ameliorate any negative effects of the development, or alternatively entrench positive trends. If the third step can be accomplished prior to the initial change, then the proposed development can be altered a priori to minimize the negative impacts of the development and enhance the positive ones, reducing the necessity of corrective measures after the fact.

A social impact analysis should begin with a profile of the population of the community or area concerned. The statistics for this profile can usually be found within national census data, if they exist, or alternatively in other municipal plans particularly land use plans. Official land use plans usually contain population projections which estimate future population characteristics of the community based on historical data, and which should be taken into consideration in any proposed development to determine what demographic impact the proposed changes are likely to produce. If the population consists of young families, then a development catering to an older population segment is likely to have major implications in terms of the required changes to infrastructure, services and community facilities in general, like hospitals and other institutions.

In developing countries, this kind of data is often either absent or of a too general nature to allow detailed analysis at a local or regional level. Local population projections based on national statistics are fraught with difficulty, and prone to error, but in most cases it is better than no analysis at all. What planners are attempting here is to arrive at a basic understanding of the existing population structure, so that the potential impacts of proposed developments on that population can be estimated. It may be necessary to search church records or undertake a sample census in small communities where no organized database exists in order to make such an estimate. These latter methods usually produce crude results, but do supply some sense of a community's population structure.

In addition, such tools as Butler's Attitude/Behavior Index (Butler, 1974) and Doxey's Irritation Index (Doxey, 1976) are useful for organizing survey instruments or interview protocols to determine the local impacts of tourism development. These surveys provide anecdotal information about how local people are responding to the change in population makeup, or to other changes produced by tourism development, with all of its attendant stresses.

More sophisticated techniques, using computer programs, can also be employed to perform this type of analysis. Synthetic computer models can be used to introduce or remove various structural parameters in order to analyze different hypothetical scenarios. These models are particularly effective in understanding the impact of new construction in a particular landscape, or of the removal of such features as large tracts of forest. But such methods are costly, and remain unavailable to many countries, especially in the developing world.

Many communities are so enthusiastic about a proposed development that their time-frame for construction does not allow a complex analysis based on large-scale data gathering prior to development. This often creates the need to develop a database both large enough to be of use, but not so large that its analysis becomes daunting to the analyst, on which a social and cultural analysis can be completed in a relatively short period of time. Planners working in developing countries and remote areas have for some time been accustomed to this necessity, and have developed a method known as Participatory Rural Appraisal (PRA), to collect and analyse data. (Chambers, 1992; 1994) This approach involves a multitude of methods, including traversing the community in order to get some type of mental map of the area, and interviews and short surveys of the local population, to determine attitudes, perceptions and local knowledge. Beyond focusing on research technique, the major purpose of the PRA approach is to begin the process of public involvement and 'ownership' of the project, or the outcome of the research. The PRA website (www.ids.susx.ac.uk/particip/index.html) sums up PRA as a group of approaches and methods which enable local people to share and analyze their understanding of their social, political and physical environment, and to plan, monitor and evaluate the development in that environment. This provides a philo-sophical and practical framework for development which corresponds to the basic orientation of this book.

This section has provided a brief outline of some of the fundamental theoretical concepts and practical methods available to those attempting a social impact analysis of the tourism project, whether existing or hypothetical. What should be apparent from this brief discussion is that all of the techniques cited are predicated on the assumption that what is the most important aspect of the process is the learning on the part of those engaged in it about themselves and their environment. Most of the methods that are used in such a process as PRA are not very sophisticated, and can have relevance in many situations. Communities may also come to feel the need to deploy other more sophisticated techniques, developing a larger database and more detailed analysis to inform their actions. It is important to understand that the analysis does not substitute for the taking of decisions, but can only form a basis on which decisions are taken. Those in positions of power and responsibility often expect data analysis to 'reveal' a rational decision, and become frustrated when this does not occur. All decisions are political in nature, but the quality of those decisions can be enhanced by the availability of good and relevant information, as well as by the use of sound decision-making practices which are truly partici-patory in nature. It is in this area that issues surrounding the life values described by McMurtry (1999) must become a central focus of analysis. Life values stand in contrast to money values, which are made paramount in conventional social impact assessments. In many instances, money values have become a surrogate for life values, which – as McMurtry has pointed out – are not only completely different from, but often in opposition to money values.

ENVIRONMENTAL ANALYSIS

Tourism is often thought of as a sustainable alternative to primary and extractive industries, such as mining, fishing and forestry, which transform raw material into finished goods and in the process change those resources permanently. The input commodities are finite, and once used or permanently changed cannot be exploited again. Often this extractive process produces by-products which add to the levels of pollution of the water and air that humans depend on for their existence. Extractive industries also destroy habitats supporting a variety of species, thereby reducing biodiversity. However, there are fundamental decisions that society must make when confronted with competing interests in the use of resources. Table 6.4 sets out the resources which are competed for, the methods available for allocating them, and the competing uses to which they can be put.

Table 6.4   Resources, Use and Allocation

Resources	Method of Allocation	Competing Uses
– soil	– planning	– agriculture
– atmosphere	– economic markets	– forestry
– water	– individual behavior	– housing
– minerals and geological resources	– institutional behavior	– recreation and green spaces
– flora	– public policy	– industry
– fauna		– wildlife
		– natural habitats
		– mineral and aggregate extraction
		– transportation and utility
		– waste disposal

This table outlines the combination of factors which comprise the decision-making process relating to the use of natural resources for recreation or other purposes. Often, governments will want to maximize the benefits of resource use, and it may be incumbent on the tourism planner to demonstrate the economic return of their favored use of a particular resource. This is often more difficult for the tourism planner than it might be for the forester, for example, who can calculate the amount of potential return from an area of forest simply by multiplying the number of board feet it contains by the market price of the wood, minus the costs of production. Tourism planners often have to estimate economic returns by using obtrusive measurement techniques such as 'shadow pricing' and 'willingness to pay' models, as discussed previously (see Rollins & Wistowsky, 1997).

Whether or not primary resources fare better when used for tourism is a debatable notion. It is estimated, for example, that utilizing a lion in the Serengeti for tourism purposes produces considerably more revenue over time than it would if the habitat it depended upon was cleared for agriculture, thereby reducing the number of animals available to be seen by tourists, or even eliminating the population altogether. An equivalent argument applies for whale-watching off Canada's west coast. On the other hand, tourism often brings with it large numbers of tourists producing human waste, which is often released into the environment untreated, causing severe ecological harm, and sometimes – as in the case of coral reefs – even destroying whole ecosystems.

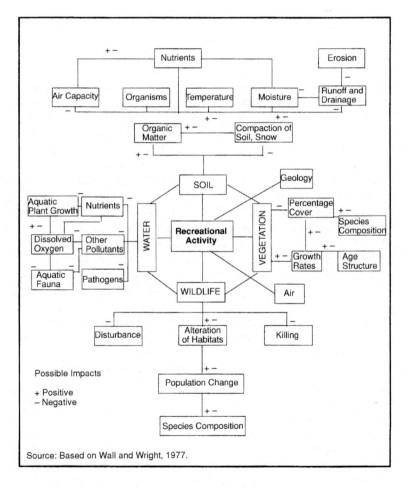

Figure 6.3   Recreational Impact Interrelationships

While this debate will doubtless continue for some time, one thing is clear: using natural resources for tourism purposes is not without costs or damage to the environment. People trudging around an environmentally sensitive area may have just as devastating an effect on the landscape as would the agricultural cultivation of that land. However, proper management and monitoring can extend the life of such areas, and can even be sustainable in the long-term. While tourism may take longer to destroy an area's natural resources, they can be destroyed nonetheless if proper monitoring and management are not adhered to. Mathieson and Wall (1982: 131) provide a framework for monitoring outdoor resources in use for tourism and recreation purposes.

Figure 6.3 lays out the fundamental concerns associated with the recreational use of the environment. Each resource – water, wildlife, vegetation and soil – can be affected by recreational use. There are specific components connected to each resource which contribute to the sustainability of its use, and which need to be constantly monitored for change. If, in the monitoring of these elements, the condition of the resource is seen to deteriorate, then practices can be employed to address this problem. Resting an area and constructing elevated pathways are examples of such measures. In the case of built environments, and in relation to pollution by motor vehicles, public transport provision can be of benefit. A particular difficulty in the ongoing monitoring process is to determine which change is the result of recreational use, and which would have come about in the absence of tourist activity, due to natural processes.

While it cannot generally be expected that tourism planners will have the academic background necessary to conduct a study of these factors, they must nonetheless understand the fundamental structure of each component so that they can collaborate with those responsible for carrying out such work. It is also often necessary for a tourism planner to present the results of any monitoring to the relevant policy-setting body, so a sound overall understanding of what remedial action might be indicated is required on his or her part. The concept of 'carrying capacity', particularly in its ecological and physical senses, is fundamentally related to the type of research suggested by Figure 6.3.

THE CONCEPT OF CARRYING CAPACITY

The environmental analysis envisioned by Figure 6.3 examines the impact of resource use on the ecology of an area devoted to tourism and recreation, attempting to determine both the long- and short-term implications of that use. This often necessitates an estimation of the carrying capacity of the area concerned. While it is a useful concept, it has proved difficult for researchers and planners to use in a practical way. Unlike rangeland management, for example, which simply determines how many animals can be supported by the amount of fodder grown on the land, carrying capacity for recreation and tourism purposes is not a single variable, but is a function of a variety of interacting variables, making an accurate estimation very difficult, if not impossible. Other techniques, such as the Recreation Opportunity Spectrum, Limits to Acceptable Change, and the Social Learning Model have been substituted for carrying capacity analysis (see Stankey, McCool, Clark and Brown, 1999). While these methods involve less quantitative analysis than does the framework of carrying capacity – and are therefore less precise – they incorporate the social dynamics of human use which do not need to be taken into account when estimating carrying capacity for rangeland purposes.

Shelby and Haberlein have developed an approach to the estimation of carrying capacity for recreational purposes. Their method incorporates concepts of rangeland management with the approach outlined by Stankey et al. (1999), discussed above. Shelby and Haberlein's method utilizes a descriptive and an evaluative component, in which 'carrying capacity is the level of use beyond which impacts exceed acceptable levels specified by evaluative standards'. (Shelby and Haberlein, 1986: 13) A descriptive component develops and implements management and impact parameters for each site based on the evaluative component which outlines the type of experience required by visitors and the evaluative standards which have previously been set. Shelby and Haberlein (1986: 13) set out a more detailed description of this framework, in Table 6.5.

Shelby and Haberlein's schema is not unlike the method Stankey et al. (1999) deploy to deal with recreational carrying capacity. Both models utilize a management and development approach, rather than the mathematical ratio model used in rangeland management. Both recognize the perceptual and social component of identifying carrying capacity, as well as the physical and ecological necessities of sustainability. Generally, recreational carrying capacity is concerned with not one but four major categories of analysis: physical, ecological, perceptual, and economic.

The idea of physical carrying capacity relates to such issues as the built environment which is used to support the use of a recreational

Table 6.5   Carrying Capacity Framework

Descriptive Component
Describes how a recreation system works, including physical and biological characteristics and human and nonhuman use patterns.

Management Parameter	*Impacts*
Elements of the recreation system which managers can manipulate. These include amount of use (use level) as well as the way an area is used (e.g. redistributing use in time or space, or changing use practices).	Elements of the recreation system affected by the amount or type of use. The type of impact determines the type of capacity (ecological, physical, facility, or social).

Evaluative Component
Defines how an area should be managed and specifies how much impact is too much.

Management Objectives	*Evaluative Component*
Defines the type of experience or other outcomes that a recreation setting should provide.	Specifies acceptable levels of impact in terms such as minimum, maximum or optimum.

Source: Shelby and Haberlein, 1986

resource. It may, for example, take into account the necessary quantity of ramps for launching boats, the number which can be launched in a certain period, where there are suitable bodies of water for such uses. Similarly, ski lifts would come within this frame of reference in relation to the carrying capacity of terrain used for downhill skiing.

Ecological carrying capacity relates to the effects of direct use of the natural environment for tourism and recreation purposes. It is this dimension which closely resembles the original notion of carrying capacity that was generated for rangeland management. This category attempts to determine how much use an area or environment can endure before it can no longer regenerate itself. The model of Wall and Wright, 1997, discussed earlier, is useful here for identifying the critical elements to be measured and monitored.

The issue of perceptual carrying capacity is often not considered. It is precisely this issue which makes the idea of carrying capacity so difficult to apply in recreational and tourism settings, and yet it is this issue also which often determines the success or failure of a tourism destination. A tourist in a remote national park who is expecting to experience solitude, and instead encounters hundreds of people using the same resource, may quickly become disillusioned due to such a violation of the perceptual carrying capacity of the area concerned. However, those attending a rave or rock concert would feel that the event was not successful if they were not crowded together with fellow revelers. So, perception of carrying capacity is specific both to the activity concerned and to the culture of which it forms a part.

Finally, the issue of economic carrying capacity must also be examined. Governments, who are often major actors in providing anchor facilities like national parks, art galleries and museums, tend to demand financial self-sufficiency from these facilities in today's fiscally cautious environment. This puts pressure on a facility to ettract ever more visitors, which may be antithetical to some of the other priorities entailed in the idea of carrying capacity outlined above. An analysis of economic carrying capacity must include its effect on those other aspects of it. The issue of the public good, as well as the role of a facility as a stimulant to the private sector, should also be considered in this analysis. It may be unfortunate, but economic carrying capacity may be given greater weight in the decision-making process than its counterparts, particularly where government is making the decisions. It is nonetheless absolutely necessary for tourism planners to point out to public officials that there are other important measures of carrying capacity, in addition to economic concerns, which need to be part of the equation.

GEOGRAPHICAL INFORMATION SYSTEMS

A recent development which has enormous potential for the monitoring of carrying capacity and the evaluation of sites for tourism and recreation purposes is the geographical information system (GIS), a tool made possible by recent advances in computer technology. Where researchers were once limited to the construction of overlay maps for examination by hand, GIS now allows data to be manipulated instantaneously, creating new mapping configurations and answering hypothetical questions in seconds, if not less. This tool allows the manipulation of much greater quantities of data, and a much more elegant and sophisticated analysis, than more traditional manual techniques. However, there is a downside to this methodology. GIS is highly labor-intensive, and much labor and money is required to collect and enter the initial data which drive the technology. With the proliferation of satellite and remote-sensing methods of data collection, this tool should become less laborious and more user-friendly in the future.

In summary, there are three elements critical to completing the environmental impact component of the program and product development and feasibility assessment stages of the model, outlined in Figure 6.1. The first is the identification of a baseline against which change can be measured over time. Often, projects are begun without due consideration for this priority. If this is the case, then the planner is limited to taking a snapshot of a given moment, leaving the community without the ability to estimate future changes based on historical data. Tourism planners must explain the importance of collecting baseline data, and press decision-makers to allow adequate finances and time to be devoted to this stage in the process. Certainly, there are many examples of jurisdictions which have come to understand the importance of this necessity after the fact, when they have wanted answers to questions which have depended on understanding the condition of the environment before development began. The second critical element in the process is the ability to distinguish between human-induced and natural change. The ideal method for making this assessment is through the use of comparison plots, if the site in question is a natural area. The setting aside of such areas as control sites is an ideal solution to this problem. Finally, an ability to incorporate all of the complexities in an overall analysis is important. Planners are often constrained by limited budgets and other factors, thus having to use only a few surrogate measures to monitor a given situation, when a full array of measures would provide a more comprehensive picture. However, it is better to undertake an incomplete assessment than no assessment at all.

TOURISM PLANNER AS SOCIAL CRITIC

Much of this chapter has focused on techniques of analysis. However, I want to stress that the tourism planner should not fall into the trap, as many do, of believing that planning is solely about the analysis and interpretation of data. On the contrary, tourism planning also involves social critique. In fact, the tourism planner must see his or her role as that of the facilitator of a broad and inclusive social debate, about not only the merits and potential outcomes of the project concerned, but also about the long-term vision of the community, and the positive and negative consequences for those who will be directly affected by tourism development.

The role of social critic removes the analyst from the realm of detached scientific investigator, which requires the researcher to maintain a healthy degree of distance from the subject being studied. Rosaldo suggests that 'social criticism involves making complex ethical judgments about existing social arrangements'. (Rosaldo, 1994: 178) He states further that 'social critics should be meaningfully connected with, rather than utterly detached from, the group under critique'. (Ibid., 1994: 179) No longer can we perpetuate the idea of the social scientist as the detached, impartial observer. Rosaldo goes on to state that:

> Rather than work downward from abstract principles, social critics work outward from in-depth knowledge of a specific form of life. Informed by such conceptions as social justice, human dignity, and equality, they use their moral imagination to move from the world as it actually is to a locally persuasive vision of how it ought to be. Because different communities differ in their problems and possibilities, such visions must be more local than universal.

> (Ibid., 1994: 183)

The appropriateness of any tourism development must be seen in light of the aspirations of those who will live with the development in the long term. There are no objective standards on which to judge good or bad development, although there are certain types of development which most will agree have severe shortcomings. That said, the factors that distinguish between good and bad tourism development emerge substantially from local circumstances and taste. It is therefore necessary for the tourism planner to engage the public meaningfully in the analysis and critique of the proposed development. It is not an acceptable tactic, in my view, for a planner to assume the role of tourism expert, with a preconceived set of ideas about what is good and what is bad for the community concerned, and then to proceed solely on his or her own analysis. The role of the planner is to help a community to undertake the assessments outlined in this chapter, and then to engage the community in a discourse utilizing the resulting information leading to a decision.

7 Case Studies in Tourism Planning

INTRODUCTION

This chapter presents three case studies designed to demonstrate the theories and techniques outlined in Chapters 5 and 6. It will become evident that each case focuses on a few of the techniques described, rather than incorporating all equally. In real life, each situation is unique and requires a customized approach to planning. It is when tourism planners use a cookie-cutter approach to all problems that difficulties often arise. Most tourism developments, from the perspective of either the entrepreneur or the community, nevertheless encounter issues that are likely to be common to all cases. These usually include: concerns with supply and demand; cost-benefit analysis; cost-unit analysis; establishing a range of fees and charges for the product that the market will bear, and the economic impact of the development upon those who will assume the costs, both physically and financially. In addition, there are likely to be issues of process and resource allocation, such as who defines the vision on which development is based, and how decisions are made when there are conflicting views and opinions.

All development represents what economists call 'opportunity costs' – that is, once a resource has been allocated and used for one purpose, society forgoes its use for some other, perhaps equally important purpose. There are also two major practical concerns of tourism analysis: the evaluation and selection of suitable resources for the facility or activity being planned; and the identification and management of the conflicts between users of the same resource. Finally, in parts of the world where traditional cultures are involved, tourism planners must grapple with the consequences of the commodification of culture. It is in this domain that tourism development can have drastic effects on people's everyday lives and even on their basic construction of reality. Tourism development has too often changed the living patterns of communities without giving much thought to the consequences of those changes. This is illustrated by the short discussion in Chapter 1 of the Ladakhis and the Canadian composite community scenario also presented in that chapter.

This chapter examines several case studies in light of the issues outlined above. Each case study represents an attempt to deal with a number of the issues raised in this book. While it will be evident that the processes deployed in each case are focused on certain areas and not on others, the studies were chosen because it was felt that their planning activity had proceeded in a way that was generally consistent with the values outlined in this text. In each case, a concerted attempt was made to take the welfare of the community and the environment into account, rather than only the interests of profit maximization. Attempts were made, in other words, to incorporate much of the philosophy outlined in the preceding chapters of this book. Fundamentally, these cases saw attempts to institute a planning process that recognized the partnership between the producer (the environment or culture), the supplier (the tourism industry), and the consumer (the tourist), as depicted in Figure 5.3. Thus, each case discussed approaches tourism development from a systems perspective.

It is important to identify examples of tourism development that give proper attention to the various subsystems within the planning process and their relation to each other. These cases provide living examples of developments which recognize the fact that change to one subsystem produces changes throughout the entire process. Moreover, examples of tourism planning that challenge the 'value program' (McMurtry, 1999) on which tourism is constructed are most instructive. As tourism planners and communities construct more holistic tourism projects, case studies demonstrating the implementation of these new values are important. Each case discussed here recognizes the potential impacts on all those concerned, whether they are directly involved in a development or affected by inevitable changes to the social and natural environment in which they live. It is important to remember that people living in communities dominated by tourism are part of the project whether they wish to be or not, simply by virtue of where they live. Each of the development processes examined in these case studies recognizes that fact, and have based their planning process upon it. In these case studies, tourism development is viewed as part of the overall social and natural environment in which it exists. The value of individual and social life seems to provide the basis on which tourism is initiated and managed.

CASE STUDY: GOLDEN, BC, AND KICKING HORSE MOUNTAIN
RESORT (KHMR)

Introduction

The Town of Golden is located in the interior of British Columbia,
Canada. It is nestled in the Rocky Mountains, surrounded by a
natural area which is sought out by visitors for its unique, spectacular
scenery. The Rocky Mountains provide a world-class resource for
skiing and other recreational pursuits, both active and passive. The
area is adjacent to the trans-Canada highway, which is used heavily
by tourists traveling through the Rocky Mountains to the west coast
of Canada. In the past many of those tourists hurried past Golden to
get on to other destinations, but now they have a reason to stay.
Golden sits approximately halfway between the two major airports
of Calgary, Alberta, to the east, and Kelowna, BC, to the west. The
journey takes four hours by bus or car from either airport to Golden.
At the time of writing, Golden does not have an international airport,
but it does have a small facility that could be expanded for this
purpose. There are other skiing facilities of equal quality located
between Golden and each airport.

Golden is a home to approximately 5,000 people. It is adjacent to,
but politically separate from, a more rural area known officially as
Area A. Golden provides many basic services to the residents of Area
A, including schools, an indoor recreation infrastructure, health
services and the usual variety of retail stores found in a small rural
town of this type. Area A is located between the Town of Golden,
including the bench lands, known as such because they are the flat
lands which lie at the base of the mountain, and where the resort
development is situated.

Initially, the economic condition of Golden and Area A relied
mainly on forest products and railroading. Forestry stabilized after the
closing of the mill at Donald in 1995. There has been significant
development in wood products, particularly in post beam and wood
processing, but not sufficient to support the entire population. As a
Community Impact Report concluded,

> there has been a strengthening of the tourism/hospitality industry
> in the region which now includes everything from providing
> accommodation and meals to those driving through the mountain
> parks, to providing bed and breakfast or lodge accommodation to

those interested in paragliding, river rafting and backcountry skiing.

(West Coast CED Consulting Ltd, 2001: 17)

Tourism in the area is about to increase because of a new development on a local section of the Rockies. An international corporation, Kicking Horse Mountain Resort (KHMR) is developing a section of the mountain, including an international ski area. While the ski runs have been established for some time as a local facility, the corporation plans to expand the existing number of runs, develop a restaurant at the top of the mountain and a ski village, mainly consisting of hotels and other amenities, at its base. A gondola which carries passengers up the mountain has been put in place to increase the numbers of skiers who can be accommodated. Table 7.1 sets out the proposed developments for this expansion.

This development will transform the area from being the site of a primarily local recreational facility into a regional, and even perhaps international, tourism destination. With the development of the gondola and the mountain-top restaurant, in particular, and the additional ski runs and base lodge housing, KHMR will attract increasing market attention. It is projected (Westcoast CED Consulting Ltd, 2001) that over 100,000 skiers will visit the mountain ski resort on an annual basis. While this may fall within the range that the projected facilities can be expected to handle without great difficulty, visitors will not pass through evenly throughout the week or year, and this could cause periodic congestion. The majority of visitors will come at weekends and during holidays, which could place stress on the capacity of both the resort and the community itself. It is expected that the new facilities will produce an economic benefit to the area of approximately eight million dollars per year (Ibid, 2001), with about half of that being generated within the Town of Golden itself.

Since the new facilities at KHMR will be located in Area A, none of the resulting tax revenues generated will be collected by the Town of Golden, although many of the site's visitors and workers will receive services from the town. A problem of equal importance, perhaps, is the fact that Area A has no official municipal plan or zoning scheme in place to control or accommodate the expected growth. Many of the residents of Area A are philosophically against restricting growth, and there is a strong sense that if you own land you should be able to do with it what you wish, without government

Table 7.1 Summary of the KHMR Facilities at Full Build Out

Facility	Notes	Numbers
9 ski lifts	Gondola, 6 new chair lifts, 1 existing chair lift, 1 grip tow	128,750 skiers 225,000 visitors
2–3 hotels	Total of 442 rooms in two or three hotels in the 3–5 star range	884 bed units
1 mountain-top restaurant	A mountain top 'Eagle's Eye' restaurant and lookout with a gift shop at the top of the gondola	
4 bed & breakfast units	Owner operated units	32 bed units
150 Condotel units	1- and 2-bedroom units, some managed as hotel units and some as timeshares	450 bed units
363 residences	298 town homes and 65 single family chalets	1,582 bed units
Commercial areas	Ski related services and private retail services in the first 10 years, with the provision for future expansion as demanded	25,000 sq. ft. Provision for 55,000 sq. ft. if required
Employee housing	Up to 17 rental apartments near gondola base on leased land (not included in bed count)	
Employees	Full and part time employees with ski area, hotels and other	320 employees 20% from Golden

Source: Westcoast CED Consulting Ltd., 2001, Community Impact Report for the Town of Golden BC. p. 8.

186

restriction. Understandably, the municipal council and residents of Golden are quite concerned about this approach to development, given that the already planned resort (KHMR), and the inevitable tourism businesses which will undoubtedly cluster around this new development, will have a direct impact on their daily lives.

The consultation

As a first step towards resolving some of these issues, the Town of Golden Department of Economic Development undertook to complete a planning process to deal with any relevant issues arising from the proposed development; consultation with the community was a centerpiece of this process. This consultation process consisted of representation from a wide variety of individuals and groups, which included members of the councils of both municipalities. The basic process was summarized in a public relations brochure (Golden Strategic Planning Process 2001–2006, 2001) distributed by the Department of Economic Development prior to the conference, which constituted the focus of the second stage of the process. This second stage followed a series of weekly public information sections constituting Stage One. A short description and outline of the objectives for each of these stages was presented to the conference delegates in the brochure as they arrived at the conference. The process for the study was contained in the brochure as outlined below:

Stage One
A series of weekly public information sessions were offered throughout March, April, May and June that brought in speakers on issues that will affect the area like growth management, planning, affordable housing, beautification and revitalization, etc. These sessions were well attended and successfully stimulated an informed discussion among the participants, preparing them for Stage Two.

Stage Two
The most important part of strategic planning involved bringing residents together in order to make recommendations on how they want their community to grow, and how they wish to direct and manage changes that are taking place. In a Stage Two workshop a comprehensive cross-section of representatives from groups, businesses, sectors, agencies, organizations and from the general public came together to make critical recommendations on these

issues. To ensure that all interested individuals had the opportunity to contribute, the workshop was planned so anyone who was a resident of the community could take part. Over the two days the Stage Two workshop involved presentations, brainstorming and interactive dialogue to engage the participation of all those in attendance, and resulted in what will be the framework for Golden's next five-year strategic plan. This work was subsequently compiled and redistributed to participants for review. Its components will be taken on by various community organizations (including local government) who will carry out the action plan for the next five years.

The section of the brochure announcing the conference demonstrates the commitment of the community to making the strategic planning process inclusive, and open to broad community participation. As part of the agenda of the conference, the larger group was broken down into sectoral groups in order to examine in detail the most critical issues that presented themselves. These groups were assigned a subject area on which to focus their attention and expertise. The subjects to be examined included; local government, health and welfare, transportation, tourism, and economics. A summary of the deliberations of the tourism sector group is presented in Table 7.3. While the motivation for planning was the imminent development on the mountain, the planning process examined all aspects of the community and its development in general, rather than examining it only from the point of view of tourism. The incorporation by Golden residents of this or any development into an overall community plan demonstrates their recognition that tourism was part of a larger system from which it could not be treated in isolation. That said, the participants were well aware that tourism was going to drive development in the immediate future, while any side-effects, both positive and negative, needed to be addressed in a coherent way. The planning process was based on the assumption that the development was essentially positive, and that any negative side-effects could be addressed through an ongoing process of planning and monitoring.

A consulting company from Vernon BC was engaged to develop and implement both stage one and two of the community consultation process and to write a strategic plan based on the information produced by these deliberations. In addition to the planning conference, which was a major feature of the process, a social and environmental impact assessment was also undertaken, providing much of the information on which the agenda of the conference was based.

The processes of research and community consultation in Golden and Area A were diverse and extensive. Nine meetings were held with the Golden Community Services Adjustment Committee (GCSAC), the community group responsible for the process. Two conference calls were also held with four external experts to define what the issues were likely to be, and which of these needed to be addressed by the research. Twenty-seven interviews were conducted with representatives from community agencies in Golden and Area A, in addition to 25 interviews with officials from nearby communities that had experienced the impacts of similar developments in the past. An analysis of relevant documents was completed, and site visits were made to Whistler, BC – the site of the largest ski resort in Canada – and interviews conducted with its officials. Numerous meetings with the community's project coordinator, staff, and the Chair of the Golden Economic Development Committee were also held in addition to the open community meeting discussed earlier held over a two and one-half day period. This conference included over 100 individuals from a variety of backgrounds and interests. It was this latter activity which brought the process to a climax. Subsequent to this forum the consulting team presented the strategic plan to a community meeting of 80 participants and officials where it was adopted.

The research and consultation addressed a number of issues in a variety of areas. Of particular concern to the research team were the environmental, social, infrastructural, economic and cultural challenges brought about by the proposed development. Forty-six potential impacts were identified and analyzed in light of the experiences of comparative communities. All of this research and analysis was assembled and discussed at the community conference – one of the last components of the research process. Of particular concern to the residents of Golden was the lack of local government cohesion – particularly the lack of planning guidelines within Area A, where most of the physical development of the project was to take place.

The community consultation produced a list of issues associated with the proposed development. Potential strategies were explored for addressing those issues in both the immediate and long term. The conference created the information on which a vision for future development of the community, including Area A, would be constructed. The report which resulted from this research consists of goals, objectives, recommendations and actions, but without the regulations to enforce them, which are usually found in more formal planning documents. The resulting ideas were subsequently reworked by the consulting team, and presented to the municipal council as part of the presentation of the final report that followed. The majority of time at the conference was devoted to sectoral group discussions, with specific issues of interest to each group addressed in accordance with the overall theme of the event. Each of these groups (local government, health and welfare, tourism, and alternative economic strategies) met in a workshop format, and subsequently presented reports at a plenary meeting outlining their deliberations. Each group was asked to follow a similar format, so that the results would be comparable. First, the groups were asked to identify the issues they felt needed to be addressed by the community, and then to set out the likely impacts of those trends from environmental, economic, social, educational, and organizational perspectives. The groups were also asked to identify what they thought were the key elements that would need to be incorporated into an overall vision statement for the town. The results of the impact discussion for the tourism sector are outlined below. While the deliberations of the other sectoral groups are not presented here, each group did indeed follow the same format. The consulting team then compiled a report including recommendations for action based on this material, and presented it to the municipal council in the form of a plan of action.

The tourism sector discussion

The tourism specific sub-sector of the conference was comprised of fifteen individuals representing a variety of interests, from tourism businesses to those identifying themselves simply as citizens, including two municipal councilors from Golden and Area A, a representative from the KHMR corporation and the proponents of the proposal itself. It is important to note that although tourism was a major issue for the conference participants, organizers intended to examine all aspects of community life and not solely the ski resort issue, so tourism was treated as a sub-sector like all of the other areas of interest.

In order to stimulate the discussion, the group was presented with a twelve-point self-assessment questionnaire. Table 7.2 presents some of the statistics resulting from the Golden sample of respondents to

Table 7.2   Basic Tourism Statistics for Golden

n = 15	Items	Mean	Mode	Std	Sum
1.	I can see the problems identified in the scenarios unfolding in our community at this very moment. (The composite scenario presented in Chapter 1)	3.2	3	1.01	48
2.	There is a person or small group of people in the community who are readily identifiable and give leadership to the tourism and community planning process.	3.6	4	0.74	54
3.	Tourism plays a predominant role in the economic life of the community.	3.87	3	0.83	58
4.	There is need for the community to be better organized to meet any tourism development needs that may arise.	4.67	5	0.62	70
5.	Tourism is a well developed industry with a long but rocky history in our community.	2.73	3	0.7	41
6.	We do not have a clear process for solving problems as they arise.	3.8	3	0.94	57
7.	Tourism development is out of control and too dominant an industry in our community.	1.6	1	0.63	24
8.	The residents do not want to see any more tourism development take place in our community.	1.87	2	0.52	28
9.	The residents and business community are not in agreement on how tourism should develop in the future.	3.13	3	0.83	47
10.	Everyone in the community needs to be involved in tourism development and not just left to the business community.	4.27	5	0.88	64
11.	Most residents would be willing to attend a community meeting to discuss an important tourism issue.	2.6	2	0.99	39
12.	If certain tourism proposals are developed by certain people in the community they are automatically opposed by others.	2.58	2	0.64	38
13.	Everyone is willing to pitch in and help when we have a tourism event.	2.4	2	1.06	36

Table 7.3 Tourism Sector Discussion Summary

Trends/Issues	Environmental Impact	Economic Impact	Social Impact	Educational Needs	Organizational Needs
Aging Pop. Ethnic Tourist mainly Asian					
Conflicts between tourists & locals.	Signage to direct users.		What are the values that need protection?	We need to identify the rules under which sharing occurs. Good host program.	People need to be happy with their community first.
Lack of education of players in the system.					
Development of Cooperation within the system.		Who pays for common facilities (trails)?		Increase in tax to support infrastructure needs to be explained to residents. Good host program.	
Education about culture and expectation of tourist.					
Infrastructure development (e.g. power).		Divide up responsibility and assessment for expenditure.	Who should pay for what needs to be negotiated? – roles!		Identify a single coordinating agency.
Service quality. Influx of seasonal employees.				Identify a single agent.	Coordinate training.
Beautification of area. Conflicting expectations between uses of resources (e.g. wetlands).	Designated access points. Make it user friendly. Need system and code of ethics.		Locals need education on how to handle influx of tourists.	Conflict resolution. Educate for environmental consideration.	

Ecotourism definition. What is Authenticity of experience? How do we maintain it? Adventure tourism. How do we keep it safe? Interconnection between activity sites.				
Unified theme. What should it be?		We need to identify what it should represent	Who and what we are. Civic pride.	Connect highway with town. Need lots of individual initiative.
Night-life. There are none at present but tourists will expect some.	Can it be industry based?	What is it worth and what are its contributions to tourism, development and local recreation?		
Family oriented activity. This is how we want to promote ourselves.	Can it be industry based? Need more culture and arts.	What is it worth and what are its contributions to tourism, development and local recreation? Need more culture and arts.		
Package rather than single activity. Not just a ski hill.			Recognition and identification.	
Coordinate between activities (front country/back country) and public/private delivery.				
Information management and marketing. Who will do it? Can it be coordinated? We need to set priorities.			Put tourism office on Trans Canada Highway.	Identify an agent. Information and discovery center is stalled. Get it going!

the questionnaire. The statistics provided in the table include the mean (arithmetic average), mode (most frequently appearing number), standard deviation (variability among responses) and sum (raw score) for each question. The statistics in the table are calculated for the group, and based on the fifteen completed responses to the questionnaire.

The questionnaire proved to be very useful in initiating discussion about the state of tourism in Golden and Area A, and in determining how people felt about the projected development of tourism in their community. Workshop participants were interested in discovering the views of their fellow participants that had led them to score each item on the questionnaire as they had. This facilitated a rich discussion of the participants' views on many aspects of tourism in the community.

The tourism sub-group then proceeded to identify issues and trends identified on the left hand column in Table 7.3. The group then identified the potential impacts of each of these trends or issues according to the key variables identified along the top of the table. This table is presented verbatim to demonstrate the thought process of those engaged in the exercise. Obviously it lacks a certain polish but is the type of thing which results from a highly participatory community consultation process where participants are simply asked to brainstorm an issue or problem.

The conference was not able to deal with all of the issues identified, and felt that some of the items did not warrant close attention at the time, which is reflected by the blank spaces in the table. In fact, the discussion implied by Table 7.3 raised more questions than it answered, suggesting that the planning process designed in Golden would be ongoing, rather than a onetime event. The matrix will continue to be worked through by town officials as the project progresses, and as further data is gathered and analyzed. Table 7.3 can provide the community concerned with a framework on which a continued monitoring process can be constructed to provide ongoing evaluation for the project.

Critique of the Golden tourism planning process

There is certainly more to be said in favor of this process than against it. The initial report of the consulting team has been accepted by the Golden Town Council and they have articulated their satisfaction with its content and direction, and believe the plan will assist them greatly as they address the major tourism development on the mountain. Although the process was fairly simple and standardized, a key component leading to its success was the genuine involvement of the citizens of Golden and Area A by the planning and research team. The process was based on the assumption that a community needs to take control of a plan that is to provide the framework for the proposed development of the resort and not leave planning solely to the development company. While the issue of the lack of planning standards and regulations in Area A was not resolved completely, this initial planning process was not designed to resolve this thorny problem, but focused instead on building relationships and getting all data and opinions on the table, without the pressure of demanding final decisions in such sensitive areas. While there is no doubt that this issue will need to be resolved in the long-term, the process employed here recognized that a permanent solution that would not divide the community had to be built initially upon trust and dialogue and therefore could not be forced into a truncated timeframe. The eventual decision regarding the lack of planning standards in Area A will need to be reached through a collective process, and not forced by a single authority.

The process used by Golden clearly demonstrates the use of both positivistic and interpretive research paradigms as outlined in Figure 6.1. Quantitative data was used in helping the participants make decisions, but no one said during the Golden process that 'the data tells us to do this so we had better do it' even though we have reservations about the inevitable outcome. In some cases decisions were made in contradiction to the indications of the positivistic research, because the community as a whole was not comfortable with moving in the direction indicated without time for broader discussion, or in some cases simply time to get used to the idea of such drastic change. However, because the analysis of these quantitative data was made available to the general public, the risks of not acting on their indications were clear and acceptable to the decision-makers.

The process also identified many issues that did not seem, on the surface, to be related to the immediate issues unearthed by the ski resort development. Whether the new development would have positive side-effects for unrelated community needs – in the form, for example of additions to the community's recreational facilities – was made part of the discussion. Dialogue was generated around the issues of poverty and affordable housing, particularly in relation to those who might be attracted to the area by employment in the tourism service industry; and around issues of how the environment might change, and potentially affect the quality of the back-country hiking and skiing enjoyed by local residents. In effect, what began as an impact study directly motivated by the development of the proposed ski resort became a general and comprehensive discussion of the community by the community, concerned with the overall development of the town and area A, and not just the site in question. It is hoped that Golden and Area A will now design and implement ongoing monitoring and evaluation procedures which will make the planning process cyclical, as suggested in Figure 5.2, rather than simply a one-off effort, as is often the case.

CASE STUDY: KENYA

Kenya and its tourism product

Tourism in Kenya is big business. For the most part, it is its number one foreign currency earner, competing with tea and coffee for that honor. The country is rich in wildlife and steeped in traditional cultures. Until recently, Kenya was for years seen as the Mecca of tourism development in Africa. This has changed somewhat since the re-entry of South Africa into the world community after apartheid ended in 1990, but in spite of the competition for tourists provided by South Africa, Kenya remains one of the main destinations of European and Asian tourists in Africa, particularly the Indian Ocean coast and the country's two major national parks, Amboseli and the Maasai Mara.

Kenya is blessed with an abundance of wildlife, world-class beaches, and traditional cultures like that of the Maasai people. This combination of people and wildlife provides Kenya with a rich resource base on which tourism relies. During the colonial period, white Kenyan colonialists founded many game reserves for sport hunting. Unfortunately, many of the lands that were set aside were the homelands of traditional peoples like the Maasai, who lived a semi-nomadic lifestyle, herding their cattle seasonally between pastures. The many reserves and national parks which tourists enjoy today began somewhat sordidly in this process of expropriation. Sindiga (1999: 71) suggests that Kenya contains 57 national parks, marine parks, national reserves, marine reserves and national sanctuaries.

These parks and reserves stretch across the whole of Kenya, and some – like the Maasai Mara – extend into Tanzania's Serengeti Plain, providing a spectacular reserve for many migratory animals and birds.

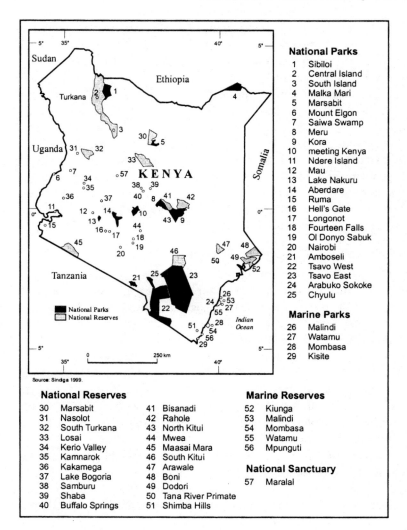

National Parks

1   Sibiloi
2   Central Island
3   South Island
4   Malka Mari
5   Marsabit
6   Mount Elgon
7   Saiwa Swamp
8   Meru
9   Kora
10   meeting Kenya
11   Ndere Island
12   Mau
13   Lake Nakuru
14   Aberdare
15   Ruma
16   Hell's Gate
17   Longonot
18   Fourteen Falls
19   Ol Donyo Sabuk
20   Nairobi
21   Amboseli
22   Tsavo West
23   Tsavo East
24   Arabuko Sokoke
25   Chyulu

Marine Parks

26   Malindi
27   Watamu
28   Mombasa
29   Kisite

Source: Sindiga 1999.

National Reserves

30	Marsabit	41	Bisanadi
31	Nasolot	42	Rahole
32	South Turkana	43	North Kitui
33	Losai	44	Mwea
34	Kerio Valley	45	Maasai Mara
35	Kamnarok	46	South Kitui
36	Kakamega	47	Arawale
37	Lake Bogoria	48	Boni
38	Samburu	49	Dodori
39	Shaba	50	Tana River Primate
40	Buffalo Springs	51	Shimba Hills

Marine Reserves

52	Kiunga
53	Malindi
54	Mombasa
55	Watamu
56	Mpunguti

National Sanctuary

57	Maralal

Figure 7.1   National Parks and Reserves of Kenya

Wildlife tourism depends largely on the 'big five' animals: elephants, lions, rhinoceros, water buffalo and leopards. While these seem to be the main attractions, other spectacular animals like the giraffe also receive considerable attention. Marine parks on the coast, mainly at Mombasa, attract a large number of tourists, particularly from Germany and other European countries. The beaches are spectacular, and the coral reefs are of world-class quality, competing with those in Australia and South America. Some refer to Mombasa as the African Riviera because of its long beach with white sand and warm water. Overlaying all of this wildlife and spectacular scenery is the culture of the people, particularly the traditional cultures of the Maasai and the Samburu. These cultures have become particularly well known since the Hollywood film *Out of Africa* was a box-office hit in the 1980s. Considering the abundance of the three ingredients of wildlife, culture and scenery, and the enormous publicity enjoyed by the country, it is easy to see why Kenya is highly sought after as a tourism destination. However, more than two decades of this very success has caused some severe problems for Kenya and its tourism industry.

The problems of Kenya and its tourism industry

The success of tourism in Kenya has created severe problems in maintaining the essence that visitors expect to find. Many of Kenya's parks and reserves have become gigantic zoos. Overuse by tourists, and a very successful biodiversity effort by the Kenya Wildlife Service (KWS), has led to some severe environmental problems and conflicts between wildlife and human beings. Many villages and crops have been destroyed, to say nothing of the loss of human life, as a result of elephants walking through inhabited villages. It is acknowledged by all those working in the area that up to 80 per cent of the wildlife exists outside park boundaries, therefore sharing space with the local human population and their domesticated animals. During times of drought, there is intense competition between wildlife and cattle for water holes, including those that lie within the boundaries of parks and reserves, even though they are supposed to be off-limits to cattle herders. The former colonialists, when they expropriated lands and dedicated them to wildlife reserves, had selected the most desirable land containing the wetlands and water holes. As a result of all of these factors, the conflict between wildlife and human beings became so acute that the local Maasai threatened to kill many of the animals unless the problem was addressed. A part of the resolution of the problem was provided by the inclusion of the local population in the tourism enterprise and its planning, so that more of its benefits would be realized in the local villages. It was felt that if the Maasai benefited directly from tourism, they would begin to see the benefits of the conservation movement and participate in it willingly.

Compounding the problems presented by the escalating number of large animal herds was the increase in the number of visitors to a few of the areas which contain these animals. More specifically, a problem was created for the KWS by the proliferation of visitors and their subsequent concentration within a few of the many available parks and reserves. The majority of tourist activity is concentrated within the Maasai Mara, the Amboseli National Park (which is adjacent to Mt Kilimanjaro) and the sea coast, mainly Mombasa. Some visitors from Amboseli to the coast stop off at Tsavo on their way, but this site does not receive an overabundance of visitors. The concentration of tourist activity is particularly interesting given the other choices that tourists could make. Kenya – particularly its northern part – contains the sites where Louis Leakey did much of his archaeological and anthropological work, often considered to be the cradle of humanity; yet few tourists visit the related sites.

Political unrest, particularly when it erupts into violence, also causes problems for the tourism industry. Needless to say, when extreme violence shows itself in any country people will forgo visits to that region in favor of more tranquil destinations. The 1997 pre-election violence in Kenya shut the tourism industry down completely in Mombasa for several months. However, while planning can deal with such issues as overcrowding, the dispersion of visitors to underused sites, and conflict between people and wildlife, it is unlikely to be able to resolve issues of violence within society in any direct way. Planning can, however, have a positive effect if the standard of living for all people is increased through a sharing of the benefits of tourism development.

The philosophy and approach of the KWS

The KWS has recognized for some time the problems associated with tourism and the role it plays in the degradation of parks and reserves. In order to try to address some of these problems, the former director of the KWS, David Western, initiated a reorganization of the KWS, and the completion of a 'conceptual' plan on which to base its future development. A central feature of the reorganization and planning exercise was to recognize the importance of the local people as stake-holders, and contributors to both the resolution of the problems discussed above and the future health of the ecosystem in the long term. Formerly, Kenya suffered from problems similar to those experienced by a number of countries that have engaged in top-down planning and ignored the needs of the local population. As Reid, Sindiga, Evans and Ongaro point out:

> In Kenya, several national parks have been created and are managed by the Kenya Wildlife Service (KWS) for the purpose of protecting the bio-diversity of the country's natural resources. While this policy can be seen as a noble goal in itself, it has often produced conflict and hardship on local people who have had to adjust their traditional patterns of living to fit this national initiative. The Kenya situation is another example of national goals conflicting with, and impacting on, local lifestyles.

(Reid et al., 1999: 60)

Prior to 1997, the KWS was constructed based on two directorates: the Bio-diversity Directorate and the Tourism Directorate. Subsequently it was reorganized, creating a third section called the Partnership Directorate, along with an administrative division. The mandate of the Partnership Directorate was to bring all stakeholders into the process. Implementing the mandate of the Partnership Directorate was a daunting task. There appeared to be no lack of good will on the part of the parties involved, but a number of historical difficulties impeded the process. Remnants of colonial administrative culture stressed top-down decision-making and hierarchical authority, even though Kenya had enjoyed independence for over three decades. Many of the group ranches relied too heavily on the KWS for the smallest of decisions, and failed to take charge of their own development. This may have also resulted from the lack of primary education among the Maasai population, and the understandable confusion resulting from the slow transition of a semi-nomadic lifestyle based on subsistence to a money-based economy. While some might argue that such a transition was tantamount to cultural genocide, the recent phenomena stemming from globalization are sure to have had an impact on the Maasai, so it was important for the transition to be directed by parties inside the process rather than by international agents, such as the many trans-national tourism companies that seemed to enjoy increasing influence throughout the country.

The establishment of the Partnership Directorate and its focus on including other stakeholders in the planning process sets a new direction for the KWS. It recognizes that increasing revenues through biological success and more tourism, will only occur if all the stake-holders, including people living in villages adjacent to parks and reserves, are included in the planning process, and receive some direct benefit from them. Two direct financial benefits will be realized by the communities directly adjacent to the parks. The first is known as the Benefits-Sharing Program, and the second is the Wildlife for Development Fund (WDF). This sharing of revenues represents a significant departure from earlier practices, when planning was basically driven from the top, and based on the needs of the national government and the biodiversity mandate of the KWS. While it can be argued that the new strategy of involving the stakeholders is still directed by the two fundamental objectives of biodiversity and tourism development, it can also be seen as a step forward for the local communities who are – and will continue to be – affected by the development of tourism sites. For the first time, those affected by tourism development are due to receive financial benefit from these initiatives. More specifically, this inclusive philosophy recognizes the rights of the local people to a share in the revenues raised by the parks and reserves under KWS jurisdiction. As a result of this recognition, a scheme for revenue sharing was developed and, although it has encountered some difficulties in implementation, it represents a breakthrough in recognizing the birthrights of the Maasai and other traditional groups living alongside parks and reserves. This is not dissimilar to the recognition in Canada of the rights of First Nations people to the resources which were expropri-ated by settlers upon their arrival in North America, or to the current present difficulties between the Australian government and the Aborigines.

Highlights of the KWS conceptual plan

The KWS publication, *Maintaining Biodiversity into the 21st Century: A Concept Paper on the Vision and Goals of Kenya Wildlife Service for the Period: 1997–2002*, commits the KWS to an inclusive vision of biodiversity and tourism development into the future. The paper sets out the mission statement of the KWS:

The Government of Kenya through the Kenya Wildlife Service holds in trust for present and future generations nationally and globally the biological diversity represented by its extraordinary variety of animals, plants and ecosystems ranging from coral reefs to alpine moorlands and from deserts to forests. Special emphasis is placed on conserving Kenya's unique assemblage of large animals found in few places on earth.

(KWS, 1999: 1)

While the mandate of the KWS maintains its clear focus on the goal of biodiversity, the strategies for implementation incorporate a wider range of objectives, including the involvement in the KWS planning process of local communities and stakeholders. The paper also notes that the

> KWS is now organized into three main goal directorates i.e. Biodiversity, Partnerships and Nature Tourism. These directorates are mainly responsible for policy matters and for the design and direction of activities. These are implemented through a field structure comprising of eight regions which cover the whole of the country including the marine areas i.e. lakes and coastline. In addition there are a number of support functions which are coordinated through the Management Services Division or directly by the Directors Office. Overall co-ordination and integration of activities is controlled through the Directors Office and the strategic planning process.

(Ibid.: 3–4)

A. The Biodiversity Directorate

Below, I paraphrase the KWS conceptual plan which suggests how it will achieve its mandate of biodiversity:

- Undertaking of specific initiatives in the field of bio-diversity conservation;
- The development of the partnership concept with communities and other stakeholders involved in or affected by conservation initiatives;
- The development of nature tourism to provide optimum utilization of the bio-diversity resources while maintaining their integrity;
- The development of internal capacity within the KWS to efficiently, economically and effectively achieve its mission.

In order to achieve the mandated biodiversity goals of the organization, I summarize the KWS document (Ibid.: 5–6) which sets out some overall strategies:

- Identifying of threats to areas of primary conservation significance;
  - Undertaking bio-diversity inventorying;
  - Development of sustainable wildlife utilization and management programs;
- Establishing an Environmental Impact Assessment Unit;
- Developing bio-diversity databases at HQ and at regional levels;
- Undertaking of specific research work in high priority areas;
- Establishing ecological monitoring programs;
- Establishing evaluation unit to monitor various programs.

In establishing the Partnership Directorate, the KWS plan states that

[w]ithout the involvement and support of the communities involved, the threats to sustainable Bio-diversity Conservation will remain high. Therefore, the main objective of the Partnership goal is to reduce Human Wildlife conflict, especially in the areas of strategic species and ecosystems. KWS will endeavour to effectively manage the conflict through the establishment of a database that will facilitate continuous monitoring and evaluation against predetermined indicators. While the majority of KWS's activities and its jurisdiction are focused within the National Parks and Protected Areas the Partnership function will be to work with:

- communities adjacent to parks and protected areas
- landowners involved in wildlife management activities
- associations and NGOs involved in wildlife conservation
- private sector

(Ibid.: 7)

In order to accomplish these objectives the KWS recognize they will need to assist their partnered communities to develop the capacity to plan, construct and manage the tourism enterprise in their jurisdictions. The Conceptual Plan speaks about building community capacity in 'preparing communities to take up the challenges that are expected to ensue from the new Wildlife Act'. (Ibid.: 7) They go on to suggest that critical to success of this change the 'KWS will endeavour to minimize the current dependency syndrome which has developed out of numerous social projects and instead concentrate on enterprise projects which build an economic and sustainable financial base for the respective communities'. (Ibid.: 7) Within this new order is the need for a change of attitude on the part of many communities from that of dependent to one that stresses ownership of the enterprise by the community which demands accountability and responsibility for the conservation and utilization of wildlife and other natural resources.

While not losing sight of their biodiversity mandate, the KWS clearly sees the importance of engaging the local community. The activities of the Partnership Directorate reach back to the mandate of biodiversity conservation for their direction. It is intended that communities and other stakeholders play a predominant role in the planning process leading to enhancement of this mandate. However, the KWS understands that unless it speaks to the needs of the people who live alongside parks and reserves, those same facilities will not be maintained and the mandate will not be achieved. Although the conceptual plan could have gone a lot further in making the community the subject of development, rather than seeing it as a means towards the goal of biodiversity development solely, the KWS has substantially increased the visibility of the producer compared with their past practices. It has yet to be seen whether this amendment to the strategy of the KWS will significantly change the environmental, social and economic situation of those who are affected by Kenya's tourism plan, but it certainly represents a welcome initiative which, at the very least, recognizes the importance of the role of local people, where previously planning tended to treat them as if they did not form a significant part of the tourism enterprise. The new approach represents a clear recognition that the old way of managing the development of parks and protected areas for tourism failed, and that new and inclusive strategies were needed if the twin objectives of biodiversity and a successful tourist industry are to be achieved.

B. The Tourism Directorate

The conceptual plan of the KWS also reconstituted the tourism function as part of its strategy. The plan set out four specific objectives for the Tourism Directorate:

- To diversify to new parks hitherto not visited
- To diversify tourism activities beyond parks
- To maximize economic benefits to KWS, communities and Kenya as a whole

- To minimize negative environmental impact from tourist activities

(Ibid.: 9)

To achieve these objectives the KWS suggested that it would focus on investing in the areas of infrastructure, product quality, training, accommodation, and marketing, setting out in some detail how they would approach each area.

C. *The Partnership Directorate*

Perhaps of most interest is the final part of the KWS conceptual plan, which sets out the framework according to which local community plans from experimental communities in and around the Amboseli region will be undertaken. Each of the seven Maasai group ranches (the official designation of Maasai communities) was invited to submit documents outlining plans for biodiversity conservation and tourism development – and particularly for the establishment of nature reserves. Each submission was required to follow the following planning category guidelines:

1. Objectives – including the development of an overall direction for development which takes into account the Strengths, Weaknesses, Opportunities and Threats (SWOT) for the group ranch;
2. Goals – including the identification of initiatives to achieve the objectives that result from the SWOT analysis;
3. Strategies – including activities that will build the capacity of the community to engage in tourism and biodiversity development, in addition to harmonizing their activity with that of the KWS.
4. Integrated plans – incorporating those of other stakeholders, to enhance harmonious working relationships;
5. Capacity building – developing ideas which contribute to the building of self-reliance in group ranch management, and towards financial self-reliance; identifying training requirements for a variety of skills;
6. Nature tourism activities – developing strategies for marketing and attracting visitors, and for diversifying products; planning the development of new accommodation for visitors;
7. Review of assets and priorities – the completion of inventories of group ranch assets, including wildlife, land available for

      development as tourist accommodation or for wildlife; the
      evaluation and ranking of those assets;

8. Integration of plan and budget – the matching of resources to plans;

9. Action plans – each plan identifying its objectives and listing activities to accomplish those objectives; all plans providing starting dates, performance indicators, assignment of responsibilities and projected completion dates for the project;

10. Activities schedule – all activities and sub-activities listed and ordered in the sequence necessary to allow for other projects to be completed.

These plans were to be submitted to the KWS, to expatriate NGOs and to foreign governments as part of a funding effort. One such pilot project was commissioned, and stands as the flagship for the KWS's conceptual planning initiative. That project is the Kimana Group Ranch reserve, adjacent to the Amboseli National Park and in sight of Mount Kilimanjaro.

Kimana

In 1993 the Conservation of Bio-diverse Resource Areas (COBRA) project was established through a number of expatriate funders, notably USAID, in cooperation with the KWS. The specific mandate of the project was to increase the socioeconomic benefits deriving from conservation and the sustainable management of wildlife and other natural resources to communities living alongside protected areas in Kenya. As Knegt points out,

> The proposed project was to provide financing for technical assistance, short- and long-term training and material support to help KWS establish and operate an effective *Community Wildlife Service*. The Community Wildlife Service was established to institutionalize a 'community conservation' approach in which the KWS would improve its relationship with communities in key biodiversity areas and engage as 'partners in conservation'. This should be accomplished by reducing the negative impacts of wildlife on the communities and increasing the economic benefits, through: direct sharing of park and reserve revenues; small-scale community development projects; and financial and technical assistance.

(Knegt,1998: 50)

The Kimana Group Ranch was selected as a pilot project under that program (see map in Figure 7.2 for location of the Kimana Group Ranch).

Kimana is a Maasai community, located next to the Amboseli National Park, which has established a nature and wildlife reserve on its group ranch property for tourism purposes. It has also constructed a resort hotel, complete with a kitchen that can compete

Figure 7.2   Amboseli National Park and Kimana Group Ranch

in quality with the other resorts in the Amboseli National Park area. In fact, Kimana is a miniature version of Amboseli, complete with a similar array of animals and facilities. In addition, there are a number of Maasai villages located on the property, adding a cultural experience to the visit. It is operated by the Kimana Group Ranch council for the benefit of the members of the community. It is hoped by the KWS that the Kimana reserve will accommodate some of the animals that have overflowed from the Amboseli park. The KWS and the Kimana council hope that many of the visitors who would otherwise invade the already overcrowded Amboseli will visit Kimana instead. Although Kimana has been successful in those terms, it has not, at the time of writing, generated the level of revenue that was originally anticipated. It is still in its early days, and only time will tell whether it will be successful or not.

Critique of the KWS initiative

Kenya provides a case study of a large national organization that was successful in its original mandate. In fact, the KWS was perhaps too successful in attracting tourists to its parks and reserves, and in its efforts at biodiversity development. As problems emerged – particularly for communities adjacent to the parks – the KWS needed a set of plans which would deal with the concerns of local communities and other stakeholders, without losing sight of its original mandate. The recognition that local communities need to be part of the planning process, and to benefit from any development, is a step forward for an organization like the KWS, which is dominated by professionals from within natural sciences whose mandate is exclusively focused on the issues of biodiversity. While the KWS still relies heavily on their ongoing scientific research, they also take advantage of the interpretivist and constructivist side of the planning process, as outlined in Chapter 6.

While the primary focus of the KWS on biodiversity is unquestionably laudable, it must be accompanied by an equal emphasis on the goal of community development. This can only be accomplished either by a concerted effort on the part of the KWS, or through the establishment of a new agency with community development as its central focus. Until the goal of community development is given equal attention to that of biodiversity, the attempt at strengthening biodiversity is likely to stagnate. Regardless of how this effort is institutionalized, tourism should be seen as the means to achieving both goals. The present KWS mandate of biodiversity will be best achieved through partnering with communities and other tourism stakehold-ers that are adjacent to natural areas. By working in partnership, people will come to realize the importance of local flora and fauna to their welfare, and will be much more willing participants in their preservation. The way in which biodiversity has traditionally been emphasized has made people feel that they are secondary to wildlife. True partnership will not come about until the people of the area are convinced that their welfare is central to any tourism development, rather than being seen as subordinate to their husbandry of wildlife on behalf of others.

The establishment of the Partnership Directorate was important in dealing with this problem. It not only gave a symbolic signal to communities that the KWS took their problems seriously, but also provided the KWS with a framework for finding solutions. Unfortunately, however, it is not clear that staff employed within the new division have the necessary skills in community development to meet the demands of the conceptual plan. Most of the staff within the Partnership Directorate have been reassigned from the other two divisions, and they therefore have a professional bias towards the natural sciences or business, rather than community development. A different set of skills is required for this new function, and it is unclear whether they are possessed by the personnel in the newly-formed Partnership Directorate.

The KWS has initiated an immensely important process by adopting the partnership project in its mandate, and by implement-ing it in Kimana through the COBRA pilot project. It is only a focus on communities themselves that will produce sustainable increases in biodiversity – the main goal of the KWS.

CASE STUDY: BERMUDA

Since Bermuda inspired Shakespeare to write *The Tempest*, and Queen Victoria's daughter Princess Louise paid an extended visit in 1883, it has become a pre-eminent holiday destination for tourists around the world.

Bermuda is a singular island in the Atlantic, 600 miles off the coast of North Carolina, USA. It was formed some 110 million years ago by volcanic action, and emerged from the water approximately 70 million years later. The volcanic island is ringed by a coral reef, which captured decaying sediment and other soil-building materials which now provide cover to the island. Often described as resembling 'a string of pearls', because the land mass and the reef between them form a complete elliptical chain, Bermuda's surface area, of little more than 20 square miles, is easily navigated by motor scooter, ferry, bus or on foot. In fact, while Bermuda is very small in terms of both population and land mass, by all North American and European standards, it has a public transportation system which would be the envy of many large North American cities; every part of the island is accessible by bus or ferry. Early in the twentieth century Bermuda operated a railway which ran from one end of the island to the other. Because of an absence of spare parts, the railway was dismantled and the track taken up during the late 1940s. Its remnant is an island-long walking and hiking trail, which not only adds to the public transit system but provides a stimulating form of recreation for residents and visitors alike. This attention to public transit has allowed the Bermudian government to maintain one of the strictest automobile policies in the world, resulting in a relatively clean environment. Households are limited to one car, and visitors are not allowed to rent them. Mopeds are available, but the excellent public transport system obviates the need for them.

Travelers arriving by sea or sky are immediately captivated by the spectacular turquoise waters, stretches of sandy beaches, and by the sheer natural beauty of this tiny island. Bermuda is perpetually warmed by the currents from the Gulf Stream, which makes its climate very predictable, with temperatures in February and March averaging 17°C, and approximately 30°C during the summer months. These temperatures are certainly attractive to North American travelers, particularly in the winter months.

But it is not just the pleasant temperatures that make Bermuda a favorite tourism destination with North American and European visitors. In most heavily developed tourism destinations, particularly small island states, tourists are kept in a bubble away from the everyday life of the local inhabitants, but this has not been the case in Bermuda. As McDowall observes,

> tourists in Bermuda are visitors. They spilled down the Furness-Withy gangways or into the jaunty pastel-coloured taxis at the airport and then melted into Bermuda society ... visitors were invited into a huge Bermuda living room and left to their own devices. All that was asked was that they abide by the decorum of the place and leave it as clean and peaceable as they had found it.

> (McDowall, 1999: 124–5)

Unlike many islands in the Caribbean to the south, tourists in Bermuda are invited to join in the day-to-day activities of the locals, and are not walled off in a remote resort complex. The island remains a British colony, after a referendum seeking secession in 1995 was thoroughly defeated. As a result, many of the cultural traditions and lifestyles are similar to the social practices of visitors themselves. Bermuda does not have the searing poverty of many of the islands farther south, which often creates discomfort for visitors.

The population of the island is 60,000-strong, with 60 per cent of it being of African descent, as against 40 per cent deriving from Europe. While this may seem like a small population, it translates to 3,160 people per square mile. It is argued that Bermudians enjoy the highest standard of living in the world, as measured by literacy rates, educational attainment, life expectancy and the relative absence of poverty and crime (see McDowall, 1999). Hamilton is the largest city, with a population of 3,000, although its main street and shopping district appear similar to any North American shopping plaza. Of course, because it is a tourism destination it possesses an abundance of fine restaurants and a wide array of consumer outlets.

Bermuda is unlike many of the tourism destinations south in the Caribbean because of its lack of absolute poverty. Unions have traditionally been strong in Bermuda, and the Bermuda Industrial Union has worked tirelessly to secure wages and working conditions for tourism workers which are well above the poverty line, no matter how that standard is measured. For example, there is a mandatory 15 per cent gratuity added to all hotel and dining charges. Strong unions have been seen by some as a constraint on the process of rejuvenation within the tourism industry, while others see unionism as a positive contribution to its attractiveness. On the positive side, high crime rates and extreme and evident poverty have been avoided, contributing to the general feeling of security found in Bermuda. Decent wages and tight union policies in the tourism industry have contributed to the civility of the tourism enterprise. On balance union strength has contributed to the maintenance of a fairly tranquil society – in spite of occasional racial tensions – which, in these times of heightened concern about terrorism, is a valuable asset for a tourism destination.

Tourism in Bermuda

Tourism in Bermuda relies on history as one of its differentiations from the Caribbean islands further south. The first community was founded following colonization by the British in 1612. The historic town of St George's has been designated a World Heritage Site by UNESCO. On the opposite tip of the island, Bermuda's seafaring history can be explored at the Maritime Museum, on six acres at the Royal Naval Dockyards. Fort St Catherine, a strategic defense garrison built by the British in 1614 rounds out the official historical infrastructure. All of Bermuda's cities, as well as the smaller villages and towns, provide a very clean and architecturally pleasing environment to the visitor. In contrast to many island destinations, virtually no parts of Bermuda are off-limits to tourists.

Bermuda Tourism also relies on a wealth of golf courses for their tourism focus and, although expensive, they are magnificently groomed and arguably among the best in the world. The harbor facilities are also quite adequate for both the private yachts and cruise ships, either visiting the island or making their permanent home there.

Bermuda is home to numerous historic shipwrecks, and diving and snorkeling opportunities in the clearest waters in the western Atlantic. The colorful coral reefs provide a spectacular backdrop for fish, sea turtles, and a wealth of exotic marine life. An abundant supply of fish provides angling to the Bermuda tourism experience. The myth of the Bermuda triangle certainly adds to the mystery and attractions of the island.

Bermuda has always been attractive to tourists, but it was not until the 1970s that it had its heyday as a tourist destination. Its best year was probably 1987, when it attracted 631,314 visitors. Arriving tourists enter either by air or by cruise ship. However, Bermuda has set limits on visits by cruise ship to five or six per year. In this way the island avoids being inundated by excessive numbers of visitors at any given time.

An important feature of tourism in Bermuda is the schedule of festivals and events which have been created for both citizens and visitors. Fashion shows, international road races, weekly Gombey dance performances, a national art gallery, heritage walking tours and a weekly performance of the Scottish highland regiment, at noon on Monday, all contribute to the experience of the visitor. Bermuda has created a coordinated program of events for tourists, and not just left visitors to their own devices. Many of these events also provide recreation to Bermudian residents.

Challenges to Bermuda's tourism industry

In spite of what appears to be an idyllic setting for tourism, guaranteeing its pre-eminence in the global marketplace, Bermuda's tourism industry is in decline, due to a number of factors. Competition in general has increased throughout the world within the tourism market, in association with the deregulation of the airline industry initiated by Ronald Reagan, and with economic globalization. When airlines were regulated, flights were generally priced by the mile; now it is just as inexpensive for North American travelers to travel to distant locations like Europe, or farther south to the Caribbean, as it is to travel 500 miles to Bermuda. Deregulation has meant that, for the same price, the traveler now has more potential destinations to choose from.

Bermuda has also been criticized – and indeed has criticized itself – for not maintaining its properties to the level necessary to justify the relatively high cost of a visit. Through visitor research Bermuda has found that 'Bermuda is too expensive for the value it offers'. (Bermuda Alliance for Tourism, 2001; 11) If the island's tour operators are to continue attracting their traditional, high-end target group of visitors (defined as those with household incomes in excess of US$125,000) then facilities and services will need to be improved.

As things stand, a number of large hotels have either closed down or are in the process of diversifying their operations. The Marriott Hotel has closed completely, and is in the process of being redeveloped into condominiums. The Belmont Hotel is renovating most of its property to create condominiums, while maintaining a small section as a hotel. Such developments represent a necessary rationalization of the industry, which will also allow other hotels and accommodation units to take a larger share of the market.

Bermudian tourism now faces challenges from other parts of the business sector. Because of what some would argue are liberal corporate tax laws, Bermuda has become very attractive to North American insurance and financial firms. While this is healthy for the economy as a whole, it provides serious competition to the tourism industry, particularly for labor. This new form of employment pays better and is more glamorous to young Bermudians than the seasonality and low-end jobs offered by employment within tourism. While this seems positive on the surface, it does open up the possibility that low skilled jobs, on which many residents depend, may be lost to the economy completely if the tourism industry is considerably reduced.

Strategic planning

The decline of tourism over the last decade has shaken tourism officials out of their complacency. The culture of the tourism industry in the past was to provide the product in the sure knowledge that lucrative business would follow; in a sense, the strategy was supply-driven. This approach to tourism development is no longer appropriate, and the industry has been quick to take action. What emerged during the late 1990s was the development of a partnership among the various stakeholders within the tourism industry dedicated to implementing a planned approach to this critical problem. An organization called the Bermuda Alliance for Tourism (BAT) was created to plan and manage Bermuda's tourism industry out of decline. The government of Bermuda and the hotel industry were the main partners in the system, but places at the table were also occupied by union officials and other interested parties. An outline of the organizational structure of the Bermuda Alliance for Tourism is shown in Figure 7.3.

This partnership produced a strategic plan which, it was hoped, would guide the tourism industry back to the pre-eminence it once enjoyed. It is this partnership and its plan which makes Bermuda an important case study. The Bermuda Tourism Strategy (Bermuda Alliance for Tourism, 2001) takes the strengths, weaknesses, opportunities and threats (SWOT) approach to planning. Each of these factors is used as a basis for analysis throughout the process. The Bermuda Tourism working group further subdivides their analysis by visitor category, believing that each separate group possesses dissimilar needs, requiring different responses. The numbers of arrivals for each visitor sector group in 1999 were as follows: cruise visitors – 196,000; individual leisure visitors (arriving by air) – 207,000; business group visitors – 76,000; individual business travelers – 41,000.

With the Bermuda Tourism Strategy (Bermuda Alliance for Tourism, 2001) in place, the BAT established three basic questions on which analysis would focus:

- What best depicts to the tourist what Bermuda is all about?
- What are the needs of visitors to Bermuda?
- How can Bermuda improve the experiences to the variety of tourists it attracts?

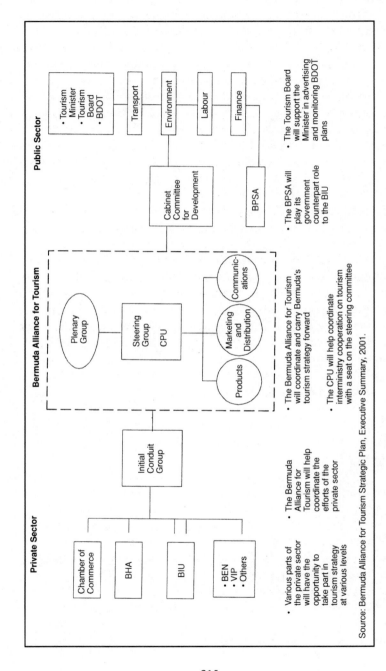

Figure 7.3　The Role of the Bermuda Alliance for Tourism within the Tourism Industry

215

The response to the first question would produce an understanding of the foundation on which the Bermuda tourism project would be built in the future. Figure 7.4 outlines that foundation.

These 'anchors' of Bermuda's tourism project were developed at a series of workshops conducted by BAT. The strategic plan goes on to identify the key needs of the four visitor sectors under the categories of planning, selection, on-island, and post-trip (see Figure 7.4). Factors which will make selection of Bermuda by group visitors easier were outlined for each category. These needs were identified by ongoing research, and through focus groups organized by the travel industry. Surveys were conducted at the airport, and at other strategic points on the island, to incorporate visitor perspectives. Finally, the BAT brainstormed the question 'How can Bermuda improve the different visitor experiences?' The results of this brainstorming exercise produced recommendations for action and implementation.

These recommendations will provide the focus for the BAT's activities over the next few years. Decisions about market segments, and improvements to programs and facilities, are contained in the plan. Short-term goals include: physical plant upgrades; an employee training program; transportation improvements; increasing the number of signature events which characterize what Bermuda tourism is about; development of a technology platform which incorporates internet and other new and emerging technologies; improvements to safety and cleanliness. Long-term goals include: the development of an overall island plan; a Hamilton development plan; improvements to the St George's World Heritage Center; enhanced recreational facilities at the Dockyards; the creation of a national center; better management of the balance between cruise ship and air arrivals.

The plan also discusses in some detail a number of other issues, including: a schedule of activities and programs to increase the number and quality of experiences for each of the visitor segments identified above; a number of unresolved issues requiring resolution by public organizations; an overview of the guiding principles for a short-term sales and marketing plan; an overview of the guiding principles for a long-term sales and marketing plan. This list of issues led to a consensus on key areas of the plan, including the development of a vision statement for Bermudian tourism; overall sales and marketing objectives; the identification of a number of channels for communications distribution, and a budget proposal.

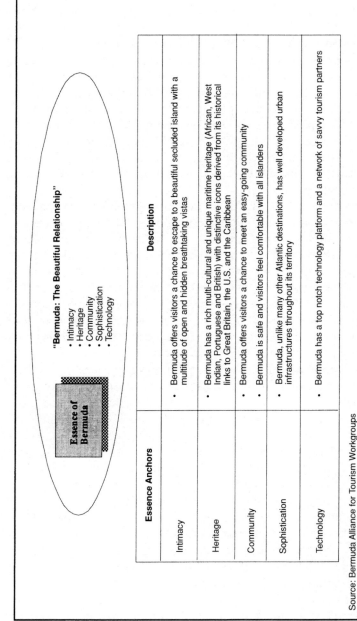

"Bermuda: The Beautiful Relationship"

- Intimacy
- Heritage
- Community
- Sophistication
- Technology

Essence of Bermuda

Essence Anchors	Description
Intimacy	• Bermuda offers visitors a chance to escape to a beautiful secluded island with a multitude of open and hidden breathtaking vistas
Heritage	• Bermuda has a rich multi-cultural and unique maritime heritage (African, West Indian, Portuguese and British) with distinctive icons derived from its historical links to Great Britain, the U.S. and the Caribbean
Community	• Bermuda offers visitors a chance to meet an easy-going community • Bermuda is safe and visitors feel comfortable with all islanders
Sophistication	• Bermuda, unlike many other Atlantic destinations, has well developed urban infrastructures throughout its territory
Technology	• Bermuda has a top notch technology platform and a network of savvy tourism partners

Source: Bermuda Alliance for Tourism Workgroups

Figure 7.4   Anchors of the Essence of Bermuda

Critique of the Bermudian plan

The development of the BAT and its subsequent strategic plan is an example of planning involving many of the parties on the island with an interest in tourism. Bermuda's strategic tourism plan focuses as robustly on the process of planning as it does on the outcome of the plan. It strongly represents the perspectives of government and the hospitality industry, however, it may not take into account sufficiently those of the general public. This may prove to be the plan's Achilles heel. Greater inclusion of the general public in this discourse might have produced innovative solutions that may not have been apparent to those officially closest to the action. There may be many unidentified interests that can also produce new entrepreneurs in the tourism system if they are encouraged through a process enabling wider public involvement.

Nevertheless, Bermuda's current tourism planning activity provides a clear example of a community of interest in crisis coming together in a coordinated and planned way to address a set of problems. Research, both positivistic and interpretive, is a central feature of the process. It is to be hoped that the process will be ongoing, and not just provide a one-off burst of activity in response to a crisis. The research process has created some very useful categories on which monitoring can be based, while the structure is now in place and can be augmented in the long-term. While the Bermudian process does not follow exactly the research process outlined in Chapter 6, it does adapt features of it to its own situation. It is important to note that the research and planning process must not only be technically correct, but must also fit the personality, and – perhaps more importantly – the levels of skill, of the members of the community to implement. Finally, it is to be hoped that BAT will broaden the process to include those community groups that were not originally involved in it. This will maintain the high level of acceptance of tourism that has traditionally prevailed on the island.

With the recognition that additional plans are needed for Hamilton the main city and the other smaller towns and villages throughout the island, planning in Bermuda is recognized as a cyclical process. In many tourism planning exercises, planning is devoted to solving a specific problem. This does not appear to be the case in Bermuda. Ongoing planning is an important recognition of the need for constant attention to the health of the tourism system which will not only assist Bermuda in rejuvenating its tourism industry, but will also continue to provide a very agreeable environment to its citizens. Whether by accident or through the pressure of public opinion, tourism has not dominated the social framework of Bermuda, even though it accounts for a large part of the economy. Unlike many small island states which embrace tourism as a dominant industry, Bermuda has created a project which benefits both tourists and citizens alike. In the final analysis, the judgment of the success of tourism development in Bermuda has not been made solely according to economic criteria, but has been considered from a broader social perspective. Questions such as who benefits from tourism, and who pays the costs, have been an ongoing part of the discourse within Bermudian society.

ANALYSIS OF THE CASE STUDIES

The three cases discussed in this chapter provide the reader with examples of the planning principles outlined in Chapters 5 and 6. Although each case study has employed the various theories and techniques to greater and lesser degrees in its planning activities, each has embraced the spirit of the principles enunciated in this text, and developed tourism in dialogue with the people most likely to be directly affected by its nature. Certainly, the Maasai have at last been brought into the planning process, after decades, if not centuries, of neglect. It has been recognized that the mandate and values of the KWS will not be furthered without the support of the people who live in the vicinity of its parks and reserves, and alongside the animals it is attempting to protect.

The Town of Golden is faced with a potentially overwhelming ski resort development (KHMR), which may change the nature of the town fundamentally. While welcoming this new development, Golden has initiated a planning process which attempts to maximize the positive side-effects of this development while minimizing its potential social and environmental costs. The planning process initiated by the Town of Golden, whether intentionally or not, came to examine many aspects of life in the community which are not usually found in a planning exercise that is mandated to deal with a specific developmental issue. A central lesson to be learned from this case seems to be that negotiating the terms on which planning will focus is very important. Communities like Golden are too often prone to follow too closely the planning precedents set by other similar towns. All communities are unique in their construction and social conditions, and one town's terms of reference for a study cannot be simply passed on to another community. While this point may seem self-evident, it is clear that many towns depend too much on the experiences of their neighbors, and do not negotiate sufficiently the conditions of their planning framework. An in-depth discussion, forming part of the process of setting up the terms of reference for a planning study within a community is a rich learning experience for that community, and should not be bypassed.

Both of these case studies demonstrate the implementation of Friedmann's concept of social learning (see Friedmann, 1987). Here the planning framework stresses the central position of the citizen in the process. It links knowledge to action – a central feature of Friedmann's construction of social learning. This process relies as much on broad-based interpretation of the meaning of the data to those who live in the community as it does on the expert analysis which is often a part of the process.

In the case of Golden, the discourse and the social learning it produced initiated social action. The recommendations of the research and the subsequent plan, if implemented as directed in that plan, will produce a fundamental change in the structure of decision-making in regard to the future development of the KHMR. The plan recommends continued exploration of the possibility of unifying the governance of the Town of Golden with that of Area A. If this political unification were to come to fruition, the basis for planning and continued growth would be on a more secure footing. Both costs and benefits would be equally shared, and the negative impacts to existing communities could be ameliorated more easily. This recommendation and others demonstrate that tourism planning not only differs in the process but also in substance. Issues of governance, as well as development concerns, are legitimate areas of interest within tourism planning. Due to the nature of tourism as an enterprise, and its pervasiveness in many rural areas, community tourism planning must adopt a comprehensive outlook. Issues of economics, environmental concerns and social impacts must necessarily be considered by a tourism planning exercise, in addition to the usual focus on physical development – and in Golden's case, matters of governance and regulation as well.

While the Kenya Wildlife Service included its own version of Friedmann's social learning model in its concept paper, it also represents a demonstration on the part of the Maasai of Friedmann's concept of radical planning. In order for the Maasai to become part of the KWS's planning process, they had to threaten to kill some of the large animals which represented a serious threat to the safety of the area's inhabitants. This caught the attention of the KWS, and acted as a catalyst in widening the scope of its planning to include other stakeholders. It could be argued that the process provided the KWS with a social learning experience as the Maasai became forceful in their demands for inclusion in the planning and decision-making processes of the KWS. This was forcefully reflected upon by David Western, Director of the KWS, when he talked in his book, *In the Dust of Kilimanjaro* (1997), about the Maasai and their cattle economy as an integral part of the ecosystem, acting in harmony with the environment, rather than to the detriment of local flora and fauna. The KWS concept paper was built on the blending of positivist, interpretivist and constructivist research and not just on positivist research which often pervades this type of planning. To the credit of the KWS, it was able to break from tradition and revamp an organization which not only made the various stakeholders part of the decision-making process, but also bestowed many of the economic benefits resulting from tourism upon them.

While tourism development in Bermuda does not demonstrate the same kind of commitment to the inclusion of all citizens in the planning process, as with the other two examples, it does demonstrate the organization of the government and the industry into a working group to plan and manage themselves out of a state of decline. In many cases, this is often done by discarding the fundamental principles on which a society has been built, in order to serve the economy. In Bermuda's case this clearly did not occur. Instead, its actions demonstrated the implementation of what Friedmann would designate as the 'policy analysis' model of development, in which the tourism plan is organized from the top down – in that the government and the industry dominate the decision-making process – while the union movement was nevertheless not excluded from the process completely. The industry knows that it cannot violate any agreements it has made with labor, so the unions are somewhat protected in the process, without having an equal number of seats on the BAT. The participation strategy used in the Bermuda plan may be closest to the 'informing' or 'consultation' stage of the continuum as identified in Arnstein's model (see Arnstein, 1969). Here, there is no pretence of providing citizens with full access to the decision-making process and then acting contrarily by informing or consultation with people who are supposed to be in control of the outcome. What is important in the Bermuda case is to recognize that it implemented a participation framework which was consistent with the overall theoretical model of the planning process. In many planning projects, planners promise a participation model which is not consistent with the fundamental theory on which the process is constructed. Figure 5.1 outlines which participation strategy is generally appropriate for each of the overall theoretical approaches presented by Friedmann. While most planners and lay people alike may want to argue that the social reform and policy analysis approach is clearly inferior to any process which includes wide-ranging public discussion, I believe there are times when this is not the case, and Bermuda may be one of those cases in which social reform or policy analysis is appropriate. I would make this argument for two reasons. First, the issue for Bermuda is one of rejuvenation of the industry, and not of drastic development departing from the established nature of the local industry. This may not have been true if there had been a proposal in the planning project to incorporate a facility which departs drastically from what is presently in the system, like a casino. If that were to be part of the plan, then a different and perhaps more social learning oriented approach would be necessary. A casino has been talked about informally, but has not formed part of any proposal. This also demonstrates the flexibility needed by the planner to adopt a different theoretical approach to the planning process when the environment changes. As it stands, however, the present project in Bermuda does not include the proposal of a casino, so the citizen participation approach adopted may be satisfactory. The second reason why a relatively limited degree of citizen involvement may be acceptable is that the citizens of Bermuda are clearly in favor of tourism, and have historically demonstrated satisfaction with tourism as it has historically evolved. The present planning process, from the citizen's point of view, is merely a matter of 'tinkering' with the nature of tourism on the island, which is already accepted by the population.

These case studies demonstrate the importance of planning for tourism development. Tourism planning is not just a technical and physical activity, but is as much social and political. Obviously, tourism affects the lives of those living alongside tourism attractions, and it is therefore necessary to include them in the planning of any tourism project. Unlike that of many other economic sectors, tourism's product brings people into the community: the more successful the attraction, the more extensive will be the problems of congestion and pollution with which the community will have to deal. Given that tourism is an ever-changing system, planning must be ongoing, rather than addressing a set of problems in a one-off fashion. Tourism planning must try to project the problems that are likely to occur in the future as a result of decisions made in the present.

8 The Integration of Tourism within General Development

INTRODUCTION

This book concludes with a discussion of the integration of tourism into the overall development strategies, at the local, regional and national level. It addresses how countries or communities which play host to failing tourism projects or those which require rejuvenation can retrospectively deploy the principles outlined in this text.

This last chapter outlines the basic approaches to tourism development, based on the issues outlined in the preceding chapters. Tourism is seen by many communities as one economic development strategy among the many available to them. There remains, of course, a question as to whether any economic development at all is desired within the community. If the answer to that question is no, then much of what is contained in this text will obviously be of no interest. However, in most cases the answer to the above question is not determined until much of the process of discussion advocated in this text has been completed. Moreover, this book views the local debate about tourism and its implementation as having a larger purpose: namely, that of building a variety of capacities within communities. The tourism plan provides an opportunity to articulate a vision for the community, as well as the identification of the sacrosanct community values which need protecting. That in itself is a worthwhile goal.

THE INTRICACIES OF TOURISM DEVELOPMENT

This book demonstrates the value of tourism development to nations and communities in need of economic revitalization. In fact, it has gone beyond that initial assertion to suggest that tourism can engender greater understanding between people who come into contact through travel, if devised and implemented properly. The conception and implementation of a tourism project must be the prerogative of the community concerned, and constructed so as not only to preserve and protect the values and culture of the community, but actually to enhance them. I have also explored the problems and pitfalls of tourism for communities which are not in control of the planning and management of development. Tourism is neither inherently positive nor inherently negative, as its critics would have us believe. What constitutes its success or failure is how it is planned and managed, and who controls that development. If left to the vagaries of the market alone, tourism developments will emerge without any consideration of the conditions of the social and natural environment in which they are located. This form of development will simply produce more of the same types of tourism development which have been criticized throughout this text. Status quo planning is bound to produce the same problems over again and any developments that emerge in this way will certainly not constitute examples of sustainable tourism development. While many tourism attractions have been successful and maximized profits for their owners, they have not always lived up to the expectations of the people who live with the development on a day-to-day basis, and have in fact often had a negative impact on their environment.

These problems have motivated the development of planning models that place the community clearly in charge of the planning process. Why, then, has tourism been such a disruptive force in many communities, in both developed countries and LDCs? A partial answer to this question is that tourism has been consistently developed according to agendas that come from outside the tourism communities, which give no priority to the welfare of those communities as their guiding principle. Moreover, communities are rarely organized to deal collectively with such a complex initiative as tourism development. While large corporations and most small businesses are well organized and have the skills to tackle these initiatives, communities often lack the expertise and organizational skill necessary to create an overarching structure to control the direction of tourism development. Communities often expect the national government to supply some of that direction; but national governments have their own agendas, which may be quite different, and which may conceivably conflict with local interests. For example, local and regional development requires different processes and foci than does the goal of raising foreign currency in order to pay down foreign-held debt. Most community members see the former goal as clearly in their interests, while the latter is a concern of the nation-state. Pressures exerted by such international organizations as the IMF and World Bank can overshadow any interest a national government may have in local development.

In addition to the large-scale issues outlined above, Ed Mahoney – in a keynote address presented at the 'Beyond City Lights' conference held in Toronto, Canada, in February 2000 – listed eight reasons why community tourism often fails. I interpret and summarize them here:

- No collective vision of tourism or monitoring of its performance.
- No incorporation of tourism in a pro-active way into community plans. Tourism is viewed as separate and it is not usually cooperatively developed.
- A great diversity of attractions, events and products that should be packaged, made accessible and communicated to target markets is not developed in that way. It is often the case that this type of systematic development does not occur.
- A diversity of cultural organizations with different missions, philosophies, markets, and marketing sophistication needs to be recognized. Most importantly, tourism marketing needs to recognize a plurality of market segments.
- The recognition that there exists a diversity of stakeholders and markets that we do not know as well as we should.
- The creation of marketing products and strategies that are designed for their own aggrandizement and not for their ultimate effect on target markets.
- Entrepreneurs and planners are busy doing more of what they have been doing rather than what they should be doing to make tourism successful.
- Adhering to the maxim that if you don't have a worthwhile tourism product, or it is not of good quality, do more and more fancy advertising.

Mahoney makes many important points. The fact that communities often do not develop a vision of their desired future is a critical failing – and one that this book has stressed throughout. Even if such a vision is developed, this is often done in isolation from the wider community by the business sector, which clearly cannot represent the collective aspirations of the entire community. If there is a vision of the future and an accompanying strategic plan, it is often not consistent with or incorporated into the general, more comprehensive plan of the community or region. In the developed world there is often no requirement for the tourism sector to undertake a plan under the guidelines set by an official plan. Local governments view tourism in a similar way to other retail industries, and therefore treat it under a generic commercial designation. Given the distinctive nature of tourism, which brings a variety of people into a given community and thereby introduces stresses and tensions into the environment which would otherwise not exist, tourism should not be treated in this generic fashion, but should be allocated a distinct category for the purposes of planning and regulation. This distinct designation would demand that tourism development be addressed in an official community plan, rather than leaving the decision to plan or not up to the prerogative of progressive local officials. In LDCs the requirement for planning may be even more critical. In most cases, tourism planning in LDCs is non-existent. Planning should here include, at least, the establishment of a desired direction of change, an environmental and social impact assessment – including an analysis of who will benefit and who will lose out from any activity, and of what role the local population will play in its development and management – and the inclusion of an ongoing monitoring and evaluation plan.

Mahoney also points out that tourism projects within communities are often unrelated to each other, and fail to add up to a well defined cluster of attractions; they often comprise a number of parts which do not form an integrated product that can be clearly defined and articulated to a target market. This is mainly the result of a plethora of organizations in the community, each creating its own event, which are developed for reasons outside tourism. Music and other cultural festivals are often created by community groups for their own artistic interests, and not initially as a tourism project. However, with the passage of time these festivals become well known regionally, nationally, or internationally because of their high quality and uniqueness, which causes their adoption to the purposes of tourism. Such events will stimulate other development in the community, which may equally be generated for a variety of reasons. The coordination and management by the whole community of such events for the purposes of tourism may cause antagonism. Obviously sponsors of one event may desire more attention than they think they are being accorded by the organizers. This also relates to Mahoney's point that tourism operators become jealous of such personal accomplishments as their brochures and, consequently, spend time and money on such pet projects while neglecting other parts of their enterprise which may need more attention or resources.

While this may simply reflect human nature, tourism is in most cases no longer a 'hobby' business, but a full-time occupation. As such, there is a need to approach community tourism development with the same intensity as with any other business.

Finally, Mahoney raises the issue of transparency. He argues, quite rightly, that, in the absence of a high quality project, tourism operators will attempt to overestimate the merit of their product by less than honest advertising, often in the form of glossy brochures. Inevitably, this practice leads to customer dissatisfaction and to the long-term failure of the attraction. The experience of Bermuda outlined in Chapter 7 demonstrates one successful approach in rejuvenating a declining tourism industry. The first initiative, in Bermuda's case, was a process of self-examination, producing an honest analysis of weaknesses to overcome and strengths to build upon. It would have been quicker and easier simply to pour more money into marketing, in the hope of turning the situation around immediately. Thankfully, those responsible for tourism in Bermuda did not take the quick and easy route. Instead, they brought together all the actors in the system and created a new vision for their industry, spending time on issues of organization and self-examination. There is no substitute for ongoing planning, monitoring and evaluation of a tourism project. Furthermore, this planning and evaluation must be coordinated with the wider assessment of the project's role in the larger community or national picture. Tourism, as stressed throughout this book, must be considered in relation to other potential or actual developments, and to environmental and social interests in the local and national communities involved. To view tourism in isolation from this larger picture is clearly a mistake which will eventually lead to failure.

Tourism relies on a wide variety of systems external to its own operations. The transport infrastructure is critical to success: the most pristine national park in the world will not be visited by a viable number of tourists if access to it is too difficult. With the possible exception of activities for the adventurous tourist, most destination sites need an infrastructure including running water and sanitation. As the dominant age among tourists increases, travelers will require yet more lavish infrastructure. Safety will also become a more central concern, as the media continue to provide sensational coverage of the many conflicts occurring around the world.

We witnessed a drastic decline in the numbers of travelers immediately following the attack on the World Trade Center in New

York, which severely affected the airline industry. Tourists are very wary of visiting parts of the world where their safety is not assured. National governments, working in concert with local communities must address some of these infrastructure and safety issues. However, they must be addressed with the community as a whole in mind, rather than just the tourist. If the latter approach is taken, it will further enhance antagonisms between the developed and developing countries – and between the host and guest in the tourism equation. One of the significant features of the Bermuda plan is that tourists temporarily become a part of the society they enter, rather than being separated from it. This is easier to accomplish in a place like Bermuda, where there is a short cultural distance between the host and guest, but all destinations can attempt to shorten that cultural distance, and work on the same basic principle. Violence against tourists is usually an extension of the general violence found within a society. Bermuda has a low crime rate, and this may be one reason why violence against tourists, while not non-existent, is very low. In situations where violence is high, however, programs to decrease violence against tourists must only be implemented as part of an effort to lower the incidence of violence in the society as a whole. To act otherwise is not only futile, but will be seen as giving preferential treatment to outsiders, and as demeaning to local residents – often a cause of some violence in the first place. If differential treatment occurs, violence directed against tourists is likely to increase, thereby working against the original goal. Generally, tourism must be seen by the local population as benefiting them. If the allocation of resources to the tourism project only benefits the tourist or offshore owner, then antagonism will increase, leading to overt or covert resistance. Such resistance would of course be detrimental to both the tourism enterprise and the day-to-day lives of local citizens.

Most communities construct a public service according to their long-term requirements and allocate resources based on social demography and expressed needs of the population. However, when a community is forced to reconsider its raison d'etre – as has recently been the case in many communities whose economy was once dependent solely on the natural resource extractive industries, and where an influx of new immigrant populations has changed fundamental demographic patterns – the original public services may no longer fit the needs of the new population. Tourism generally attracts a young workforce. Given their long-standing operation, many of the extractive industries are served by a mature workforce. Health service requirements for these two population types may be quite different, for example. As a result, additions to local services will need to be made, or services may even need to be changed completely. Training for a transition from an economy based on extractive industries to one based on service industries will also be required; it should not be assumed that a worker from one sector can make an easy transition to another. The transition to tourism often fails because of inadequacies in training, which includes a psychological adjustment as well as an upgrading of job-specific skills. In LDCs there may be needs as fundamental as providing skills that are associated with the transition from traditional economic practices, such as direct commodity exchange, to a money-based economy. In this case, it will be necessary to focus on such skills as reading, writing and numeracy, as well as the skills specific to tourism itself (see Reid and Sindiga, 1999). This itself is no easy task, and must form part of a larger strategy instituted by the national government, probably with help from NGOs and the international community. It would need to be accomplished in association with some larger goal of national transformation, incorporating tourism development as one of its objects but not driven solely by that sector. Training would not be an isolated technical project, but would ideally relate to the social, cultural and political institutions of the society as well. Many traditional societies are constructed on kinship relations, or other fundamental forms of social organization which are substantially altered through the transition to a monetized economy. This type of transformation must be approached with great caution, and not simply propelled by the desire on the part of the few for tourism development.

CRITERIA FOR TOURISM DEVELOPMENT

The community tourism research completed by myself and others has demonstrated the ingredients necessary for the successful and sustainable development of community tourism. They include:

- Community involvement
- Community organization
- An accurate and honest assessment of the community's resources and possible tourist attractions, both human and physical

- A comprehensive plan developed from a long-term vision
- A transparent marketing plan
- A program of events appealing to local residents as well as visitors
- The recruitment, training and recognition of volunteers
- The deployment of outside resources without the surrender of control of the development

Many of these points seem self-evident, but they are often overlooked by communities impatient to begin developing a project in order to attract tourists and start generating income. To ensure the durability of a project, tourism development must be carefully considered and not rushed.

Community involvement seems the most self-evident of these priorities. However, many communities both define community involvement too narrowly and include only the business population in their deliberations; or otherwise they assume that all members of the community see things the same way as the business person. Tourism promoters are sometimes surprised to find out that there is usually a wide range of opinions and feelings about developments of this nature. It is often wrongly assumed that non-business members of the community are not interested in what the business community does. This is a great mistake which can cause considerable damage to the initial stages of the project being planned. These problems can easily be avoided by involving communities in the process – the most fundamental ingredient of successful tourism development. It has been demonstrated many times that the psychological 'ownership' of a tourism project by local citizens, which protects their value system and builds on their heritage, is critical to success. Citizens must see themselves and their history as represented by whatever product eventually emerges. If it is alien to the history of the area, local citizens will feel that their heritage has been neglected and, perhaps worse, fraudulently portrayed for the sake of commerce. Many rural communities take great pride in displaying their agricultural history to an urbanized clientele often unaware of such rural roots and traditions. Communities once dependent on the land or water for their economic existence are anxious to use tourism as, among other things, a means of telling their story to the outside world. Tourism is often a mechanism for preserving part of a local culture that is in danger of being lost forever. Various sectors of the community must be involved in determining what the theme of a tourism development is to be, and how that theme will be organized and portrayed to the outside world.

Coupled with this imperative is the need to organize the community so that it can contribute in a meaningful way to the direction of planning. Again, it is assumed by many planners and community officials that communities are sufficiently and naturally organized to take part meaningfully in a tourism planning exercise. This assumption has, however, been proved false on many occasions. Relying on such a mistaken assumption, planners have been sorely disappointed when public meetings have been called to discuss a project and few residents have attended to express their opinions. A planning manual titled *Visiting Your Future: A Community Guide to Planning Rural Tourism* (Reid et al., 2001) outlines a step-by-step method for organizing a community so that it can participate meaningfully in a tourism planning process. It also outlines a provisional 'table of contents' for any community-driven tourism plan. Below, I have paraphrased this list from the original manual.

1. Introduction
Provide a history of the community focusing particularly on tourism development. Describe the predominant features of the tourism project as it exists at present.

2. Vision, goals and objectives
Determine what we want our community to look like in the future. Outline the goals and objectives to reach that state from a tourism perspective.

3. Strengths and weaknesses of existing tourism
Outline the features and themes that give strength to the tourism project in the community. Discover the weaknesses in the product or tourism planning process.

4. Physical and human inventory
List and describe the major attributes in the community that will be incorporated into the tourism project. Both human and physical features should be addressed.

5. Recommendations for action
Items that need to be created or completed should be listed here and ranked according to importance. These may range from attracting new businesses to improvement or completion of the tourism planning process, the creation of new special events or a

town beautification plan (each community will have different needs and will set out different actions). This section answers the question WHAT needs to be done to accomplish the objectives.

6. Organizing the tourism planning process or system
Develop and outline an organizational structure that will implement this plan and monitor the system over time. This component should include people who represent all stakeholders including community and non-business groups as well as tourism operators.

7. Implementation of strategic plan
This component focuses on HOW the recommendations will be completed. Not only does it establish the implementation procedure but also the time frame for completion and WHO will be responsible for the action. Also included is a procedure for monitoring progress on implementation as well as the tourism planning system in general.

(Ibid.: 5)

This planning process contains some of the items identified earlier as important ingredients in the success of community tourism development. Creating a long-term vision – not only for tourism development but for the general development of the community – is of paramount importance. By examining the community as a whole, participants in tourism planning will need to fit any project into the overall development direction of the community, as established by local citizens and through their structures of governance. The planning process also calls for the itemization of the physical and human resources of a community that can be exploited in the development of tourism. Inventories of this nature are notorious for quickly becoming outdated, so this part of the planning process needs to be updated continually.

Finally, a word needs to be said about who might undertake such a planning exercise. Modern society has become accustomed to employing professional consultants to work on behalf of communities, or of the businesses proposing the development. While this is a widely accepted method for undertaking such plans, I would advocate the actual involvement of local people in the day-to-day aspects of the planning process whenever possible; many of the relevant research projects can be completed by local groups. The final preparation of the research results and of certain portions of the plan itself can be undertaken by local people, for example. There is really nothing, except for the most technical areas such as statistical data analysis, which necessarily needs outside expertise. Local planning departments and other community institutions are capable of designing and implementing this type of exercise. For those who are nervous about their expertise, hiring a consulting firm to act as a coach in the process is also an option which may be very successful. Not only will this ensure that the plan is completed; it will also leave the community with the skills needed to undertake such activities in the future, without outside help. This approach gives expression to the idea of community capacity building. The *Community Guide* mentioned above is designed for communities to implement when planning tourism development using their own human resources.

One of the principles of a tourism plan should be a commitment to slowing the leakage of money from their community – meaning, in this case, providing attractions and events that encourage local people to stay and spend money in their own community. Activities and events which have value in terms of local recreational needs, as well as from the point of view of tourism, provide an added advantage to living in a tourism community. In many tourism communities this benefit is not realized. Many communities have become so congested that the locals prefer to actually leave the area during peak times. The overall goal of tourism should be to enhance community life, not to inadvertently constrain it. This means that tourism development plans must be considered and evaluated in light of the overall priorities of a community. Certainly, one way of accomplishing this objective is to use local citizens as volunteers in the tourism sector; in rural areas in particular, tourism cannot exist without the use of volunteers. Many festivals and special events which are part of the tourism product require labor, and much of this can be provided by willing volunteers. In fact, volunteering for tourism events can be a recreational experience for local residents. Like other areas of tourism development, however, the proper recruitment, training and public recognition of volunteers is important to success.

In most rural communities, particularly in LDCs and in certain urban settings, large-scale tourism development requires outside resources, but a balance must be struck. Naturally, outside investors will not invest without certain guarantees and some control. But tourism communities have been so anxious to secure these investments that they have tended to give up too much control, so that they no longer dictate the basic goals of development. Great care and ample community discussion must be devoted to this concern. Communities need to understand what they are giving up and what they are getting in return, and to be comfortable with those arrangements. Analysis must be undertaken over the long term, and not focused only on the immediate economic returns.

Marketing and advertising packages need to be considered when designing tourism development. After all, it is these methods that communicate the image of the community to the outside world. The importance of designing a package that truly represents what is offered by the community cannot be overstated. Some tourism communities and destination sites have overstated their attractions and facilities, to the consternation of both visitors and citizens alike. Wels (2000) has outlined how Europeans have designed an image of Africa that fits their romantic perceptions of that continent, but not necessarily in keeping with how Africans see themselves. Advertising Africa with posters of bare-breasted African women is a misrepresentation of what Africa is all about, and an affront to fair-minded people everywhere.

BUILDING SUSTAINABLE COMMUNITY TOURISM

Building a sustainable tourism product, whether at a national or community level, requires adherence to a few basic principles, which have been outlined throughout this book. Perhaps the most important is the empowering of the people whose daily lives will be most affected by a development. Representing the inhabitants accurately is critical in this respect. Artificiality will not last in the long run. The accurate representation of the product to the outside world, and in the case of a tourism development to the local community, is very important. Sufficient accommodation and a diversity of attractions, in addition to an adequate transport network, are of obvious importance here. Tourism developments – particularly in rural areas – need the assistance of partnerships and other forms of cooperation between the various actors within the system. This cooperation can focus the efforts of those involved on organizational and practical issues such as staff and volunteer training. Finally, but perhaps most importantly, good tourism planning must dedicate itself to environmental and social protection. It is the role of the planner to point out to the community, or to the advocate of a particular development, any weaknesses in a proposal that may cause damage to the environment or social system of the community involved in the plan.

In order to build a sustainable worldwide tourism enterprise, attention must be focused at the global, regional and local levels. More specifically, the development of an integrated tourism enterprise, embracing as its fundamental goal the enhancement of the lives of the members of the community, and not just the maximizing of profits for trans-national corporations, must form the central focus of such efforts. Failure in this area may spell the demise of the tourism industry, as well as of many unsuspecting communities around the world.

The tourism industry of the future will be built through a reliance on comprehensive planning, which will view development from a holistic rather than sectoral perspective. This point of view will be driven by a locally developed vision for development, and not by the need for increased profits or revenues for foreign-owned corporations or national governments. It will be based on bottom-up globalization, rather than on the corporate variety. This means control will remain at the local level, while engaging partners from outside the community. Tourism, like many other areas of contemporary life, is controlled by global forces directed by capitalism. Citizens at the local level have lost control of their daily lives. While globalization has produced some important and useful outcomes for humanity, it has also left communities and local people feeling very vulnerable and exploited. Corporate globalism has destroyed local communities and individual ways of life in favor of homogenization. Just as we are jeopardizing genetic diversity throughout the world by the overexploitation of the natural environment, so are we also endangering social and cultural diversity through indiscriminate commercial development, including tourism. The tourism industry must think beyond the immediate drive for increased profits and consider the social, cultural and environmental implications of its actions.

Bibliography

Arai, S. M. 'Benefits of Citizen Participation in a Healthy Communities Initiative: Linking Community Development and Empowerment'. *Journal of Applied Recreation Research*, 21(1), 1996: 25–44.

Arnstein, S. R. 'A Ladder of Citizen Participation'. *American Institute of Planners Association Journal*, 35, 1969: 216–24.

Ashley, C. *Tourism Communities and the Potential Impacts on Local Incomes and Conservation*. Research Discussion Paper No. 10. Windhoek: Directorate of Environmental Affairs, Ministry of Environment and Tourism, 1995.

Ashley, C., and E. Garland. *Promoting Community Based Tourism Development: Why, What and How?* Research Discussion Paper No. 4. Windhoek: Directorate of Environmental Affairs, Ministry of Environment and Tourism, 1994.

Barber, B. R. *Jihad vs McWorld: Terrorism's Challenge to Democracy*. New York: Ballantine, 1995.

Beck, U. *What is Globalization?* Cambridge, UK: Polity Press, 2000.

Bello, W. 'Structural Adjustment Programs: "Success" for Whom?' In *The Case Against the Global Economy*, Jerry Mander and Edward Goldsmith (eds). San Francisco: Sierra Club Books, 2000: 285–96.

Berger, D. *Wildlife Extension: Participatory Conservation by the Maasai in Kenya*. Nairobi: African Centre for Technology Studies, 1993.

Bermuda Alliance for Tourism. *Strategy Document (Executive Summary)*. Bermuda: Bermuda Department of Tourism, 2001.

Biddle, W. W., and L. J. Biddle. *Encouraging Community Development: A Training Guide for Local Workers*. New York: Holt, Rinehart & Winston, 1968.

——*The Community Development Process: The Discovery of Local Initiative*. New York: Holt, Rinehart and Winston, 1995.

Brecher, J., J. B. Childs and J. Cutler. *Global Visions: Beyond the New World Order*. Boston: South End Press, 1993.

Brown, F. *Tourism Reassessed: Blight or Blessing?* Oxford, UK: Butterworth-Heinemann, 1998.

Butler, R. W. 'Social Implication of Social Change'. *Annals of Tourism Research*, 2, 1974: 100–11.

——'The Concept of a Tourism Area Cycle of Evolution: Implications for Management of Resources'. *Canadian Geographer*, 24, 1980: 5–12.

Canadian Pacific Hotels and Resorts. *Annual Report*. Toronto: Canadian Pacific Hotels and Resorts, 2000.

Carnival Corporation. *Annual Report*. Miami: Carnival Corporation, 2000.

Cary, L. J. (ed.). *Community Development as a Process*. Columbia, MO: University of Missouri Press, 1970.

Chambers, R. *Rural Appraisal: Rapid, Relaxed and Participatory*. Sussex, UK: Institute of Development Studies, Discussion Paper 331, University of Sussex, 1992.

——*Paradigm Shifts and the Practice of Participatory Research and Development*. Sussex, UK: Institute of Development Studies, Working Paper 2, University of Sussex, 1994.

Clawson, M., and J. L. Knetch. *Economics of Outdoor Recreation*. Baltimore: Johns Hopkins University Press, 1966.

Club Mediterranee. *Annual Report*. Paris: Club Mediterranee, 2000.

Cohen, E. 'A Phenomenology of Tourism Experience'. *Sociology: The Journal of the British Sociological Association*, 13(2), 1979: 179–201.

Cox, R. W. 'The Global Political Economy and Social Justice'. In *The New Era of Global Competition: State Policy and Market Power*, Daniel Drache and Meric S. Gertler, eds. Montreal and Kingston: McGill-Queens University Press, 1991: 334–50.

Culler, J. 'Semiotics of Tourism'. *American Journal of Semiotics*, 1, 1981: 127–40.

Cummings, H., G. Kora and D. Murray. *Farmers' Markets in Ontario and Their Economic Impact*. Guelph, ON: School of Rural Planning and Development, University of Guelph, Canada, 1999.

de Croo, H. 'Liberalization, Air Transport: Why Europe Needs a Common Policy'. *Viewpoint*, 1(2), 1994.

Dos Santos, T. The Structure of Dependency. *American Economic Review*, 60(21), 1970.

Douglas, D. *Community Economic Development in Canada*, Vol. 1. Toronto: McGraw-Hill Ryerson, 1994.

Doxey, G. 'When Enough is Enough: The Natives are Restless in Old Niagara'. *Heritage Canada*, 2(2), 1976: 26–7.

Drache, D., and M. Gertler. 'The World Economy and the Nation-State: The New International Order'. In *The New Era of Global Competition: State Policy and Market Power*, Daniel Drache and Meric S. Gertler, eds. Montreal and Kingston: McGill-Queens University Press, 1991: 3–25.

Dryzek, J. S. 'Critical Theory as a Research Program'. In *The Cambridge Companion to Habermas*, Stephen White, ed. New York: Cambridge University Press, 1995.

Falk, R. 'The Making of Global Citizenship'. In *Global Visions: Beyond the New World Order*, Jeremy Brecher, John Brown Childs and Jill Cutler, eds. Boston: South End Press, 1993.

Frank, A. G. *Capitalism and Underdevelopment in Latin America: Historical Studies of Chile and Brazil*. New York: Monthly Review Press, 1967.

Freire, P. *Pedagogy of the Oppressed*. London: Penguin, 1990.

Friedmann, J. *Planning in the Public Domain*. Princeton University Press, 1987.

——*Empowerment: The Politics of Alternative Development*. Cambridge, Massachusetts: Blackwell Publishers Ltd, 1995.

Four Seasons Hotels and Resorts. *Annual Report*. Toronto: Four Seasons Hotels and Resorts, 2000.

George, W. 'Globalization and Sustainable Development: The Role of Tourism'. Unpublished paper, School of Rural Planning and Development, University of Guelph, Canada, 2002.

Golub, H. 'Travel and Tourism Creates Jobs'. *Viewpoint*, 1(1), 1994: 9–16.

Graton, C., and P. Taylor. *Sport and Recreation: An Economic Analysis*. London: E and F. N. Spon, 1985.

Guess, R. *The Idea of a Critical Theory: Habermas and The Frankfurt School*. London: Cambridge University Press, 1987.

Harrison, J. 'Thinking About Tourists'. *International Sociology*, 16(2), 2001: 159–72.

Harvey, D. *Spaces of Hope*. Berkeley: University of California Press, 2000.

Hersey, P. *The Situational Leader*. California: Centre for Leadership Studies, 1984.

Hettne, B. *Development Theory and the Three Worlds*. Second edition. London: Addison, 1995.

Hilton Hotels Corporation. *Annual Report*. Beverly Hills, CA: Hilton Hotels Corporation, 2000.

Hirshman, A. O. *The Strategy of Economic Development*. New Haven, CT: Yale University Press, 1958.

Hopkins, J. *Signs of the Post-Rural: Marketing Myths of a Symbolic Countryside*. Geografiska Annaler B., 80(2), 1998 : 65–81.

Huntington, S. P. *The Clash of Civilizations and the Remaking of World Order*. New York: Simon & Schuster, 1997.

Innskeep, E. *Tourism Planning: An Integrated and Sustainable Development Approach*. New York: Van Nostrand Reinhold, 1991.

Jaakson, R. 'Exploring the Epistemology of Ecotourism'. *Journal of Applied Recreation Research*, 22(1), 1997: 33–47.

Jackson, E. L., and T. L. Burton (eds). *Leisure Studies: Prospects for the Twenty-First Century*. State College, Pennsylvania: Venture Publishing, 1999.

Jacobs, J. *Cities and the Wealth of Nations: Principles of Economic Life*. New York: Random House, 1984.

Jung, C. G. *The Basic Writings of C. G. Jung*. New Jersey: Princeton University Press, 1990.

Kenya Wildlife Service. *Maintaining Biodiversity into the 21st Century: A Concept Paper on the Vision and Goals of Kenya Wildlife Service for the Period: 1997–2000*. Nairobi: The Kenya Wildlife Service, 1997.

Knegt, H., *Whose (Wild)life? Local Participation in Wildlife-Based Tourism Related Activities Under the Kenya Wildlife Services Partnership Programme*. Master's Thesis in Development Studies at the Catholic University of Nijmegen, The Netherlands, 1998.

Leakey, R., and R. Lewin. *People of the Lake: Mankind and its Beginnings*. New York: Avon Books, 1978.

Lengkeek, J. 'Leisure Experience and Imagination: Rethinking Cohen's Modes of Tourist Experience'. *International Sociology* 16(2), 2001: 173–84.

Macy, J. *Mutual Causality in Buddhism and General Systems Theory: The Dharma of Natural Systems*. New York: State University of New York Press, 1991.

Mander, J. 'Facing the Rising Tide'. In Mander and Goldsmith (eds). *The Case Against the Global Economy*: 3–19.

Mannell, R. C., and D. G. Reid. *Treating the Work–Leisure Relationship as a Personality Variable and Lifestyle Indicator*. Paper presented at the National Parks and Recreation Association Conference, Cincinnati, Ohio, October 1992: 15–18.

Marriott International Inc. *Annual Report*. Washington, DC: Marriott International Inc., 2000.

Mathieson, A., and G. Wall. *Tourism: Economic, Physical and Social Impacts*. London: Longman, 1982.

Martinussen, J. *Society, State and Market: A Guide to Competing Theories of Development*. Halifax: Fernwood Publishing, 1997.

McDowall, D. *Another World: The Rise of Modern Tourism in Bermuda*. New Jersey: Macmillan, 1999.

McIntosh, R. W., C. R. Goeldner and J. R. Ritche. *Tourism: Principles, Practice and Philosophies*. Seventh edition. Chichester, UK: John Wiley, 1995.

McMurtry, J. *Unequal Freedoms in the Global Market as an Ethical System*. Toronto: Garamond Press, 1998.

——*The Cancer Stage of Capitalism*. London: Pluto, 1999.

Meethan, K. *Tourism in Global Society: Place, Culture, Consumption*. New York: Palgrave, 2001.

Mill, R. C., and A. M. Morrison. *The Tourism System: An Introductory Text*. Englewood Cliffs, New Jersey: Prentice Hall, 1985.

Minnesota Extension Service. *A Training Guide for Rural Tourism Development*. Minnesota: University of Minnesota, 1991.

Mitchell, C. J. A. 'Entrepreneurialism, Commodification and Creative Destruction: A Model of Post-Modern Community Development'. *Journal of Rural Studies*, 14(3), 1998: 273–86.

Mowforth, M., and I. Munt. *Tourism and Sustainability: New Tourism in the Third World*. London: Routledge, 1998.

Myles, J. 'Post-Industrialism and the Service Economy'. In *The New Era of Global Competition: State Policy and Market Power*, Daniel Drache and Meric S. Gertler, eds. Montreal and Kingston: McGill-Queens University Press, 1991: 351–66.

Norberg-Hodge, H. 'The Pressure to Modernize and Globalize'. In Mander and Goldsmith (eds). *The Case Against the Global Economy*: 33–46.

Nurske, R. *Problems of Capital Formation in Underdeveloped Countries*. Oxford: Blackwell, 1953.

Ontario Ministry of Tourism. *Premier Ranked Tourism Destinations*. Toronto: Queen's Printer, 2000.

Overton, J., and R. Scheyvens. *Strategies for Sustainable Development: Experiences from the Pacific*. Sydney: New South Wales Press, 1999.

Pearce, D. *Tourism Development*. UK: Longman, 1989.

Polanyi, K. *The Great Transformation*. Boston, MA: Beacon Press, 1957.

Prebisch, R. 'Five Stages of My Thinking on Development'. In *Pioneers in Development*, G. M. Meier, and D. Seers (eds). New York: Oxford University Press, 1984.

Ralston Saul, J. *On Equilibrium*. Toronto: Penguin Viking, 2001.

Reid, D. G. *Work and Leisure in the 21st Century: From Production to Citizenship*. Toronto: Wall and Emerson, 1995.

——'Rural Tourism Development: Provincial/State Issues'. In *Tourism and Recreation in Rural Areas*, Richard Butler, Michael Hall and J. Jenkins (eds). London: John Wiley & Sons, 1998: 69–80.

Reid, D. G., and E. van Dreunen. 'Leisure as a Social Transformation Mechanism in Community Development Practice'. *Journal of Applied Recreation Research*, 21(1), 1996: 49–65.

Reid, D. G., and J. FitzGibbon. 'An Economic Evaluation of Municipal Recreation Expenditures: A Preliminary Report'. *Journal of Applied Recreation Research*, 16(2), 1991: 244–55.

Reid, D. G., A. M. Fuller, K. M. Haywood and J. Bryden. *The Integration of Tourism, Culture and Recreation in Rural Ontario*. Toronto: Queen's Printer, 1993.

Reid, D. G., N. Lee, A. Phillips and J. Duggan. *Guelph/Wellington Tourism Study Report*. Guelph, ON: School of Rural Planning and Development, University of Guelph, 1995.

Reid, D. G., H. Mair and J. Taylor. *Rural Tourism Development: Research Report*. Guelph, ON: School of Rural Planning and Development, University of Guelph, 2000.

Reid, D. G., H. Mair, W. George and J. Taylor. *Visiting Your Future: A Community Guide to Planning Rural Tourism*. Guelph, ON: Ontario Agriculture Training Institute, 2001.

Reid, D. G., and I. Sindiga. 'Tourism and Community Development: An African Example'. *World Leisure and Recreation*, 41(2), 1999: 18–21.

Reid, D. G., I. Sindiga, N. Evans and S. Ongaro. 'Tourism, Bio-Diversity and Community Development in Kenya'. In *Ecotourism Development in Eastern and Southern Africa*, Donald G. Reid (ed.). Harare: Weaver Press, 1999.

Rifkin, J. *The End of Work: The Decline of the Global Labor Force and the Dawn of the Post-Market Era*. New York: G. P. Putnam's Sons, 1995.

Roberts, H. *Community Development: Learning and Action*. Toronto, ON: University of Toronto Press, 1979.

Rocha, E. M. 'A Ladder of Empowerment'. *Journal of Planning Education and Research*, 17, 1997: 31–44.

Rojek, C., and J. Urry (eds). *Touring Cultures: Transformations of Travel and Theory*. London: Routledge, 1997.

Rollins, K., and W. Wistowsky. 'Benefits of Back-Country Canoeing in Ontario Wilderness Parks. *Journal of Applied Recreation Research*, 22(1), 1997: 9–31.

Rosaldo, R. 'Subjectivity in Social Analysis'. In *The Postmodern Turn: New Perspectives on Social Theory*, Steven Seidman (ed.). New York: Cambridge University Press, 1994.

Rosenstein-Rohdan, P. 'Problems of Industrialization of Eastern and South-Eastern Europe'. *Economic Journal*, 1943: 279.

Ross, M. G. *Community Organization: Theory, Principles, and Practice*. Second edition. New York: Harper & Rowe, 1967.

Rostow, W. W. *The Stages of Growth*. Cambridge: Cambridge University Press, 1960.

Rothman, J. 'Three Models of Community Organization and Practice, Their Mixing and Phasing'. In *Strategies of Community Organization*, F. M. Cox, J. L. Erlich, J. Rothman and J. E. Tropman (eds). Itasca, IL: F. E. Peacock, 1979: 25–45.

Sanders, I. T. 'The Concept of Community Development'. In *Community Development as a Process*, L. J. Cary (ed.). Columbia, MO: University of Missouri, 1970: 9–31.

Schuller, T. 'The Complementary Roles of Human and Social Capital'. *ISUMA, Canadian Journal of Policy Research*, 2(1), 2001: 18–24.

Schuurman, F. J. (ed.). *Beyond the Impasse: New Directions in Development Theory.* London: Zed Books, 1993.

Seidman, S. 'The End of Sociological Theory'. In Seidman (ed.), *The Postmodern Turn: New Perspectives on Social Theory*, Steven Seidman (ed.). New York: Cambridge University Press, 1994.

Shelby, B., and T. A. Haberlein. *Carrying Capacity in Recreational Settings.* Carvallis Or: Oregon State University Press, 1986.

Sindiga, I. *Tourism and African Development: Change and Challenge of Tourism in Kenya.* Hampshire, UK: Ashgate, 1999.

Smith, A. *Economic Impact Analysis of Sport Fishing on the Upper Grand River: A Methodology.* Thesis presented to the School of Rural Planning and Development, University of Guelph, Canada, 1997.

Stankey, G. H., S. F. McCool, R. N. Clark, and P. J. Brown. 'Institutional and Organizational Challenges to Managing Natural Resources for Recreation: A Social Learning Model'. In *Leisure Studies: Prospects for the Twenty-first Century*, Edgar L. Jackson and Thomas L. Burton, eds. State College, Pennsylvania: Venture Publishing, 1999: 435–50.

Starwood Hotels and Resorts Worldwide. *Annual Report.* White Plains, New York: Starwood Hotels and Resorts Worldwide, 2000.

Statistics Canada. *International Travel 2000.* Ottawa: Statistics Canada, 2000.

Stebbins, R. A. 'Serious Leisure: A Conceptual Statement'. *Pacific Sociological Review*, 25, 1983: 251–72.

——'Casual Leisure: A Conceptual Statement'. *Leisure Studies*, 16, 1997: 17–25.

——'Antinomies in Volunteering – Choice/Obligation, Leisure/Work'. *Loisir et Société*, 23(2), 2000: 313–24.

Sumner, J. *Sustainability and Rural Communities in the Age of Globalization: Can We Learn Our Way Out?* Guelph ON: Ph.D Dissertation, Rural Studies Program, University of Guelph, 2002.

Sutherland, P. 'Traveling with the GATT: Abiding by the New Rules of Trade'. *Viewpoint*, 2(1), 1994: 17–24.

Town of Golden. *Golden Strategic Planning Process 2001–2006.* Conference Brochure, presented by the Town of Golden at the 2001 Community Conference.

Transformative Learning Centre. *Fourth International Conference on Transformative Learning*, Ontario Institute for Studies in Education, University of Toronto, 2001.

Urry, J. *The Tourist Gaze: Leisure and Travel in Contemporary Societies.* London: Sage, 1990.

van den Bor, W., J. M. Bryden, and A. M. Fuller. *Rethinking Rural Human Resource Management: The Impact of Globalization and Rural Restructuring on Rural Education and Training in Western Europe.* Wageningen, NL: Mansholt Institute, 1997.

van der Duim, R., J. Caalders, A. Caordero, L. van Duynen Montijn, and N. Ritsma. *Developing Sustainable Tourism: The Case of Manuel Antonio and Texel.* Wageningen, NL: Wageningen University and Research Centre, 2001.

Vaughan, D. R., H. Farr, and R. W. Slee. 'Estimating and Interpreting the Local Economic Benefits of Visitor Spending: An Explanation'. *Leisure Studies*, 19, 2000: 95–118.

Veblen, T. *The Theory of the Leisure Class: An Economic Study of Institutions.* New York: Mentor Books, 1953.

Wall, G., and C. Wright. *The Environmental Impact of Outdoor Recreation.* Waterloo, ON: Department of Geography, University of Waterloo, Canada, 1977.

Walsh, R. G. *Recreation Economic Decisions: Comparing Benefits and Costs.* State College Pennsylvania: Venture Publishing, 1986.

Wearing, S., and J. Neil. 'Refiguring Self and Identity through Volunteer Tourism'. *Loisir et Société*, 23(2), 2000: 389–419.

Weaver, D. *Tourism Management.* Brisbane: John Wiley & Sons Australia Ltd, 2000.

Wels, H. *A Critical Reflection on Cultural Tourism in Africa: The Power of European Imagery.* Proceedings of the ATLAS Africa Cultural Tourism Conference, Mombasa, Kenya: 2000: 55–66.

West, C. 'The New Cultural Politics of Difference'. In Seidman, ed., *The Postmodern Turn.*

Westcoast CED Consulting Ltd. *Community Impact Report for the Town of Golden BC.* Golden BC: Golden Community Services Adjustment Committee, 2001.

Western, D. *In the Dust of Kilimanjaro.* Washington: Island Press/Shearwater Books, 1997.

Wight, P. *Environmentally Responsible Marketing of Tourism. In Ecotourism: A Sustainable Option?* Chichester: John Wiley & Sons, 1994.

Wilkinson, P. *Tourism Policy and Planning: Case Studies from the Commonwealth Caribbean.* Elmsford, NY: Cognizant Communication Corp., 1997.

Wilson, E. O. *The Future of Life.* New York: Alfred A. Knopf, 2002.

White, S. (ed.). *The Cambridge Companion to Habermas.* New York: Cambridge University Press, 1995.

World Bank. *World Development Report 1991: The Challenge of Development.* New York: Oxford University Press, 1991.

World Commission on Environment and Development. *Our Common Future.* New York: Oxford University Press, 1987.

World Tourism Organization. *Tourism Market Trends.* Madrid: World Tourism Organization, 1997.

WTTC/WEFA Group Research Report. 'World Travel Forecast: 1995 and Beyond'. *Viewpoint*, 2(1), 1994: 67–9.

Ziffer, K. *Ecotourism: The Uneasy Alliance.* Washington: Conservation International, Ernst & Young, 1989.

http://www.wttc.org/mediaCentre/WTTCForecastsStrongForthQuarter0812002.htm

Index

Compiled by Sue Carlton